How to Do Library Research

How to Do
Library Research

Second Edition

ROBERT B. DOWNS
CLARA D. KELLER

University of Illinois Press
Urbana Chicago London

Library of Congress Cataloging in Publication Data

Downs, Robert Bingham, 1903–
How to do library research.

Includes index.
1. Reference books—Bibliography. 2. Libraries—
Handbooks, manuals, etc. I. Keller, Clara D., 1934–
joint author. II. Title.
Z1035.1.D68   1975   011′.02   74-28301
ISBN 0-252-00449-3
ISBN 0-252-00535-X pbk.

Preface

The preparation of a reasonably concise guide to library research, the objective of the present manual, requires compromises. It is obviously impossible to cover any field exhaustively, if the size of the work is not to get completely out of hand. A restriction to basic references, therefore, is a first consideration. Also, a middle course must be followed among the several publics for whom the book is intended: the general researcher, the scholar and specialist, the college student, and others who have reason to use libraries for the investigation of particular topics.

Grateful acknowledgment is made to a number of University of Illinois Library and Graduate School of Library Science staff members who gave valuable advice in the selection of reference works in specialized subjects: Nancy D. Anderson, Mathematics Librarian; John W. Beecher, Agriculture Librarian; George Bonn, Professor of Library Science and specialist in scientific and medical literature; Leonard Coburn, Engineering Librarian; Elisabeth B. Davis, Biology Librarian; Cathleen C. Flanagan; Professor John T. Flanagan; Edward F. Hess, Jr., Law Librarian; Marguerite S. Kaufman, Art and Architecture Librarian; Jean Lokke, Physical Education Librarian; William McClellan, Music Librarian; Barbara C. Sergent, Home Economics Librarian; and Harriet W. Smith, Geology Librarian. Elizabeth C. Downs assisted with bibliographical searching and editorial work.

Special appreciation is due to Deloris Holiman, who prepared the manuscript for publication.

ROBERT B. DOWNS
CLARA D. KELLER

Contents

1
America's Libraries

From the point of view of the consumer, library methods and techniques in the United States are the most advanced of any area of the world. Liberal concepts of library use, such as free circulation of books, open shelves, bibliographical tools, reference and research services, and similar aids to the reader, are mainly of American origin. Types of libraries have been developed here to meet almost every conceivable need. Thus, despite certain shortcomings, the American library system has become a bulwark of democratic society, widely emulated abroad.

Though libraries vary widely in size, in the clienteles they are designed to serve, and in the scope of their collections, they are planned, with few exceptions, to meet the informational, cultural, and recreational requirements of their users. Furthermore, basic patterns of library organization differ little, despite the seeming complexity of individual institutions.

No longer valid is the old stereotype of the library as a mausoleum of culture, dark and forbidding, filled with gloomy, silent tiers of bookshelves and backbreaking furniture, remote from the daily lives and interests of the people. In the past twenty-five years, public, college, and school libraries have experienced a revolution. Adapting to their special needs modern architecture, good lighting, efficient ventilating equipment, comfortable and attractive furniture, and pleasing color schemes, they have tended increasingly to become bright, cheerful, informal, and lively community centers. An atmosphere of service and eagerness to please pervades them.

ROLE OF THE LIBRARIAN

The public image of the librarian has been distorted by cartoonists and other popular humorists. The spinsterish, vinegarish individual in their caricatures bears little resemblance to reality. Librarianship is a highly diversified profession, attracting men and women of varied abilities and interests, extrovert and introvert personalities, those who enjoy working with people and others who prefer to work with books behind the scenes—in short, the wide range of differences one would normally expect in a profession whose practitioners number some 125,000 in the United States alone.

The word "librarian" covers a multitude of activities, duties, and functions. Merely sampling its broad scope, in public libraries we find librarians of small village libraries containing a few hundred volumes and operated by a single person and bookmobile librarians providing rural library service, and at the opposite extreme the New York Public Library with its millions of volumes, millions of readers, and staff of more than 2,000. In the field of education, the range is from elementary, junior and senior high school, and junior college libraries—not infrequently oneman operations—to large senior college and great university libraries. To these major groups we may add the thousands of librarians serving federal and state governmental agencies, American libraries abroad in United States military bases and Information Service libraries, and the special libraries of such giant corporations as DuPont and General Motors. All these professional workers are called "librarians," though they are performing functions as various as those of general practitioners and specialists in the medical sciences, who are blanketed under the term "doctors."

In order for a layman to know what kinds of assistance to expect from members of a library staff, it may be noted that the most common divisions of duties in a library organization are these: *Acquisition librarians* are responsible for procuring books, periodicals, newspapers, pamphlets, films, recordings, maps, and so forth, to add to the library's resources. The competent acquisition librarian is an expert on the book market, knows the trends in publishing, can provide information on publishers and prices and what books are in print, is a judge of the best editions, and has reliable data on the value of out-of-print, old, and rare books.

Catalog librarians classify and catalog all material received by the library, to enable the reader to find what the library has on a given subject or by a certain author, or a particular book by its title. The cataloger is expert on the most efficient and productive use of the library's card catalog, and is ready to assist readers who may encounter difficulties in locating their references, who are puzzled by the dictionary arrangement of the catalog, or who need an explanation of the mysteries of library classification.

Public service librarians may fill any one of several kinds of positions: (a) *Circulation librarian,* who helps readers to find the books they want, supervises the use of the book collection, arranges book loans for home use, and maintains circulation records. (b) *Reference librarian,* whose thorough knowledge of encyclopedias, dictionaries, yearbooks, bibliographies, periodical and newspaper indexes, and similar reference works usually produces answers to the most obscure and complex queries. The successful reference librarian has a phenomenal memory, possesses intuition as to where hidden facts may be unearthed, and enjoys the spirit of the chase. (c) *Readers' advisor,* commonly found in public libraries, who offers "personalized library service," working with individual library users in the preparation of reading programs and the compilation of reading lists on virtually any topic, and giving general guidance to library patrons who wish to read with a purpose. (d) *Subject specialists,* who administer special subject divisions of the library, for example, science and industry, business and economics, fine arts and music, language and literature. The divisional librarian customarily has had formal training as well as experience in his or her field, is familiar with its literature, and is ready to render expert aid to readers concerned with particular topics.

The foregoing summary necessarily omits many of the specialized activities and concerns of modern-day librarians. In a great majority of cases, these individuals have entered the library profession because they have a liking for people, plus an attachment to books and a keen realization of the benefits which books and libraries can confer on their users; all are united in their dedication to the proposition that the combination of books and people is fundamentally important.

TYPES OF LIBRARIES

The student of American library resources soon becomes aware of the many types of libraries to be found in the United States and of their varying facilities for research purposes.

Standing at the top of our system of libraries, from the point of view of advanced study and research, are the university libraries. The most obvious characteristic of a university, distinguishing it from other educational institutions, is its research activities, and these activities are naturally reflected in the development of its library. Using quantitative standards only, 68 university libraries in the United States now hold more than 1,000,000 volumes each and ten others are approaching that figure. On the basis of membership in the select Association of Research Libraries, eighty-three United States university libraries possess resources of considerable importance to the scholar and research worker.

Comparable to the best of the university libraries are the collections found in a small group of institutions known as reference libraries, privately endowed and controlled and not ordinarily affiliated with any educational institution. Leading examples are the J. Pierpont Morgan Library and New York Public Library (Reference Department) in New York City, the John Carter Brown Library in Rhode Island, the American Antiquarian Society Library in Massachusetts, the Folger Shakespeare Library in Washington, the Peabody Institute Library in Baltimore, the John Crerar Library and Newberry Library in Chicago, the Linda Hall Library in Kansas City, and the Henry E. Huntington Library in California. None of these institutions, except the New York Public Library, is among the largest in the nation, but from the point of view of the rarity and value of their collections they rank at the top.

Also of prime significance are libraries associated with the federal government, a group which has grown rapidly in the past generation and has become increasingly important in many fields. Standing at the top of the system is the Library of Congress, with its approximately 16,000,000 volumes, probably the world's largest library, holding notable collections in many fields. In addition to the national library, which the Library of Congress is for all practical purposes, virtually every branch of government has a library of its own pertaining to its specialized interests. Among these are some of the world's leading libraries in their areas, for example, the National Library of Medicine, containing 1,500,000 volumes, the National Agricultural Library of comparable size, and collections equally comprehensive and rich in their fields for education in the Department of Health, Education and Welfare, for geology in the Geological Survey, for military science in the Army Library, for labor in the Department of Labor Library, for economics in the Department of Commerce Library, for international law and relations in the Department of State Library, and scores of others.

Another category of governmental libraries contains those belonging to the individual states. State libraries have been established in all the fifty states. Many of the states also possess library extension agencies, legislative reference libraries, supreme court libraries, state archives, and historical commissions. From the viewpoint of research, the state libraries, archival agencies, and law libraries are important chiefly for newspaper files, state government publications, executive, legislative, and judicial archives and manuscripts, law, and local history.

As a type, public libraries are among the most common, numbering more than 7,000. An example is to be found in every city and town of substantial size in the country. Twenty-four public libraries own over 1,000,000 volumes each, and as many more contain from 500,000 to 1,000,000 volumes. With a few exceptions, these institutions are less useful to the advanced student and scholar than one would assume from their size. The principal reasons for this fact are that public libraries must serve the needs of large numbers of general readers who may not require highly specialized materials, and public libraries must do an excessive amount of duplicating for their branches and to meet the demands of the large clienteles served. The exceptions are such atypical institutions as the Boston and New York public libraries, and specialized collections in the Cleveland, Detroit, and several other outstanding public libraries.

The term "special libraries" is applied to a numerous and diverse lot of organizations. By its nature, the special library is designed to serve a restricted clientele for a special and limited purpose. The most common type, business and industrial libraries, is concentrated in large cities and industrial centers. The emphasis is almost invariably on current material and up-to-date information, and such libraries seldom contain much retrospective or background literature. Their resources may or may not be available to outside users. A second division of special libraries is those owned by societies, associations, and similar organizations. For example, bar associations have established law libraries and medical associations, medical libraries for the use of their members. The Engineering Societies Library of New York is one of the country's foremost engineering libraries. Association libraries are often highly specialized and are therefore of first-rate value to research workers in the fields covered by them.

Finally, two large groups of libraries belong to educational institutions: college and school libraries. Junior and senior college libraries number about 2,500, but, except for a handful which have developed collections in special subjects, they are unequipped to meet the needs of the scholar. Research is quite outside the scope of the nation's 50,000 or more elementary and secondary school libraries.

NATURE OF LIBRARY COLLECTIONS

In thinking and speaking of libraries, one naturally visualizes a collection of books. Modern libraries, however, are by no means limited to books. Books make up a large part of most collections, but they are only a part of a scholar's requirements. In a good number of fields, serial literature is regarded as even more essential, particularly in technology and the sciences, including general and specialized periodicals, learned and technical journals, the transactions of academies, societies, museums, observatories, universities, and institutions of all sorts. A general university library, for example, needs 10,000 to 20,000 current journals to keep abreast of research activities and developments.

Another great body of research material is government publications. There are not only the documents of the federal government, but also of the individual states, counties, and municipalities, of foreign governments, and of such international organizations as the United Nations.

The last of the major categories of research materials is collections of manuscripts. Manuscripts are of fundamental importance to scholars in many fields, but most essential in history and literature.

Separately printed books, serials, government publications, and manuscripts are the principal types of resources for research. By no means, however, do they exhaust the varieties of records being accumulated by libraries today. To illustrate, the Library of Congress reports millions of maps, microreproductions, motion pictures, music and recordings, photographs, prints, slides, broadsides, and posters. Every large library makes liberal provision for such nonbook research materials.

As one examines the materials for research in various disciplines, many of them fall into well-defined patterns. For most of the sciences, the literature of mathematics is basic. In the biological, chemical, and physical sciences the essential materials are complete sets of specialized journals, followed by transactions of societies and institutions in these fields. Ranking third in importance are monographic publications, handbooks, and encyclopedias. In the applied sciences of medicine, surgery, and chemical technology the situation is the same. In short, the zoologist, the botanist, the chemist, and the surgeon are concerned first of all with the journals in their fields; therein they learn most promptly about the latest discoveries and investigations.

In the so-called "earth sciences"—agriculture, geology, paleontology, mineralogy, geography, and geophysics—the journal literature is also highly important, but is supplemented extensively by government publications, for example, the innumerable reports of geological surveys and a steady stream of agricultural publications.

Scanning the research materials needed by social scientists—historians, sociologists, economists, educators, political scientists, lawyers—the diversity of forms is much greater than for the biological and physical sciences. In addition to numerous journals and society proceedings, government publications are necessary, as are published archives, laws, treaty collections, court reports, maps, newspaper files, census reports, and other statistical compilations. Separately published books and monographs bulk large in the total.

From the viewpoint of the general library, the largest single classification is language and literature. Periodicals devoted to language and literature studies are relatively few and the great mass of research materials is in book form.

In another category, the fine arts and their applications, journals and other serial publications are numerous, but other kinds of material are equally necessary, notably monumental collections of sources, prints, slides, photographs, sheet music, music recordings, and architectural drawings.

The last of the great fields is philosophy and religion, whose literature is used not only for theological study and research, but also for ancient and medieval history and literature. In this area, books, journals, and society transactions are present in great numbers. As an example, for the history and doctrines of Christianity, a large body of collected sources, scriptural commentaries, council decisions, and similar records has grown up.

DISTRIBUTION OF AMERICAN LIBRARY RESOURCES

The distribution of materials for library research in the United States is uneven. The chief concentrations are to be found in the northeast, the north-central west, the southeast, and the Pacific southwest. By contrast the southwest, Rocky Mountain area, and northwest are less adequately equipped with research library collections.

By states, the heaviest concentrations of books are to be found in New York, California, and Massachusetts, in that order, with Ohio, Illinois, District of Columbia, and Pennsylvania trailing not far behind. At the opposite end of the scale, the states with fewest books are in the sparsely populated northwest and southwest: New Mexico, South Dakota, Wyoming, North Dakota, Idaho, and Nevada. Viewed by regions, the northeast quarter of the nation possesses almost two-thirds of all the books held by libraries in the United States, or according to the most recent count 495,000,000 compared to 286,000,000 volumes.

It is thus apparent that scholars and research workers in certain areas of the country are handicapped by the absence of adequate resources close at hand and must depend upon richer libraries elsewhere. The ready availability of library materials in photoreproduction is helping to alleviate the shortage. Also of value are a number of regional and national programs of library cooperation to improve access to library resources.

ONE HUNDRED NOTABLE AMERICAN LIBRARIES

Where are the leading collections for advanced study and research in American libraries? The question is asked repeatedly by librarians, college and university faculty members, graduate students, research workers for business and industry, and others contemplating an exhaustive investigation of a subject.

In the nature of things, it is improbable that any library can ever acquire an absolutely complete collection in any large field, and the odds are against its doing so even in a segment of that field. Nevertheless, there are library collections so outstanding in value and so comprehensive in scope that they are naturally turned to first by the scholar and the specialist.

In choosing the first 100 libraries in the United States whose resources are most noteworthy, a basic list is the institutional membership of the Association of Research Libraries, totaling eighty-three. To these might be added selected public libraries holding in excess of 1,000,000 volumes each, and certain specialized reference libraries which do not meet the particular criteria for Association of Research Libraries membership. Following this selection procedure produces the following list, arranged by types of libraries and with brief annotations for the guidance of prospective users:

UNIVERSITY LIBRARIES (by size of collections, 1971–72 statistics)

1. *Harvard University Library*, Cambridge, Mass. The world's largest university library, with 8,707,822 volumes. Collections of major importance are maintained in law, medicine, business administration, public administration, zoology, theology, archeology, ethnology, and Chinese and Japanese literature.

2. *Yale University Library*, New Haven, Conn. Second largest American university library, with 5,993,856 volumes. Holds specialized collections in medicine, theology, drama, law, music, natural history, forestry, German, English, and American literature, colonial and Western Americana, and other fields.

3. *University of Illinois Library*, Urbana. Largest state university library, with 4,992,391 volumes. Outstanding collections include classical literature, all periods of English literature, American humor and folklore, Abraham Lincoln, Latin American history, Slavic literature, and all branches of science and technology.

4. *Columbia University Library*, New York City. 4,448,350 volumes; strong in law, medicine, architecture, engineering, geology, education, psychology, philosophy, music, American history, Russian, Chinese, and Japanese languages and literature, and international relations.

5. *University of Michigan Library*, Ann Arbor. 4,332,518 volumes; noteworthy collections in medical history, music, political science, labor, law, transportation, engineering, business administration, and American history.

6. *University of California*, Berkeley. 4,153,936 volumes; special strength for California history, western Americana, Mark Twain, Latin American colonial history, architecture, chemistry, biology, East Asia, engineering, forestry, geology, music, physics, and law.

7. *Cornell University Library*, Ithaca, N.Y. 3,888,634 volumes; special collections: English and French revolutions, witchcraft, Dante, Petrarch, China and Southeast Asia, Icelandic literature, Brazil, German literature, American history, the Reformation, history of science, and New York regional history.

8. *Stanford University Library*, Stanford, Calif. 3,721,343 volumes; has Hoover collections on war, revolution, and peace, also special collections on Isaac Newton, music, nineteenth- and twentieth-century English and American literature, American history and constitutional law, transportation, education, ichthyology, biological and mineral sciences.

9. *Indiana University Library*, Bloomington. 3,344,141 volumes; significant special collections relate to Abraham Lincoln, Daniel Defoe, English history 1668–1731, American folklore, Indiana history, War of 1812, William Wordsworth, American Revolution, and de Lafayette; also, has Lilly Library of rare books relating to English and American literature, medicine, and science.

10. *University of Minnesota Library*, Minneapolis. 3,245,740 volumes; special collections: classical literature, South Asia, early Western Hemisphere exploration, world commerce to 1800, seventeenth-century English history, Scandinavian history and literature, magic, historical children's books, law, public administration, and the principal sciences.

11. *University of Chicago*, Chicago, Ill. 3,212,296 volumes; leading collections in language and literature, law, political science, history, economics, education, sociology, psychology, physical and biological sciences, Lincolniana, modern poetry, Near and Far East, history of Kentucky and Ohio Valley, and religion.

12. *University of California Library*, Los Angeles. 3,164,328 volumes; departmental libraries for agriculture, art, biomedicine, chemistry, education, engineering, geology, industrial relations, law, meteorology, music, physics, and theater arts; also, William Andrews Clark Library devoted to English culture, seventeenth to nineteenth centuries, architecture, urban planning, and Oriental literature.

13. *University of Texas Library*, Austin. 2,734,595 volumes; notable special collections in English and American literature,

American poetry, southern Americana, Texas history, and Latin American history, especially Mexican.

14. *Ohio State University Library,* Columbus. 2,670,984 volumes; special collections: American literature, Cervantes, Reformation history, Spanish drama, history of medicine, Civil War, Hawthorne, James Thurber.

15. *University of Wisconsin Library,* Madison. 2,517,796 volumes; specialized collections for agriculture, engineering, education, medicine, geology, geography, and law; rich also in economics, history of science, political science, socialism and labor, Scandinavian literature, and Gaelic history and literature.

16. *Northwestern University Library,* Evanston, Ill. 2,433,420 volumes; special collections: Bolivian history, French Revolution, Spanish plays, Johnson-Boswell, Africana, anthropology, Japanese politics and government, twentieth-century English and American literature, and World War II.

17. *Princeton University Library,* Princeton, N.J. 2,412,871 volumes; particular strength in classical literature, Orientalia, European medieval and Renaissance manuscripts, colonial and western Americana, American Civil War, and Victorian novelists.

18. *University of Pennsylvania Library,* Philadelphia. 2,410,933 volumes; noteworthy sections on medieval history, Inquisition, Shakespeare, Spanish drama, Italian and Spanish Renaissance literature, Benjamin Franklin, history of chemistry, economics, and South Asia.

19. *Duke University Library,* Durham, N.C. 2,333,382 volumes; special collections: American South, Chinese history, Italian history, French literature, Latin Americana, Philippiniana, folklore, tobacco, history of medicine, Reformation, and English and American eighteenth- to nineteenth-century literature.

20. *New York University Library,* New York City. 2,175,680 volumes; special collections: economics, American literature, Robert Frost, Belgian literature, Hegel, Victorian novel, psychology, and numismatics.

21. *Johns Hopkins University Library,* Baltimore, Md. 1,993,113 volumes; special collections: art, Bibles, economic classics, seventeenth-century English literature, French, German, Icelandic,

Scandinavian, and Mongolian literature, slavery, Swiss history, and trade unions.

22. *University of Washington Library*, Seattle. 1,928,298 volumes; special collections: Pacific northwest and Alaska, Far East, drama, fisheries and oceanography, forestry, and geography.

23. *University of North Carolina Library*, Chapel Hill. 1,894,-132 volumes; special collections: history of American South, North Caroliniana, history of the book, Napoleonic period in France, George Bernard Shaw, Thomas Wolfe, Spanish drama, and Latin Americana.

24. *Michigan State University*, East Lansing. 1,867,236 volumes; special subjects: history of veterinary medicine, horticulture, western Africana, American labor movement, apiculture, Lincoln, history of printing, agricultural machinery, and twentieth-century American theater.

25. *University of Virginia Library*, Charlottesville. 1,777,936 volumes; special strength for Virginia and southeastern United States history, English and American literature, international law, history of printing, Chinese literature, music, classical literature, voyages and travels, and optics.

26. *University of Iowa Library*, Iowa City. 1,672,927 volumes; special collections: Leigh Hunt, Abraham Lincoln, American Indians, typography, Iowa authors, and history of hydraulics.

27. *University of Pittsburgh Library*, Pittsburgh, Pa. 1,664,234 volumes; special collections: early transportation, western Pennsylvania history, modern American and English drama, Stephen Foster, Hervey Allen, Mary Roberts Rinehart, and educational history.

28. *University of Missouri Library*, Columbia. 1,639,261 volumes; special collections: advertising, crime and criminology, western Americana, and classical literature.

29. *University of Kansas Library*, Lawrence. 1,639,070 volumes; special collections: ornithology, economics, Kansas history, travel, European history, Irish literature, Spanish plays, history of women, botanical history, Renaissance, and Chinese classics.

30. *Syracuse University Library*, Syracuse, N.Y. 1,637,442 volumes; numerous special collections: Balzac, Stephen Crane, Gus-

tave Flaubert, Frederic Goudy, Averill W. Harriman, early works in science and economics, John Cowper Powys, Oneida Community, Walt Whitman, and Walter De la Mare.

31. *Rutgers University Library*, New Brunswick, N.J. 1,584,529 volumes; special collections: agricultural history, nineteenth-century English literature, New Jersey history, American almanacs, Defoe, Cobbett, Freneau, Noah Webster, Walt Whitman, and Joyce Kilmer.

32. *University of Colorado Library*, Boulder. 1,570,251 volumes; special collections: English drama, Rocky Mountain regional history, Central European history, medieval history, twentieth-century British literature, music, silver, metallurgy, and mountaineering.

33. *University of Florida Library*, Gainesville. 1,550,486 volumes; special collections: Floridiana, West Indies, Latin Americana, Caribbean, dance music, and theater.

34. *Pennsylvania State University Library*, University Park. 1,547,593 volumes; special collections: American literature, Australian art and literature, Bibles, American gift books, Latin American sociology, Pennsylvania history, Joseph Priestley, and Renaissance.

35. *University of Southern California Library*, Los Angeles. 1,524,066 volumes; special collections: American literature since 1850, cinema, international relations, education, philosophy, oceanography, and marine biology.

36. *Case-Western University Library*, Cleveland, Ohio. 1,476,629 volumes; special collections: bookplates, French Revolution and Napoleonic period, chemistry, geology, German language and literature, medieval history, Auduboniana, history of nursing, and history of printing.

37. *Brown University Library*, Providence, R.I. 1,428,298 volumes; specialized holdings for American poetry and plays, Dante, Abraham Lincoln, Walt Whitman, John Hay, Napoleon Bonaparte, Rhode Island history, Latin Americana, Italian literature, mathematics, and Egyptology; affiliated is John Carter Brown Library on early history of the Americas.

38. *Wayne State University Library*, Detroit, Mich. 1,405,035

volumes; special collections: science, philology, medicine, law, labor, folklore, Judaica, Michigan history, and children's literature.

39. *Southern Illinois University Library*, Carbondale. 1,400,000 volumes; special collections: Abraham Lincoln, Walt Whitman, James Joyce, D. H. Lawrence, Irish Renaissance, Ecuador, private presses, and American expatriates.

40. *University of Maryland Library*, College Park. 1,394,629 volumes; special collections: agriculture, American history, music, chemistry, engineering, Maryland, mathematics, and physics.

41. *University of Arizona Library*, Tucson. 1,393,772 volumes; special collections: fine arts, drama, southwestern Americana and anthropology, and private presses.

42. *Louisiana State University Library*, Baton Rouge. 1,391,141 volumes; special collections: history of lower Mississippi Valley, Civil War, rural sociology, Romance philology, sugar technology, petroleum engineering, plant pathology, micropaleontology, and Louisiana history.

43. *Massachusetts Institute of Technology Library*, Cambridge. 1,383,492 volumes; special collections: early history of aeronautics, civil engineering, electricity and magnetism, nineteenth-century glass manufacture, early works in mathematics and physics, microscopy, shipbuilding and naval history, and spectroscopy.

44. *Washington University Library*, St. Louis, Mo. 1,371,232 volumes; special collections: German language and literature, Romance languages and literature, classical archeology and numismatics, history of architecture, Mississippi Valley travel and exploration, and Eugene Field.

45. *University of Utah Library*, Salt Lake City. 1,311,772 volumes; special collections: Utah history, western Americana, social sciences, and Judaica.

46. *University of Rochester Library*, Rochester, N.Y. 1,232,324 volumes; special collections: early children's books, Thomas E. Dewey, nineteenth-century horticulture, Washington Irving, Henry James, Mark Twain, Thurlow Weed, and western New York state history.

47. *University of Kentucky Library*, Lexington. 1,216,049 volumes; special collections: English chapbooks, 1750–1850, French drama, 1600–1900, graphic arts, Kentucky authors, dime novels, southern and Ohio Valley history, Civil War, tobacco, western travel, and Spanish drama.

48. *University of Oklahoma Library*, Norman. 1,201,372 volumes; special collections: Oklahoma and Indian history, history of science and technology, Bible, and business history.

49. *Joint University Libraries*, Nashville, Tenn. 1,197,932 volumes; departmental collections for biology, chemistry, geology, and physics.

50. *University of Cincinnati Library*, Cincinnati, Ohio. 1,190,-741 volumes; special collections: Restoration drama, American Indians, modern Greek, classical languages, literature, archeology, chemistry, geology, and geography.

51. *University of Nebraska Library*, Lincoln. 1,185,429 volumes; special collections: Anne of Brittany, French Revolution, fine bindings, William of Ockham, Samuel Taylor Coleridge, and private presses.

52. *University of Georgia Library*, Athens. 1,158,047 volumes; special collections: Confederate imprints, Georgiana, and southern history.

53. *University of Connecticut Library*, Storrs. 1,154,172 volumes; special collections: Chilean history and literature, José Toribio Medina, modern German drama, early American periodicals, French Renaissance, and little magazines.

54. *University of Oregon Library*, Eugene. 1,146,199 volumes; special collections: Pacific northwest, early printed books, English and American literature.

55. *Temple University Library*, Philadelphia, Pa. 1,142,862 volumes; special collections: Joseph Conrad, Walter De la Mare, Richard Owen, and business history.

56. *Tulane University Library*, New Orleans, La. 1,120,836 volumes; special collections: George W. Cable, Lafcadio Hearn, Huey Long and Louisiana politics, early Louisiana history, southern history, economic history, and Swiss history.

57. *Dartmouth College Library*, Hanover, N.H. 1,064,907 vol-

umes; special collections: French, German, and English plays, American calligraphy, bookplates, Don Quixote, Italian dialects, mountaineering, New England railroads, New Hampshire history, polar regions, skiing, Spanish civilization, and Spanish plays.

58. *University of Notre Dame Library*, South Bend, Ind. 1,054,-533 volumes; special collections: Dante, Hiberniana, South America, and medieval history.

59. *Oklahoma State University Library*, Stillwater. 1,048,241 volumes; special subjects: agriculture, animal husbandry, engineering, entomology, chemistry, mathematics, Civil War, and Russian history, 1905–17.

60. *Brigham Young University Library*, Provo, Utah. 1,025,200 volumes; special collections: Victorian literature, Middle American linguistics, Welsh and Icelandic literature, Herman Melville, William Wordsworth, western Americana, Mormon history, and Robert Burns.

61. *Purdue University Library*, Lafayette, Ind. 1,011,430 volumes; special collections: English and American literature, glass, industrial management, Indiana authors, Charles Major, Bruce Rogers, New Harmony Community, Indiana history, and technology history.

62. *University of Tennessee Library*, Knoxville. 1,007,995 volumes; special collections: Estes Kefauver, Tennesseana, nineteenth-century American fiction, Cherokee Indians, early voyages and travels, Congreve, and radiation biology.

63. *Emory University Library*, Atlanta, Ga. 1,000,000 volumes; special collections of Wesleyana and Methodist history, Civil War history, southern literary history, southern economic history, Confederate imprints, and American history.

64. *Boston University Library*, Boston, Mass. 941,109 volumes; special collections: Americana, Lincolniana, history of chemistry, African studies, philatelic literature, and Methodist church history.

65. *Florida State University Library*, Tallahassee. 922,623 volumes; special collections: maps, early Americana, Florida history, music, and children's literature.

66. *Washington State University Library*, Pullman. 892,658

volumes; special collections: Pacific northwest history, western Americana, and human relations.

67. *Iowa State University Library*, Ames. 891,309 volumes; special strength in journals in basic and applied fields of physical and biological sciences.

68. *St. Louis University Library*, St. Louis, Mo. 890,140 volumes; special collections: George Edward Follansbee, Pierre Jean DeSmet, Jesuitica, Vatican manuscript library microfilms, automatic merchandising, and Academy of Science of St. Louis.

69. *Catholic University of America Library*, Washington, D.C. 849,723 volumes; special collections: anthropology, architecture, arctic botany, canon law, Catholic Americana, Celtic, Greek, and Latin, library science, maps, nursing, medieval studies, patristics, Portuguese and Spanish, psychology, Semitics, and theology.

70. *Texas A. and M. University Library*, College Station. 768,-366 volumes; special strength for agriculture, veterinary medicine, physical sciences, engineering, nuclear engineering, transportation, water, and hydrology.

71. *Georgetown University Library*, Washington, D.C. 722,632 volumes; special collections: Carnegie Endowment for International Peace Library, Washingtoniana, Germanic language and literature, classical literature, archeology, political history, international law, Spanish American books, and public speaking.

72. *Howard University Library*, Washington, D.C. 665,659 volumes; special collections: Afro-Americana, Southeast Asia, and theater.

73. *Wesleyan University Library*, Middletown, Conn. 657,217 volumes; special collections: twentieth-century poetry, nineteenth-century Methodist literature, classics, and rare editions of English literature.

PUBLIC LIBRARIES (by size of collections)

74. *New York Public Library*, New York City. 7,375,545 volumes including branches); constitutes the third largest American library and one of the most important. It has scores of noteworthy special collections, among them sections devoted to early

Americana, art and architecture, economics, music, Orientalia, theater history, Slavonic and Judaic literature, English and American literature, science and technology, genealogy, maps, prints, and newspapers.

75. *Chicago Public Library*, Chicago, Ill. 4,796,473 volumes; special collections: Civil War, Franco-German War, American Indians, Western travel, World's Columbian Exposition, Chicago, 1893, and patents.

76. *Los Angeles Public Library*, Los Angeles, Calif. 3,824,897 volumes; special collections: accounting, American Indians, California and southwest, cookbooks, criminology, Czechoslovakia, Theodore Dreiser, genealogy, Mexicana, orchestral scores, printing, shorthand history, theater, women's suffrage, and World Wars I and II.

77. *Cleveland Public Library*, Cleveland, Ohio. 3,273, 948 volumes; special collections: White collection of folklore, Orientalia, chess and checkers, and others on architecture, baseball, Cleveland history, early children's books, Judaica, philately, tobacco, and British, French, and Latin American history.

78. *Boston Public Library*, Boston, Mass. 3,092,424 volumes; numerous special collections, including Shakespeareana and other Elizabethan literature, Spanish and Portuguese literature, history of printing, theater, music, women, mathematics, navigation, Americana, West Indies, Benjamin Franklin, George Washington, and John Adams.

79. *Brooklyn Public Library*, Brooklyn, N.Y. 2,951,407 volumes; special collections: chess and checkers, Civil War, costume, education, fire protection, early juveniles, and Walt Whitman.

80. *Cincinnati Public Library*, Cincinnati, Ohio. 2,703,696 volumes; special collections: Cincinnati and Ohio Valley, Bible, religion, art and music, genealogy and local history, Lafcadio Hearn, and Mississippi River Valley.

81. *Free Library of Philadelphia*, Philadelphia, Pa. 2,661,957 volumes; numerous special collections in art, music, business and industry, literature, social sciences, history, and rare books.

82. *Buffalo Public Library*, Buffalo, N.Y. 2,628,589 volumes;

special collections: American sheet music, Bruce Rogers, costume, early railroad surveys, Huckleberry Finn, literary autographs, Shakers, and private presses.
83. *Enoch Pratt Free Library*, Baltimore, Md. 2,219,965 volumes; special collections: American Negro poetry, Baltimore views, book illustration, bookplates, insurance, H. L. Mencken, Edgar Allan Poe, political cartoons, philately, and war posters.
84. *Milwaukee Public Library*, Milwaukee, Wis. 2,145,825 volumes; special collections: trans-Mississippi history, American history, patents, genealogy, and religion.
85. *Carnegie Library of Pittsburgh*, Pittsburgh, Pa. 2,143,225 volumes; special collections: architecture and design, costume, Cromwelliana, Pittsburgh newspapers, trade catalogs, Wales, women, and World War I.
86. *Detroit Public Library*, Detroit, Mich. 2,108,301 volumes; special collections: automotive history, midwestern history, cookery, exploration, genealogy, labor, metal work, music, Negroes in performing arts, patents, and slavery.
87. *Public Library of the District of Columbia*, Washington, D.C. 2,104,195 volumes; special collections: Washingtoniana, illustrators, and Georgetown material.
88. *Seattle Public Library*, Seattle, Wash. 1,496,061 volumes; special collections: aeronautics and Pacific northwest Americana.
89. *St. Louis Public Library*, St. Louis, Mo. 1,430,042 volumes; special collections: human justice, philosophy, architecture, costume, ethics and religion, Methodist church, genealogy, historical children's books, and patents.

REFERENCE LIBRARIES (alphabetically arranged)

90. *American Antiquarian Society Library*, Worcester, Mass. 750,000 volumes; special collections: newspapers, American imprints before 1820, Americana to 1876, early American juveniles, early American cookbooks, genealogy, United States local history, American almanacs, bookplates, circus memorabilia, American fiction to 1875, Hawaiiana, directories, western narratives, psalmody, songsters, and early American sheet music.

91. *Center for Research Libraries,* Chicago, Ill. 2,715,000 volumes; special collections: chemical and biological serials, college catalogs, foreign newspapers, state documents, foreign dissertations, and textbooks.

92. *Folger Shakespeare Library,* Washington, D.C. 250,000 volumes; special collections: Shakespeare, Shakespeare's contemporaries, and history of English civilization in sixteenth and seventeenth centuries.

93. *Henry E. Huntington Library,* San Marino, Calif. 480,000 volumes, 3,000,000 manuscripts; special collections: incunabula, American history and literature, western Americana and Californiana, British history and literature, and history of printing.

94. *John Crerar Library,* Chicago, Ill. 1,100,000 volumes; special collections: medicine, aeronautics, physiology, bacteriology, pediatrics, chemistry, physics, geology, botany, zoology, engineering, cremation, cookbooks, and international congresses and expositions.

95. *Library of Congress,* Washington, D.C. 15,660,523 volumes; book collections are encyclopedic in character, but strongest in history, public law and legislation, political and other social sciences, language and literature, science and technology, music, incunabula, Oriental and Slavic literature, and bibliography.

96. *Linda Hall Library,* Kansas City, Mo. 500,000 volumes; special collections: science and technology, including serials, history, incunabula, sixteenth- to nineteenth-century books, and seventeenth- to eighteenth-century journals.

97. *National Agricultural Library,* Washington, D.C. 1,500,000 volumes; worldwide coverage, currently and retrospectively, of agriculture and related biological and chemical sciences.

98. *National Library of Medicine,* Bethesda, Md. 1,500,000 volumes; comprehensive coverage, currently and retrospectively, of world literature for medicine and related fields.

99. *Newberry Library,* Chicago, Ill. 925,000 volumes, extensive printed and manuscript holdings related to humanities and social sciences; special collections include American Indian, history of printing, incunabula, art, music, American and English history

and literature, Portuguese discovery and exploration, Renaissance in England and Europe, French history to 1794, Philippine Islands, cartography, and genealogy.

100. *Pierpont Morgan Library*, New York, N.Y. 70,000 volumes; special collections: medieval and Renaissance manuscripts, incunabula, autograph letters and documents, bookbindings, master drawings, Rembrandt etchings, early mezzotints, Mesopotamian seals and tablets, Egyptian, Greek, and other papyri.

SPECIAL SERVICES OF LIBRARIES

Books and periodicals needed for research, but not available locally, may often be obtained by borrowing from libraries elsewhere. An extensive system of interlibrary loans has developed among libraries in the United States. Such interchanges number hundreds of thousands of volumes each year. Loans are restricted in general to books required for research purposes. A majority of libraries follow the American Library Association's "Interlibrary Loan Code," which establishes certain rules to govern the service, and use a standard "Interlibrary Loan Request" like the one included here.

If books wanted are rare, difficult to transport, or required for long periods of time, photographic reproductions may be preferable to interlibrary loans. Least expensive, but needing a reading machine or projector for use, is microfilm, which commonly comes in 35 mm. rolls or in "microfiche" strips. The larger libraries throughout the country maintain photographic laboratories capable of supplying microfilm copies on order at about five cents per exposure. For full-size production, Xerox copies, black on white, are excellent and can also be obtained from libraries, at a cost of about ten cents per exposure. Increasingly popular in libraries are do-it-yourself coin-operated machines, making it easy and simple for the reader to produce his own photocopies of pages from books, periodicals, and other materials.

Preliminary, of course, to obtaining a book on interlibrary loan or ordering a photoreproduction of it, a copy must be located. Innumerable aids are available for the purpose. The most valuable single tool is the National Union Catalog in the Library of

A INTERLIBRARY LOAN REQUEST

REQUEST

According to the A.L.A. Interlibrary Loan Code

Date of request:

Call-No.

REFERENCE DEPARTMENT
LIBRARY
UNIVERSITY OF ILLINOIS AT URBANA - CHAMPAIGN
URBANA, ILLINOIS 61801

REPORTS: Checked by

SENT BY: Library rate

Charges $ _____ Insured for $ _____

Date sent _____

DUE _____

For use of _____ Status _____ Dept. _____

Author (or periodical title, vol. and year)

RESTRICTIONS: For use in library only

Copying not permitted

Title (with author & pages for periodical articles) (Incl. edition, place & date) This edition only

NOT SENT BECAUSE: In use

Non circulating Not owned

Verified in (or source of reference)

Estimated Cost of: Microfilm _____

Hard copy _____

If non-circulating, please supply Microfilm Hard copy if cost does not exceed $ _____

BORROWING LIBRARY RECORD:

Date received _____

Date returned _____

By Library rate

Postage
enclosed $ _____ Insured for $ _____

RENEWALS: (Request and report on sheet C)

Requested on _____

Renewed to _____
(or period of renewal)

AUTHORIZED BY: _____
(FULL NAME) Title _____

Note: The receiving library
assumes responsibility for
notification of non-receipt.

Congress, Washington, which records the locations of more than 16,000,000 books in some 2,500 American libraries. A substantial portion of the National Union Catalog has been published in book form and may be found in the principal libraries of the country. For two other types of material, extremely useful works are the *Union List of Serials in Libraries of the United States and Canada* (New York: Wilson, 1966), locating files of 157,000 periodicals in about 950 United States and Canadian libraries; and the Library of Congress's *Newspapers on Microfilm* (Washington, D.C.: Library of Congress, 1967), locating files of 21,700 American and foreign newspapers. Thousands of other finding aids are listed in Downs's *Resources of American Libraries, a Bibliographical Guide* (Chicago: Amer. Library Assoc., 1951–72).

2
Key to the Library: The Catalog

The typical library catalog is an alphabetical index in card form to the books and other publications in the library. It serves as a guide to the book collection in the same way that an index guides one to the contents of a book. The catalog is the library user's chief means of discovering and locating material in a library; without it, chaos would prevail.

The most characteristic arrangement of library catalogs is in dictionary form, with authors, titles, and subjects all filed in one alphabet, though it is not uncommon to find the cards listing subjects in a separate alphabet. With few exceptions, every book has at least three catalog entries: under the author's name, under the title of the book, and under subjects. Not infrequently, the number of cards for a single book is larger; for example, if the work deals with more than one subject, a subject card will be filed under each topic. Also, there may be additional cards for joint authors, editors, compilers, translators, illustrators, pseudonyms, and series.

The catalog card, usually printed by the Library of Congress, contains a variety of other information, such as the author's birth and death dates, edition, place and date of publication, publisher, number of pages or volumes, size of book, notes on illustrations, maps, bibliographies, and so on, and sometimes a table of contents. Also included, at the foot of the cards, are "tracings," showing the subjects under which the book is listed, and classification symbols, usually both Library of Congress and Dewey Decimal classifications.

The majority of books are by individual authors. Many publications, however, are issued by associations, societies, institutions, and governmental bodies, for example, American Medical Association, Columbia University, Ford Foundation, or the United States Bureau of the Census. In such instances, the author is considered to be the organization itself, rather than the often unknown persons who prepared the publication. Thus the library catalog contains in their proper alphabetical sequence cards for "corporate authors" or "corporate entries."

Another complication for the cataloger is anonymous works. Occasionally the author's name does not appear in a book and may or may not be discoverable. Such a book is entered in the catalog under its title, as are periodicals and newspapers and works of multiple authorship.

Following are examples of various forms of library catalog cards:

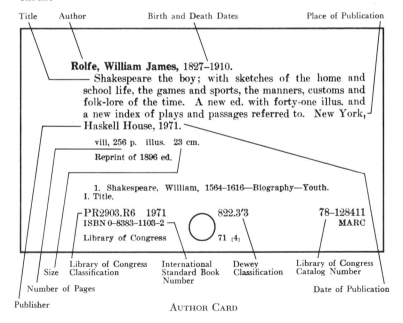

Title   Author   Birth and Death Dates   Place of Publication

Rolfe, William James, 1827–1910.

Shakespeare the boy; with sketches of the home and school life, the games and sports, the manners, customs and folk-lore of the time. A new ed. with forty-one illus. and a new index of plays and passages referred to. New York, Haskell House, 1971.

viii, 256 p. illus. 23 cm.

Reprint of 1896 ed.

1. Shakespeare, William, 1564–1616—Biography—Youth. I. Title.

PR2903.R6   1971   822.3′3   78–128411

ISBN 0–8383–1103–2   MARC

Library of Congress   71 ₍4₎

       Library of Congress   International   Dewey   Library of Congress

Size   Classification   Standard Book   Classification   Catalog Number

                            Number

Number of Pages   Date of Publication

Publisher   AUTHOR CARD

Our National Parks

Muir, John, 1838–1914.
    Our national parks. New York, AMS Press ₁1970₁

    370 p. illus., map. 23 cm.

    Reprint of the 1901 ed.

    1. National parks and reserves—U. S.   I. Title.

E160.M95   1970b   917.87′52′04   70–120568
ISBN 0–404–04516–2   MARC

Library of Congress   71 ₁2₁

Title Card

MORMONS AND MORMONISM

Mayhew, Henry, 1812–1887.
    The Mormons; or Latter-day Saints: a contemporary his-

tory. New York, AMS Press ₁1971₁

    326 p. illus. 22 cm. $12.50

    Reprint of the 1852 ed.

    1. Mormons and Mormonism.   2. Smith, Joseph, 1805–1844.
I. Title.

BX8611.M3   1971   289.3′09   71–134398
ISBN 0–404–08440–0   MARC

Library of Congress   72 ₁4₁

Subject Card

Taliaferro, William Hay, 1895–   ed.
    Medicine and the war. Edited by William H. Taliaferro.
Freeport, N. Y., Books for Libraries Press [1972, c1944]
    vii, 193 p. illus. 23 cm. (Essay index reprint series)
    Original ed. issued in series: **Charles R. Walgreen Foundation lec**tures.
    Includes bibliographies.
    CONTENTS: Historical background and introduction, by A. B.
Luckhardt.—Food and the war, by P. R. Cannon.—Chemotherapy, by
E. M. K. Geiling.—Malaria, by W. H. Taliaferro.—Insects, disease,
and modern transportation, by C. G. Huff.—Shock and blood substitutes, by A. Brunschwig.—Aviation medicine, by H. T. Ricketts.—
Neurological and psychological effects of cerebral injuries, by A. E.
Walker and W. C. Halstead.—Psychiatry and the war, by D.
Slight.—Chemical warfare, by F. C. McLean.

                    (Continued on next card)
                                                    70–37923
                    72 [4]

EDITOR CARD

Ecclesiastical History Society, London.
    Popular belief and practice; papers read at the ninth
summer meeting and the tenth winter meeting of the Ecclesiastical History Society. Edited by G. J. Cuming and
Derek Baker. Cambridge [Eng.] University Press, 1972.

    xii, 330 p. 23 cm. (Studies in church history, 8)   B***

    Includes bibliographical references.

    1. Theology—Addresses, essays, lectures. 2. Religion—Addresses,
essays, lectures.   I. Cuming, G. J., ed. II. Baker, Derek, ed. III.
Title. IV. Series: Studies in church history (London), 8.

BR141.S84   vol. 8   270′.08 s [201′.1]   77–155583
[BR50]   MARC
ISBN 0–521–08220–X

Library of Congress   72 [10–2]

CORPORATE AUTHOR CARD

Getting around Edinburgh: the complete guide for visitors.
24th ed. Edinburgh, Albyn Press ₁1971₁

   64 p. illus., maps., ports. 19 cm. £0.18   B 71–29551

   1. Edinburgh—Description—Guide-books.

DA890.E3G3 1971   914.14′45   72–183315
ISBN 0–284–79545–3   MARC

Library of Congress   72 ₁4₁

TITLE ENTRY CARD

Iowa journal of social work.
  ₁Iowa City₁ University of Iowa, School of Social Work.

    v. illus., plans. 28 cm. quarterly.

   1. Social service—Periodicals.   I. Iowa. University. School of
Social Work.

HV1.I 66   361′.005   79–613135

Library of Congress   71 ₁2₁

PERIODICAL CARD

   The library cataloger is constantly faced with decisions about
the most logical and appropriate subjects under which to enter a
given book. From this problem arises the practice of using "cross-
references," that is, referring from forms not used to those that

Ioann Damaskin, Saint
   see
Joannes, of Damascus, Saint.

LIBRARY OF CONGRESS REFERENCE

Users of depository catalogs should note that references may be to Library of
Congress secondary entries which do not appear as headings in depository catalogs.

X 71–5192

International Labor Conference.   48th,
   Geneva, 1964
      see also
   Convention concerning employment policy.

LIBRARY OF CONGRESS REFERENCE

Users of depository catalogs should note that references may be to Library of
Congress secondary entries which do not appear as headings in depository catalogs.

71

CROSS-REFERENCE CARDS

```
        Philately and philatelists,      see
    Postage-stamps--Collectors and collecting;
        Revenue-stamps




                        ◯
```

CROSS-REFERENCE CARD

are used, and from forms used to related headings where additional works are listed. A similar question arises when a choice must be made between forms of an author's name. These matters are treated in the library catalog as shown above.

In large libraries with numerous books on specific subjects, there are subdivisions under major subjects, as for example:

Water

Water — Analysis	Water — Laws and Legislation
Water — Bacteriology	Water — Physiological Effect
Water — Composition	Water — Pollution
Water — Distribution	Water — Purification
Water — Electrolysis	Water — Softening
Water — Fluoridation	Water — Underground

If the reader is interested only in the literature dealing with water fluoridation, therefore, he goes directly to that subdivision under the general heading of water, and saves a substantial amount of time that would otherwise be spent in searching through hundreds or even thousands of references irrelevant for his purpose.

CLASSIFICATION

The idea of classifying knowledge has intrigued great minds of various eras, among them Aristotle, Francis Bacon, and Thomas Jefferson. Until Linnaeus in the eighteenth century developed a scientific system of classification, botanical and zoological research was at a standstill, lacking logic and method. Classification calls for the systematic arrangement of objects, ideas, books, and so on, into rational groups or classes.

Classification as applied to libraries is intended chiefly to organize books and other materials by subject fields or types to facilitate ready access to them by library users. Theoretically, a good classification scheme should bring together everything to be found on a given subject. Practically, this goal is unattainable, because the same book may relate to several different subjects, but can only be classified in one; also, information on the desired topic will be found scattered among parts of other books, encyclopedia and periodical articles, and other sources.

A majority of libraries in the United States and Canada use the Dewey Decimal Classification, devised by a dynamic and versatile nineteenth-century American librarian, Melvil Dewey. The scheme has been revised frequently since first introduced in 1876. The essential concept of dividing all knowledge into ten major groups or classes, however, has remained unchanged. According to tradition, Dewey conceived of his ten principal classes as proceeding according to the following logical sequence:

First, a catchall class of general works, such as encyclopedias, bibliographies, and general periodicals, which do not fit into any of the other classes
Second, Philosophy (conduct of life)
Third, Religion (nature and meaning of life)
Fourth, Social Sciences (man's relations with his fellows)
Fifth, Linguistics (communication with his fellows)
Sixth, Pure Science (observation of his environment)
Seventh, Applied Science (manipulation of his environment)
Eighth, Arts and Recreation (enrichment of life)
Ninth, Literature (thoughts about life)
Tenth, History (examination of the past)

Each of the ten main classes is divided further into ten classes, for a total of 100, and each of the 100 by ten for a total of 1,000. By adding a decimal point and numbers after the first three digits, provision may be made for thousands of additional subdivisions, representing minute subjects. The major classes and principal subdivisions of the Dewey Decimal Classification are as follows:

000 GENERAL WORKS
    010 Bibliography
    020 Library science
    030 General encyclopedias
    040 General collected essays
    050 General periodicals
    060 General societies
    070 Newspaper journalism
    080 Collected works
    090 Manuscripts and rare
        books

100 PHILOSOPHY
    110 Metaphysics
    120 Metaphysical theories
    130 Branches of psychology
    140 Philosophical topics
    150 General psychology
    160 Logic
    170 Ethics
    180 Ancient and medieval
        philosophy
    190 Modern philosophy

200 RELIGION
    210 Natural theology
    220 Bible
    230 Doctrinal theology
    240 Devotional and practical
    250 Pastoral theology
    260 Christian church
    270 Christian church history
    280 Christian churches and
        sects
    290 Other religions

300 SOCIAL SCIENCES
    310 Statistics

320 Political science
330 Economics
340 Law
350 Public administration
360 Social welfare
370 Education
380 Public services and
    utilities
390 Customs and folklore

400 LANGUAGE
    410 Comparative linguistics
    420 English and Anglo-Saxon
    430 Germanic languages
    440 French, Provençal,
        Catalan
    450 Italian, Rumanian
    460 Spanish, Portuguese
    470 Latin and other Italic
    480 Classical and modern
        Greek
    490 Other languages

500 PURE SCIENCES
    510 Mathematics
    520 Astronomy
    530 Physics
    540 Chemistry and allied
        sciences
    550 Earth sciences
    560 Paleontology
    570 Anthropology and
        biology
    580 Botanical sciences
    590 Zoological sciences

600 TECHNOLOGY
    610 Medical sciences

620 Engineering
630 Agriculture
640 Home economics
650 Business
660 Chemical technology
670 Manufactures
680 Other manufactures
690 Building construction

700   THE ARTS
710 Landscape and civic art
720 Architecture
730 Sculpture
740 Drawing and decorative arts
750 Painting
760 Prints and printmaking
770 Photography
780 Music
790 Recreation

800   LITERATURE
810 American literature in English

820 English and Old English
830 Germanic literatures
840 French, Provençal, Catalan
850 Italian, Rumanian
860 Spanish, Portuguese
870 Latin and other Italic literatures
880 Classical and modern Greek
890 Other literatures

900   HISTORY
910 Geography, travels, description
920 Biography
930 Ancient history
940 Europe
950 Asia
960 Africa
970 North America
980 South America
990 Other parts of world

An example of the operation of the plan for subdivision is American literature:

810   General American literature
811   American poetry
812   American drama
813   American fiction
814   American essays
815   American oratory
816   American letters
817   American satire and humor
818   American miscellany
819   Canadian English literature

Use of the decimal point is illustrated by the classification for zoology, 591:

591.1   Animal physiology
591.2   Animal pathology

> 591.3   Animal maturation
> 591.4   Animal morphology
> 591.5   Animal ecology
> 591.6   Economic zoology
> 591.8   Microscopic zoology
> 591.9   Zoogeography

The second most widely used classification system adopted by American libraries is the Library of Congress scheme, first developed in 1897. This system adopts twenty-one letters of the alphabet to represent the principal branches of knowledge and then proceeds to subdivide further by adding second letters and numbers up to 9999. The almost infinite number of subdivisions thus achieved is a particular advantage to large research libraries, and to libraries which have ambitions to reach great size. A brief outline of the Library of Congress Classification System follows:

A	General Work—Polygraphy
B	Philosophy—Religion
C	History—Auxiliary Sciences
D	History and Topography (except America)
E-F	America
G	Geography—Anthropology
H	Social Sciences
J	Political Science
K	Law
L	Education
M	Music
N	Fine Arts
P	Language and Literature
Q	Science
R	Medicine
S	Agriculture—Plant and Animal Industry
T	Technology
U	Military Science
V	Naval Science
Z	Bibliography and Library Science

To illustrate subdivisions under the Library of Congress plan, P represents language and literature, PQ stands for Romance literature, and the numbers PQ6001-8929 are reserved for divisions of Spanish literature, thus providing immense opportunities for a detailed classification scheme for libraries with extensive holdings in the field.

A special aspect of library classification is the author number or "Cutter number" (named for its inventor) added to the subject classification. The author number is a feature of the Library of Congress system of call numbers and is generally added to Dewey numbers, especially in large libraries. Essentially, the author or Cutter number is a numerical shorthand for the author's name, assisting in arranging books alphabetically by author within a subject. It also has the advantage of assigning to each book in the library an individual and distinctive call number, not held by any other book.

3

Practical Use of Reference Books

Later in sections of this guide are listed and described briefly hundreds of reference books—comprehensive works, usually highly condensed and organized to present in convenient form large quantities of facts and other information. No attempt has been made to present an exhaustive bibliography of reference materials. Thousands of similar works exist. The prime criteria for selection were: (1) up-to-dateness; (2) coverage of subjects of current interest and importance; (3) accuracy, reliability, and thoroughness. Numerous highly specialized titles of use to scholars in a narrow field were omitted for the most part because of space limitations.

To the person who is unaccustomed to using libraries, the number of reference-type books may appear overwhelming. Naturally, there is considerable duplication, overlapping, and repetition among them, and frequently the answer to a specific question can be found in various sources. As a general rule, however, no two books are alike, and each of the titles in the ensuing sections was compiled or written to serve a particular purpose, to fill a recognized need, and to contribute something distinctive to its field.

FINDING OUT ALL ABOUT A SUBJECT
The exploration of any major subject may lead one into almost endless byways and involve the use of an extensive collection of reference tools. Assume, for example, that one wants to know

something about practically every aspect of Japan—its history, civilization, geography, government, economy, religion, population, social life, education, industry, agriculture, scientific achievements, fine arts, music, literature, and so forth. The most logical place to begin the researches would be the catalog of the library in which one is working. Under the subject of Japan and related topics, the book and periodical resources of the library would be recorded.

This first step, however, is merely the beginning of any thorough investigation. No library catalog can hope to list all the sources of information on a given subject. For background purposes, a good general work is *Japan: Its Land, People and Culture* (Tokyo: Japanese Ministry of Finance, 1964). Here are some additional references for Japan:

1. A partial record of books published in Japan will be found in the British Museum's *General Catalogue of Printed Books;* Library of Congress's *The National Union Catalog;* and the *Cumulative Book Index, a World List of Books in the English Language;* and of current Japanese imprints in the National Diet Library's *Japanese National Bibliography,* published annually since 1948. Periodicals and newspapers issued in Japan are listed in the *Newspaper Press Directory, Ulrich's Periodicals Directory, Editor & Publisher International Year Book,* and the *Union List of Serials in Libraries of the United States and Canada.*

2. Current events in Japan are covered by the *New York Times Index* and the London *Times' Index.*

3. For the Japanese language, a standard work is *Kenkyusha's New English-Japanese and Japanese-English Dictionary* (Tokyo: Kenkyusha, 1954–60, 2 v.).

4. For Japanese geography, map sources are numerous, including such standard atlases as *Life Pictorial Atlas of the World, National Geographic Atlas of the World, Rand McNally Cosmopolitan World Atlas,* and *Times Atlas of the World.* Gazetteer-type information is included in the *Columbia-Lippincott Gazetteer of the World* and *Webster's Geographical Dictionary.* Several series of guidebooks cover Japan, for example, Sydney Clark's *"All the Best" Travel Books, Fodor's Modern Guides,* and *McKay's Guides.*

Even more authoritative is the Japan Travel Bureau's *The New Official Guide: Japan.*

5. Biographical data for prominent citizens of Japan are in many general compilations; among them: *Webster's Biographical Dictionary, Biography Index, Current Biography, World Biography, International Who's Who,* and *Japan Biographical Encyclopedia and Who's Who.*

6. For background purposes and broad general treatment, encyclopedia articles on Japan, such as those in the *Americana, Britannica,* and *Collier's* are an excellent beginning, dealing with geography, history, population, economic factors, natural resources, manufactures, government, and international relations.

7. Statistical and other up-to-date information on Japan is contained in a number of yearbooks, for example: *Americana Annual, Britannica Book of the Year, Collier's Yearbook, New International Year Book, Information Please Almanac, Statesman's Year-Book, United Nations Statistical Year Book,* and *Japan Statistical Yearbook.*

8. The history of Japan is dealt with in the several series of Cambridge histories, *Ancient, Medieval,* and *Modern,* Langer's *Encyclopedia of World History,* Larned's *New Larned History for Ready Reference,* Palmer's *Dictionary of Modern History,* Keller's *Dictionary of Dates,* and the American Historical Association's *Guide to Historical Literature.*

9. Specialized reference books relating in part to Japan are available in many fields. Examples include the following:

AGRICULTURE—*Biological and Agricultural Index* and Van Royen's *Atlas of the World's Resources*

ANIMALS—Walker's *Mammals of the World*

ART—*Art Index* and *McGraw-Hill's Encyclopedia of World Art*

AVIATION—*Jane's All the World's Aircraft* and *World Aviation Directory*

COINS—Carson's *Coins of the World*

COLLEGES AND UNIVERSITIES—*International Handbook of Universities* and *World of Learning*

COSTUME AND DRESS—Hiler's *Bibliography of Costume*

ECONOMICS—*Oxford Economic Atlas of the World*

EDUCATION—*Education Index*

ENGINEERING—*Applied Science & Technology Index*

FLAGS—Carr's *Flags of the World* and Great Britain Admiralty's *Flags of All Nations*

FOLKLORE—*Funk and Wagnalls Standard Dictionary of Folklore, Mythology, and Legend*

GOVERNMENT—*Political Handbook of the World, Statesman's Year-Book*, and *Worldmark Encyclopedia of the Nations*

LABOR—International Labour Office's *Yearbook of Labour Statistics*

MEDICINE—*Index Medicus*

MOVING PICTURES—*International Motion Picture Almanac*

MUSIC—*Grove's Dictionary of Music and Musicians* and *Music Index*

MYTHOLOGY—Gray's *Mythology of All Races* and *Larousse Encyclopedia of Mythology*

POSTAGE STAMPS—*Scott's Standard Postage Stamp Catalogue* and *Standard Catalogue of Postage Stamps of the World*

RACES—Coon's *Origin of Races* and Hammerton's *Peoples of All Nations*

RAILROADS—Sampson's *World Railways*

RELIGION—Hastings's *Encyclopedia of Religion and Ethics* and *Sacred Books of the East*

REPTILES—Ditmar's *Reptiles of the World*

SCIENCE AND TECHNOLOGY—*Applied Science and Technology Index* and *McGraw-Hill's Encyclopedia of Science and Technology*

SHIPS AND SHIPPING—*Merchant Ships, World Built*

SPORTS—Menke's *Encyclopedia of Sports*

TEXTILES—American Fabrics' *Encyclopedia of Textiles*

WEATHER—Kendrew's *The Climates of the Continents*

For further research, the following bibliographies are recommended: Association for Asian Studies' *Bibliography of Asian Studies*, Herschel Webb's *Research in Japanese Sources*, Bernard Silberman's *Japan and Korea, a Critical Bibliography*, and Hyman Kublin's *What Shall I Read on Japan?*

QUESTIONS FOR THE REFERENCE LIBRARIAN

To illustrate the types of queries which can be answered on a variety of topics from standard reference books, here are typical examples of questions asked of reference librarians, and their solutions, arranged by subjects:

ABBREVIATIONS. "I want to find the symbols for the chemical elements and also symbols used in mathematics and astronomy." See Matthews's *Dictionary of Abbreviations.*

ACCOUNTING. "What is a good system of accounting to use for a retail furniture store?" See Williams's *Encyclopedia of Accounting Systems.*

ADVERTISING. "Where may I find information about mailing lists for an advertising campaign?" See Aspley's *Sales Promotion Handbook* or Melcher's *Printing and Promotion Handbook.*

AFRICA. "I want a good up-to-date summary of facts about the Ivory Coast." See the *West Africa Annual,* latest year.

AGRICULTURE. "What are the modern scientific methods for irrigation in agriculture?" See the U.S. Department of Agriculture's 1955 *Yearbook* on "Water."

AMERICAN HISTORY. "What were the boundaries of the State of Franklin, 1779–96?" See Adams's *Atlas of American History.* "Where can I find a chronological list, with brief descriptions, of early American inventions?" See Morris's *Encyclopedia of American History.*

"What were the major events of President James Madison's administration, 1810–18?" See Carruth's *Encyclopedia of American Facts and Dates.*

AMERICAN LITERATURE. "I am looking for a review of Eugene O'Neill's plays and a discussion of his influence on the American theatre." See Spiller's *Literary History of the United States.*

"Was Johnny Appleseed a real person or a fictional character?" See Herzberg's *Reader's Encyclopedia of American Literature.*

"How does American English differ from English English?"

See *Cambridge History of American Literature* chapter on "The English Language in America," H. L. Mencken's *The American Language,* and W. A. Craigie's *Dictionary of American English.*

ANTIQUES. "When and where was Sandwich glass made?" See Boger's *Dictionary of Antiques.*

ARCHITECTURE. "What buildings were designed by Sir Christopher Wren, noted seventeenth- and eighteenth-century English architect?" See Briggs's *Everyman's Concise Encyclopedia of Architecture.*

ART. "While on a trip to Alaska, I became interested in collecting Eskimo carvings. Is there a good article on the subject, with illustrations?" See *McGraw-Hill's Encyclopedia of World Art.*

"I want to see a biographical sketch of the modern American painter Andrew N. Wyeth." See *Who's Who in American Art.* "Where can I find a reproduction in color of Leonardo da Vinci's painting 'The Virgin of the Rocks'?" See *Praeger Picture Encyclopedia of Art.*

AUTOMOBILES. "How many motor vehicles have been registered in the United States each year since 1900?" See *Automobile Facts and Figures,* latest edition.

AVIATION. "What types of aircraft are being manufactured in the Soviet Union?" See *Jane's All the World's Aircraft.*

BIBLE. "What is the theological interpretation of the Holy Ghost or Holy Spirit?" See *Interpreter's Dictionary of the Bible,* Hastings's *Dictionary of the Bible,* or *Catholic Encyclopedia.* "Where in the Bible does Ruth's famous declaration 'Whither thou goest, I will go' appear?" See Strong or Young *Bible Concordance.*

BIBLIOGRAPHY. "Where can I find a list of newly published books on frontier and pioneer life?" See recent volumes of *Cumulative Book Index* or *Subject Guide to Books in Print.* "I have inherited an Old Bible, printed in London by Barker, dated 1580; what is its market value?" See *American Book Prices Current* (1957) and *Book Auction Records* (1954).

BIOGRAPHY. "Were Stephen Vincent Benét and William Rose Benét related?" See Kunitz's *Twentieth Century Authors.*

"I want to find an authoritative account of the life of James Boswell, biographer of Samuel Johnson." See the *Dictionary of National Biography.*

"Where may I see biographical data on John C. Bailar, Jr., noted chemist?" See *American Men of Science* or *Who's Who in America.*

BOATING. "I am considering buying a houseboat and want to know about different types." See Hutchinson's *All about Boats.*

CAMPS. "What public campgrounds are available in Oregon parks and forests?" See *Sunset Western Campsite Directory.*

CANADA. "Why does Canada have two official languages, English and French?" See *Encyclopedia of Canada* or *Encyclopedia Canadiana,* under "Bilingualism."

COINS. "I want to see descriptions, illustrations, and values of U.S. silver dollars from the first ones in 1794 to 1935." See Raymond's *Standard Catalogue of United States Coins* or Yeoman's *Guide Book of United States Coins.*

COLLEGES AND UNIVERSITIES. "Where can I find out about schools of forestry?" See Fine's *American College Counselor,* or *American Universities and Colleges,* or Lovejoy's *College Guide.*

"What is the general organization of the University of Paris?" See *International Handbook of Universities* or *World of Learning.*

COLOR. "Exactly what shade is the color called 'peacock blue'?" See Ridgway's *Color Standards* or Maerz and Paul's *Dictionary of Color.*

COSTUME AND DRESS. "I am writing a research paper on U.S. military costume of various periods; what are some sources of information?" See Hiler's *Bibliography of Costume.*

DANCE. "In what ballets did the famous Russian danseuse Anna Pavlova make her reputation?" See Beaumont's *Complete Book of Ballets.*

DATES. "What are some notable anniversaries falling on July 4?" See Mirkin's *When Did It Happen?*

GAMES. "Where can I find out about interesting mathematical puzzles?" See Hindman's *Complete Book of Games.*

GEOGRAPHY. "Where is Antarctica in relation to South America, Africa, and Australia?" See *Rand McNally Cosmopolitan World Atlas.*

"Where are U.S. national parks and monuments located?" See *National Geographical Atlas of the Fifty United States.*

GOVERNMENT. "Who are the chief officials of the Turkish government?" See *Political Handbook of the World* or *Statesman's Year-Book.*

INDIANS (AMERICAN). "What was the domain of the Apache Indians?" See Hodge's *Handbook of American Indians* or Swanton's *Indian Tribes of North America.*

MUSEUMS. "What art museums are there in Boston?" See Cartwright's *Guide to Art Museums in the United States,* or Faison's *Guide to the Art Museums of New England,* or *Museums Directory of the United States and Canada.*

OPERA. "I want to read a synopsis of Verdi's *Rigoletto.*" See Cross's *Complete Stories of the Great Operas,* Ewen's *Encyclopedia of the Opera,* or Kobbé's *Complete Opera Book.*

RAILWAYS. "Are there any railroads in Afghanistan?" See Sampson's *World Railways.*

REMBRANDT. "I want to read an authoritative, brief biography of Rembrandt van Rijn." See *Encyclopedia of World Art* or Bryan's *Dictionary of Painters and Engravers.*

SPACE TRAVEL. "Where can I find accounts of recent space explorations?" Check the *New York Times Index* and *Readers' Guide to Periodical Literature* for up-to-date references.

THEATER. "Which plays hold records for the longest runs on Broadway?" See the *Guinness Book of World Records.*

4
Books about Books

Statistical studies have estimated a total production of at least 30,000,000 different books since printing was invented in the mid-fifteenth century. As the flood of printed matter has risen at an ever accelerating rate, especially in the twentieth century, scholars have become increasingly concerned with the problem of "bibliographical control." Ambitious bibliographers have planned and dreamed of a complete record of all books printed throughout the world for all periods. None has remotely approached such a goal.

EARLY PRINTING

Because of the keen interest in the beginnings of printing, surviving examples of fifteenth-century books, known among bibliographers as incunabula, "cradlebooks," have been more completely recorded than any others. Approximately 37,000 different books are known to have been produced between 1450 and 1501. Catalogs and bibliographies are numerous. The most useful for general purposes are these:

British Museum Library. *Catalogue of Books Printed in the XVth Century Now in the British Museum.* London: British Museum, 1908–62. 9 v.

Valuable to the historian of printing because of its arrangement by places and printers.

Gesamtkatalog der Wiegendrucke. Leipzig: Hiersemann, 1925–
40. v. 1–8[1], A-Fredericis.

The most complete record of incunabula, based on copies
located throughout the world. Publication interrupted by
World War II and not yet resumed.

Goff, Frederick R. *Incunabula in American Libraries; a Third
Census of Fifteenth-Century Books Recorded in North Amer-
ican Collections.* New York: Bibliographical Society of
America, 1964. 798 pp.

Locates copies of 47,188 incunabula owned in America, by
institutions and private individuals.

LIBRARY CATALOGS

The printed catalogs of great libraries come closer to achieving
bibliographical universality than do any other attempts. The largest libraries, such as the British Museum, the French Bibliothèque
Nationale, and the United States Library of Congress, are far from
complete, but they are universal in scope and contain immense
numbers of books not limited as to subject, place of publication,
or date. The most important of many printed catalogs of libraries are these three: British Museum, Dept. of Printed Books.
General Catalogue of Printed Books.   London: British Museum,
1959–66. 263 v. Supplements, 1956–66. 263 v. Supplements,
1956–70, 76 v.

Bibliothèque Nationale.   *Catalogue Général des Livres Imprimés.*
Paris: Impr. Nat., 1900———. ——— v. In progress.

U.S. Library of Congress.   *A Catalog of Books Represented by Library of Congress Printed Cards Issued to July 31, 1942.* Ann
Arbor, Mich.: Edwards, 1942–46. 167 v.

Supplemented by published catalogs covering period 1942–
54, and superseded by *The National Union Catalog; a Cumulative Author List Representing Library of Congress Printed
Cards and Titles Reported by Other American Libraries,*
1952 to date, and *National Union Catalog, Pre-1956 Imprints.*
London: Mansell, 1968———. In progress, to be completed in
610 volumes. Locates copies in hundreds of American libraries.

The catalogs of the famous national libraries listed above are arranged alphabetically by authors. For listings by subjects, the two following titles are useful:

British Museum, Dept. of Printed Books. *Subject Index of the Modern Works Added to the Library*, 1881–1960. London: British Museum, 1902–66. 24 v.

U.S. Library of Congress. *Library of Congress Catalog, Books: Subjects; a Cumulative List of Works Represented by Library of Congress Printed Cards*, 1950 to date. Washington, D.C.: Library of Congress, 1955 to date. Quarterly and annual supplements.

NATIONAL BIBLIOGRAPHY

National bibliographies recording the books produced in each country are well developed for the principal nations of the world. Among the most thorough and comprehensive are the records of American books from the beginning until today. In chronological order, following is a list of the significant titles:

Evans, Charles. *American Bibliography; a Chronological Dictionary of All Books, Pamphlets and Periodical Publications Printed in the United States of America from the Genesis of Printing in 1639.* Chicago, 1903–34; Worcester, Mass.: Amer. Antiquarian Soc., 1955–59. 14 v.

A year-by-year record through 1800. Augmented by: Shipton, Clifford K., and Mooney, James E. *National Index of American Imprints through 1800: The Short Title Evans.* Worcester, Mass.: Amer. Antiquarian Soc. Barre, 1970. 2 v. Incorporates the 40,000 entries listed in Evans, with corrections plus 10,000 items. Also Bristol, Roger P. *Supplement to Charles Evans' American Bibliography* and *Index to Supplement.* Charlottesville: Univ. Press of Virginia, 1971. 636 pp., 191 pp. Lists an additional 11,282 titles.

Shaw, Ralph R., and Shoemaker, Richard H. *American Bibliography: A Preliminary Checklist.* Metuchen, N.J.: Scarecrow Press, 1958–65. 19 v.

Intended to continue Evans; covers period 1800–1819.

Shoemaker, Richard H. *Checklist of American Imprints, 1820–1827*. Metuchen, N.J.: Scarecrow Press, 1964–70. 8 v.

Roorbach, Orville A. *Bibliotheca Americana, 1820–61*. New York: Roorbach, 1852–61. 4 v.

Kelly, James. *American Catalogue of Books Published in the United States from Jan. 1861 to Jan. 1871*. New York: Wiley, 1866–71. 2 v.

American Catalogue of Books, 1876–1910. New York: Publishers Weekly, 1876–1910. 13 v.

First two volumes list books in print in 1876. Superseded by:

United States Catalog. Mineola, N.Y.: Wilson, 1900–1928. 4 v. Continued by:

Cumulative Book Index, a World List of Books in the English Language. New York: Wilson, 1928 to date.

The standard national trade bibliography of American books and of books in the English language published elsewhere. Alphabetical record by authors, subjects, and titles, with biennial, annual, and monthly supplements.

Publishers' Trade List Annual. New York: Bowker, 1873 to date. Annual.

Publishers' catalogs, arranged alphabetically. Two indexes published separately: *Books in Print: An Author-Title-Series Index.* New York: Bowker, 1948 to date. Annual. *Subject Guide to Books in Print: A Subject Index.* New York: Bowker, 1957 to date. Annual. Supplemented by: *Forthcoming Books.* New York: Bowker, 1966 to date. Bimonthly. *Subject Guide to Forthcoming Books.* New York: Bowker, 1967 to date. Bimonthly.

Paperbound Books in Print. New York: Bowker, 1955 to date.

Monthly announcement, with cumulative indexes, of books issued in paperback covers.

American Book Publishing Record. New York: Bowker, 1960 to date. Monthly.

Publishers Weekly. New York: Bowker, 1872 to date.

A weekly record of books published in the United States. Semiannual issues announce books scheduled for publication within the next six months.

Similar publications are available for the national bibliographies of England, France, Germany, and various other countries. Some of the major titles for British national bibliography, for example, are:

Pollard, Alfred W., and Redgrave, G. R. *Short-Title Catalogue of Books Printed in England, Scotland, and Ireland, and of English Books Printed Abroad, 1475–1640.* London: Bibliographical Society, 1926. 609 pp. New edition in progress.

Wing, Donald G. *Short-Title Catalogue of Books Printed in England, Scotland, Ireland, Wales, and British America and of English Books Printed in Other Countries, 1641–1700.* New York: Columbia Univ. Press, 1945–51. 3 v. New edition in progress.

English Catalogue of Books . . . Books Issued in the United Kingdom of Great Britain and Ireland. London: Publishers Circular, 1864 to date.

> Includes period from 1801 to date. Recent supplementary volumes cover from three to five years each.

British National Bibliography. London: British Museum, 1950 to date. Weekly with quarterly, annual, and five-year cumulations.

> Based on copyrighted books deposited at the Copyright Office. Classified arrangement with author, title, subject index.

British Books in Print. New York: Bowker, 1965. 2 v.

> Formerly *Reference Catalogue of Current Literature.* Records 250,000 titles of 6,800 English publishers.

British Books. London: Publishers' Circular, 1959 to date.

> Weekly record of books published. Continues *Publishers' Circular and Booksellers' Record,* 1837–1959.

BOOK PRICES

A frequent inquiry received by reference librarians concerns the market value of old, out-of-print books. The most reliable sources of information are the following titles:

American Book Prices Current. New York: Bowker, 1895 to date. Annual.

Specimen entries from *Cumulative Book Index* for September, 1972, an author-subject-title "world list of books in the English language."

An annual record of books, manuscripts, and autographs sold at auction in England, the United States, and Canada.

Book-Auction Records, 1902 to date. London: Stevens, 1903 to date. Annual.

A record of books sold at auction in British markets and principal New York auctions.

Book Prices Current, 1886 to date. London: Sergeants Press, 1888 to date. Annual.

Another record of British book auctions.

McGrath, Daniel F. *Bookman's Price Index, an Annual Guide to the Values of Rare and Other Out-of-Print Books and Sets of Periodicals.* Detroit, Mich.: Gale Research Co., 1964 to date. Based upon catalogs issued by "leading antiquarian and specialist dealers in the United States, England, and Western Europe."

Mandeville, Mildred S., comp. *Used Book Price Guide; Retail Prices of Rare, Scarce, Used and Out-of-Print Books.* Kenmore, Wash.: Price Guide Publishers, 1972. 2 v.

BOOK REVIEWS

Book reviews serve a variety of purposes, such as guiding a reader in the choice of books, for book selection in book buying by libraries and individuals, and in preparation of bibliographies. The principal guides to book reviews are the following:

Book Review Digest. New York: Wilson, 1905 to date. Monthly except February and July with annual cumulations.

Lists by authors, with subject and title indexes, selected book reviews from about seventy-five American and English periodicals, with brief excerpts.

Book Review Index. Detroit, Mich.: Gale Research Co., 1965–68, 1972 to date. Bimonthly with annual cumulations.

"Guide to book reviews appearing in all media of general circulation."

Index to Book Reviews in the Humanities. Williamston, Mich.: Phillip Thomson, 1960 to date. Annual.

Indexes reviews of several thousand book titles in each issue,

from English-language periodicals. Covers social sciences, as
well as humanities.

Moulton, Charles W.   *Library of Literary Criticism of English and
American Authors.* Buffalo, N.Y.: Moulton Pub. Co., 1901–5.
8 v.
Biographical sketches and quotations from criticisms of works
of authors from 680 to 1904. Available in an abridged edition:
New York: Ungar, 1966. 4 v. Complemented by: Tucker,
Martin. *The Critical Temper: A Survey of Modern Criticism
on English and American Literature from the Beginnings to
the Twentieth Century.* New York: Ungar, 1969. 3 v.

Curley, Dorothy N., and others.   *A Library of Literary Criticism:
Modern American Literature,* 4th ed. New York.: Ungar,
1969. 3 v.
Includes excerpts from critical material, appearing in books
and periodicals, for 289 American authors after 1904. Index
of critics.

Temple, Ruth A., and Tucker, Martin.   *A Library of Literary
Criticism: Modern British Literature.* New York: Ungar,
1966. 3 v.
Excerpts from critical writings on over 400 twentieth-century
British authors. Cross-reference index and index of critics.

Gray, Richard A.   *A Guide to Book Review Citations; a Bibliography of Sources.* Columbus: Ohio State Univ. Press, 1968.
221 pp.
Annotated list of sources of book review citations.

Contemporary Literary Criticism.   Detroit, Mich.: Gale Research
Co., 1973 to date.
Companion to same publisher's *Contemporary Authors* series.
Covers current critical writings on modern authors now
living or deceased since 1960. First volume includes about
200 authors. Cumulative indexes of authors and critics.

Science Books; a Quarterly Review.   Washington, D.C.: Amer.
Assoc. for Advancement of Science, 1965 to date. Quarterly.
Classified listing, with annotations, of new books in the pure
and applied sciences.

Technical Book Review Index. New York: Special Libraries Assoc., 1917–29, 1935 to date. Monthly except July and August.

Indexes reviews appearing in scientific, technical, and trade journals, often with brief excerpts.

BOOK SELECTION

Booklist. Chicago: Amer. Library Assoc., 1905 to date. Semimonthly, monthly in August.

Classified list of new publications with descriptive and critical annotations. Section of reference and subscription book reviews. Subject-author-title indexes cumulate semiannually and annually. Other book selection aids are:

Choice. Chicago: Assoc. of College and Research Libraries, Amer. Library Assoc., 1964 to date. Monthly except bimonthly July–August. Annual index. *Library Journal.* New York: Bowker, 1876 to date. Semimonthly except monthly July–August. Annual index.

Books for College Libraries. Chicago: Amer. Library Assoc., 1967. 1,056 pp.

"A selected list of approximately 53,400 titles based on the initial selection made for the University of California's New Campuses Program." Also from American Library Association: Pirie, James W., comp. *Books for Junior College Libraries; a Selected List of Approximately 19,700 Titles.* 1969. 452 pp. Hodges, Elizabeth D. *Books for Elementary School Libraries: An Initial Collection.* 1969. 321 pp. Lists more than 3,000 titles.

Public Library Catalog, 5th ed. New York: Wilson, 1968. 1,646 pp. Four annual supplements, 1969–72.

Classified and annotated list of nonfiction titles. Author, title, and subject index. Also from Wilson: *Fiction Catalog,* 8th ed. 1971. 653 pp. *Children's Catalog,* 12th ed. 1971. 1,156 pp. *Junior High School Library Catalog,* 2d ed. 1970. 808 pp. *Senior High School Library Catalog,* 10th ed. 1972. 1,214 pp. All have annual supplements.

GOVERNMENT PUBLICATIONS

Government publications are among the oldest of written records; in fact, it was largely to preserve them that libraries were established in ancient times. Today every nation of importance issues publications relating to its governmental activities.

In the United States, the federal government is the most prolific of all publishers, sending out a steady stream of books, periodicals, pamphlets, maps, and other materials, much of it of significant value for informational and research needs. Little of it ever appears in the regular book trade, but is listed separately in a series of publications going back to the beginning of the American nation. The principal bibliographical sources are these:

Poore, Benjamin P. *A Descriptive Catalogue of the Government Publications of the United States, September 5, 1774–March 4, 1881.* Washington, D.C.: G.P.O., 1885. 1,392 pp.

Ames, John G. *Comprehensive Index to the Publications of the United States Government, 1881–1893.* Washington, D.C.: G.P.O., 1905. 2v.

U.S. Superintendent of Documents. *Checklist of United States Public Documents, 1789–1909,* 3d ed. Washington, D.C.: G.P.O., 1911. 1,707 pp.

U.S. Superintendent of Documents. *Catalog of the Public Documents of Congress and of All Departments of the Government of the United States for the Period March 4, 1893–December 31, 1940.* Washington, D.C.: G.P.O., 1896–1945. 25 v.

U.S. Superintendent of Documents. *United States Government Publications: Monthly Catalog,* 1895 to date. Washington, D.C.: G.P.O., 1895 to date. Monthly.
Current listing of publications issued by all governmental units, arranged by departments. Monthly and annual subject indexes. The September number each year contains a list of libraries which serve as depositories of federal publications.

U.S. Superintendent of Documents. *Price Lists.* Washington, D.C.: G.P.O., 1898 to date. Nos. 1–88.
Arranged by subjects, with prices for individual publications. Frequently revised.

CIS Index: Congressional Information Service Index to Publications of the United States Congress. Washington, D.C.: Congressional Information Service, 1969 to date. Monthly with quarterly and annual cumulations.

Provides abstracts of United States congressional hearings, reports, committee prints, and other documents. Thoroughly indexed.

Several guides exist to the use of federal publications. Recommended titles are:

Andriot, John L. *Guide to U.S. Government Serials and Periodicals.* McLean, Va.: Documents Index, 1969 to date. Annual with supplements.

Up-to-date comprehensive guide to current United States government serials, periodicals, and irregular publications. Arranged alphabetically by branch of government, department, and agency; by title under agency. Agency, subject, title indexes.

Boyd, Anne M., and Rips, Rae E. *United States Government Publications,* 3d ed. New York: Wilson, 1950. 627 pp.

Useful in finding and using publications.

Jackson, Ellen P. *Subject Guide to Major United States Government Publications.* Chicago: Amer. Library Assoc., 1968. 175 pp.

Contains section on "Guides, Catalogs, and Indexes" by W. A. Katz.

Leidy, W. Philip. *A Popular Guide to Government Publications,* 3d ed. New York: Columbia Univ. Press, 1968. 365 pp.

Classified guide to about 3,000 most widely used publications.

Mechanic, Sylvia, comp. *Annotated List of Selected United States Government Publications Available to Depository Libraries.* New York: Wilson, 1971. 424 pp.

Lists about 500 items with emphasis on current materials; series or title index.

Pohle, Linda C. *A Guide to Popular Government Publications; for Libraries and Home Reference.* Littleton, Colo.: Libraries Unlimited, 1972. 213 pp.

ACTION
806 Connecticut Avenue NW., Washington, DC   20525

NOTE.—ACTION was created as an independent agency within the executive branch of government under the provisions of Reorganization Plan 1 of 1971, effective July 1, 1971, and Executive Order 11603 of June 30, 1971.

Action pamphlet.

26923   4400–2. Foster grandparent program, one part of ACTION. [Nov. 1972.] 10+[1] p. il. 4°   †   ● Item 30–A–2   AA 1.11 : 4400–2

AGRICULTURAL MARKETING SERVICE, Agriculture Dept.
Washington, DC   20250

AMS (series). †   A 88.40 : (nos.)

26924   553. Packaged fluid milk sales in Federal milk order markets by size and type of containers, and distribution method during Nov. 1971. [Apr. 1973.] 42 p. il. 4°   (Dairy Division.)

26925   554. Population data for milk marketing areas under Federal orders (based on 1970 Census) ; [by Patricia C. Nessul and Anita J. Harrison]. Mar. [1973.] cover title, 69 p. il. 4°   (Dairy Division.)   ● Item 19–A

[Fresh fruit and vegetable unloads FVUS] (series).

26926   5. Fresh fruit and vegetable unload totals for 41 cities, calendar year 1972. Apr. 1973. 83 p. 4°   (Fruit and Vegetable Division, Market News Branch.)   †   ● Item 19–A   A 88.12/31 : 5/2

AGRICULTURAL RESEARCH SERVICE, Agriculture Dept.
Washington, DC   20250

ARS (series). †   A 77.15 : (letters–nos.)

26927   NC–5. Damage to corn from pneumatic conveying [with list of literature cited ; by Do Sup Chung, Chang Joo Chung, and Harry H. Converse]. Jan. 1973. [2]+9 p. il. 4°   (North Carolina region.) [Prepared in cooperation with Kansas Agricultural Experiment Station, Mohattan, Kans.]

26928   S–8.   Annotated bibliography of nematodes of soybeans, 1882–1968 ; [by J. M. Epps and others]. Jan. 1973. cover title, 75 p. 4°   (Southern region.)

26929   W–3.   Studies on control of reed canary-grass along irrigation systems [with list of literature cited ; by V. F. Bruns]. Feb. 1973. [4]+17 p. il. 4°   (Western region.) [Prepared in cooperation with Washington Agricultural Experiment Stations.]

26930   Notes from Washington, v. 72, no. 3, Aug. 1972. [1972.] cover title, ii+21 p. 4°   (International Programs Division.)   ‡   A 77.25 : 72/3

AGRICULTURE DEPARTMENT
Washington, DC   20250

NOTE.—Requests to the Department of Agriculture for publications should include the USDA number if given in the entry.

Agriculture handbook.

26931   443. How to buy food, lesson aids for teachers. [May 1973.] cover title, 51 p. il. 4°   (Agricultural Marketing Service.) [Contents on p. 2 of cover. Issued with perforations.]   * Paper, 80c.   ● Item 3   A 1.76 : 443

26932   Changing world needs for grains in 1970's [by] Don Paarlberg, Director of Agricultural Economics, Department of Agriculture, talk prepared for presentation before CIMMYT Wheat-Barley-Triticale Workshop, El Batan, Mexico, Jan. 22, 1973. [1973.] 16+[2] p. 4°   (USDA 191–73.)   †   A 1.40 : P 11/31

Farmers' bulletin.

26933   2193. Grasshopper control ; [prepared by Western Region, Agricultural Research Service]. Revised May 1973. [1973.] 11 p. il.   * Paper, 20c.   (S/N–0100–02822).   ● Item 9   A 1.9 : 2193/6

Specimen entries from United States Superintendent of Documents' *Monthly Catalog*, listed by governmental units.

Emphasis on publications from 1967–71 with some earlier
works listed if still in print; 1,394 titles are arranged alphabetically by subject.

Schmeckebier, Laurence F., and Eastin, R. B. *Government Publications and Their Use,* 2d ed. Washington, D.C.: Brookings
Institution, 1969. 502 pp.
Describes catalogs, indexes, and bibliographies, congressional and departmental publications, etc.

Wynkoop, Sally, comp. *Government Reference Books, 1970–
1971, a Biennial Guide to U.S. Government Publications,* 2d
ed. Littleton, Colo.: Libraries Unlimited, 1972. 251 pp.
Annotated list of federal publications of reference value. Arranged by subjects with author, title, and subject index.

In addition to the federal government, the individual states,
counties, municipalities, and other governmental units print large
numbers of official publications. Bibliographical records for this
mass of material are far less complete than are those for federal
publications. One source of information is:

U.S. Library of Congress. *Monthly Checklist of State Publications.* Washington, D.C.: G.P.O., 1910 to date. Monthly. Annual index.
Limited to publications received by the Library of Congress.

The publications of British and other foreign governments are
similarly recorded in bibliographies and catalogs. The official list
of current English documents is:

Great Britain Stationery Office. *Catalogue of Government Publications.* London: H.M.S.O., 1922 to date. Annual.
Quinquennial indexes: *Consolidated Index to Government
Publications,* 1936/40 to date. London: H.M.S.O., 1952 to
date.

DISSERTATIONS

Doctoral dissertations do not ordinarily appear in the regular
book trade, but because they are assumed to be original contributions to knowledge, doctoral theses may have important reference and research value. Dissertations are listed in special bibli-

ographies. For the United States, the principal general lists are, in chronological order, the following titles:

U.S. Library of Congress. *List of American Doctoral Dissertations Printed in 1912–38.* Washington, D.C.: G.P.O., 1913–40. 26 v.

> Alphabetical and classified lists with index of subjects; covers about forty-five institutions.

Association of Research Libraries. *Doctoral Dissertations Accepted by American Universities, 1933–55.* New York: Wilson, 1934–55. 22 v.

> Alphabetical subject index; also listing by universities and author index.

Dissertation Abstracts International.   Ann Arbor, Mich.: University Microfilms, 1969 to date. Monthly.

> Continues *Microfilm Abstracts* (1935–51) and *Dissertation Abstracts* (1952–69). Author and keyword indexes cumulate annually. Retrospective index (1970, 9 v. in 11) covers 1935–69 volumes.

5
The Periodical World

In contrast to the once-and-for-all book form of publication—though revised editions may appear—there is a vast amount of publishing in periodical or serial form, daily, weekly, monthly, quarterly, annually, or irregularly. For approximately the past century, serial literature has been assuming an increasingly important place. In a number of fields, especially in science and technology, the learned and technical journals, transactions of academies, societies, museums, observatories, universities, and other institutions, and the serial publications of governments have superseded to a large extent the separately published monograph or book. Where recency of information is a prime consideration, the periodical has distinct advantages over the book. In science alone, the number of currently published journals is estimated as high as 100,000 titles.

The problem of bibliographical control of serial literature is even more complex than for books. For example, the annual production of individual magazine or serial articles numbers in the millions in comparison to perhaps 400,000 separate book titles. Three types of aids have developed to guide the research worker through the mazes of periodical literature: directories, union lists, and indexes or abstracts.

PERIODICAL DIRECTORIES
The most valuable directories of periodicals generally found in American libraries are the following:

Ayer's Directory of Newspapers and Periodicals.   Philadelphia, Pa.: N. W. Ayer & Sons, 1880 to date. Annual.

Lists about 20,000 newspapers and periodicals published currently in America; arranged by states and cities, with indexes.

Irregular Serials and Annuals; an International Directory, 2d ed. New York: Bowker, 1972. 1,130 pp.

"A classified guide to current foreign and domestic serials, excepting periodicals issued more frequently than once a year." Complements "regular" periodical directories; includes proceedings, reports, yearbooks, annual reviews, handbooks, etc.

Newspaper Press Directory.   London: Benn Bros., 1846 to date. Annual.

World list of current newspapers and periodicals, though most complete for British Isles.

Standard Periodical Directory.   New York: Oxbridge, 1964 to date. Frequently revised; limited to United States and Canada. Comprehensive periodical coverage includes house organs, government publications, yearbooks, etc. Arranged by subjects.

Ulrich's International Periodicals Directory, 15th ed.   New York: Bowker, 1973. 2 v. Biennial.

A classified guide to a selected list of current periodicals, foreign and domestic. Lists 55,000 titles; v. 1, scientific, technical, medical, v. 2, arts, humanities, social sciences, business. Title and subject index.

UNION LISTS OF PERIODICALS

Aside from the bibliographical data they contain, the principal purpose of union lists of periodicals is to locate files of specific titles in libraries. The leading example, among hundreds, is the following:

Union List of Serials in Libraries of the United States and Canada, 3d ed.   New York: Wilson, 1966. 5 v.

The latest and most monumental edition of a work first published in 1927. Locates files of 157,000 journals in 956 United States and Canadian libraries.

The foregoing union list is intended to be kept up to date and supplemented by:

U.S. Library of Congress. *New Serial Titles*. Washington, D.C.: Library of Congress, 1954 to date. Monthly and annual.

A union list of serials commencing publication after December 31, 1949. A twenty-one-year cumulation has been published: *New Serial Titles, 1950–1970*. Ann Arbor, Mich.: Xerox, 1973. 4 v. For Great Britain, the standard union list is:

British Union-Catalogue of Periodicals; a Record of the Periodicals of the World, from the Seventeenth Century to the Present Day, in British Libraries. London: Butterworth, 1955–58. 4 v. *Supplement to 1960*. London: Butterworth, 1962. 991 pp. Quarterly with annual cumulations.

PERIODICAL INDEXES

Without an index to their contents, the user of periodicals is hopelessly lost. This fact was realized nearly a century ago by William Frederick Poole and a cooperating group of American librarians, who undertook to compile the pioneer index:

Poole's Index to Periodical Literature, 1802–1907. Boston, Mass.: Houghton, 1882–1908. 7 v.

Indexes 590,000 articles in 470 American and English periodicals; subject index only.

Since Poole blazed the trail, numerous indexing and abstracting services have been established to keep track of the constantly rising tide of periodical literature. Some are general in character, but the majority relate to special subjects—agriculture, art, education, engineering, law, medicine, psychology, technology, etc. The latter group will be considered subsequently under pertinent subject headings. Of first importance in the general category are these:

Nineteenth Century Readers' Guide to Periodical Literature, 1890–1899, with Supplementary Indexing, 1900–1922. New York: Wilson, 1944. 2 v.

Author and subject index to fifty-one periodicals, mainly for period 1890–99.

Readers' Guide to Periodical Literature, 1900 to date. New York:

ACP. See Associated church press
AOA. See United States—Aging, Administration on
AARON, Henry, 1934-
  Chasing the Babe. il por Newsweek 81:67 Je 4 '73
  Tortured road to 715. W. Leggett. il por Sports Illus 38:28-30+ My 28 '73 *
AARON, Jonathan
  Essential company; Blindfold; poems. Poetry 122:67-8 My '73
AARONSON, Stuart A. See Stephenson, J. R. jt. auth.
AARONSPERE, Larry
  Overview: rural development. Environment 15:3 Ap '73
ABANDONED cars. See Automobiles—Wrecking
ABKHASIANS
  Where life begins at 100. A. Leaf. il Read Digest 102:153-62 My '73
ABORTION
  Laws and legislation
  France
  Abortion, oui! il Newsweek 81:46+ Je 11 '73
  Moral and religious aspects
  Abortion: deterrence, facilitation, resistance. America 128:506-7 Je 2 '73
ABPLANALP, Robert H.
  President's quiet creditor. il por Time 101:22-3 Je 11 '73 *
ABRAHAM, Bernard M. and Schreiner, Felix
  Low-temperature thermal process for the decomposition of water. bibliog il Science 180:959-60 Je 1 '73
ABRAHAMSON, Dean E.
  Overview: energy. Environment 15:19 Ja; 3-4 Mr '73
ACADEMICALLY talented students. See High school students, Mentally superior
ACCIDENTS
  Accidents to the aging claim 28,000 lives in 1971, disable another 800,000. Aging 219:14 Ja '73
ACCOUNTABILITY (education)
  What to tell parents about professional self-governance. Todays Educ 62:26-7 My '73
ACCOUNTANTS
  Bright future for accountants. G. E. Hall. Duns 101:125 My '73
ACKERMAN, Harry
  Spotlighting. K. V. Hostick. Hobbies 78:148 Je '73 *
ACKERMAN, Page
  Irrational optimist; interview, ed. by G. R. Shields. por Am Lib 4:281-2 My '73
ACONCHA, Leandro
  Prodigies' progress. pors Time 101:70-1 Je 4 '73 *
ACROBATS and acrobatism
  Daring young men on the flying Yangtze; Shenyang acrobatic troupe. L. Vaczek. il Sat Eve Post 245:52-5+ My '73
ACTINOMYCIN
  Estimation of the half-life of a secretory protein message. S. Grayson and S. J. Berry. bibliog il Science 180:1071-2 Je 8 '73
ACTIONS and defenses
  Courts get a flurry of job bias cases. Bus W p30 My 26 '73
ACUPUNCTURE
  Acupuncture: fertile ground for faddists and serious NIH research. B. J. Culliton; discussion. bibliog Science 178:9; 179:521; 180:1002 O 6 '72, F 9, Je 8 '73
ADAMS, Arvil V.
  Evaluating the success of the EEOC compliance process. il Mo Labor R 96:26-9 My '73
ADAMS, Margaret
  Science, technology, and some dilemmas of advocacy; adaptation of address, May 18, 1972. bibliog Science 180:840-2 My 25 '73
ADMINISTRATIVE ability. See Executive ability

* Printer's device

ADMIRAL'S cup race. See Yacht racing
ADOLESCENCE
  Psychology
  Today's adolescent. I. L. Mintz. il N Y Times Mag p88+ Ap 29 '73; Reply. P. M. Nardi. p57-8 Je 3 '73
ADOPTION
  How to adopt a Vietnamese. Newsweek 81:56 My 28 '73
ADVERTISING
  Back talk; FTC accused of unfair practices. il Newsweek 81:84+ Je 4 '73
  Europe's admen go multinational. il Bus W p52+ My 26 '73
  See also
  Radio advertising
  also subhead Advertising under various subjects, e.g. Automobile industry—Advertising
  Foreign language advertising
  Habla usted espanol? reaching the Spanish-speaking market. il Newsweek 81:94+ Je 11 '73
ADVERTISING, Newspaper
  Beware! withholding information in fear of economic reprisals; case of the Courier-post, Camden, N.J. S. J. Adamo. America 128:524-inside back cover Je 2 '73
  Peking's pique; Chinese anger at anti-Communist ads in the New York times. Time 101:61 My 28 '73
ADVERTISING, Public service
  Cause agency; Public interest communications. Time 101:76+ My 28 '73
ADVERTISING agencies
  Cause agency; Public interest communications. Time 101:76+ My 28 '73
ADVISORY committee on science and foreign affairs. See United States—State, Department of—Advisory committee on science and foreign affairs
AERONAUTICS, Commercial
  Iran
  See also
  Airlines—Iran
AERONAUTICS, Military
  Iran
  Mehrabad becomes Iran training center. Aviation W 98:61 My 14 '73
AEROSPACE industries
  Europe, Western
  Paris-Bonn agreement will lower West German Spacelab share. Aviation W 98:20 My 14 '73
AESTHETICS
  Editors' choice: coffee pots to flower pots. House B 115:137+ My '73
  Matter of taste; opinions of 20 taste makers. M. Gough. il House B 115:134-7+ My '73
AGATES
  Agate pass; Puget Sound area. H. D. Brown. Hobbies 78:127 Je '73
AGE and sex. See Aged—Sexual behavior
AGED
  AoA analyst reports older Americans fastest growing minority group. Aging 219:14 Ja '73
  See also
  Church work with the aged
  Handicraft for the aged
  United States—Aging, Administration on
  Accidents
  See Accidents

Specimen entries from *Readers' Guide to Periodical Literature* listing current articles under authors and subjects.

Wilson, 1905 to date. Semimonthly (monthly in July and August) with quarterly and annual cumulations.

The most used of periodical indexes. An author, subject, and title index to about 160 leading general magazines since 1900.

Social Sciences and Humanities Index. New York: Wilson, June, 1965, to date. Quarterly with annual cumulations.

Replaced *International Index.* New York: Wilson, 1907–March, 1965. Author and subject index to 202 periodicals in the social sciences and humanities.

Subject Index to Periodicals, 1951–61. London: Library Assoc., 1919–62. Annual.

An English index, covering the contents of about 350 British periodicals. In 1962 divided into two separate indexes:

British Humanities Index, 1962 to date. London: Library Assoc., 1963 to date. Quarterly and annual.

Indexes 280 periodicals relating to "arts and politics."

British Technology Index, 1962 to date. London: Library Assoc., 1963 to date. Monthly and annual.

Indexes technical articles in 400 British journals.

NEWSPAPERS

The importance of newspapers for reference and research is generally recognized. Older files serve as contemporary records, as registers of contemporary opinion, and as repositories of facts often too small or too local to be included in books. Every day newspapers describe events, conditions, and cultures all over the world. For these reasons, social scientists are turning increasingly to retrospective collections of newspapers as primary sources.

Reference guides for newspapers are similar to those for other types of periodical or serial publications. Two of the principal directories—*Ayer's Directory of Newspapers and Periodicals* and the *Newspaper Press Directory*—are listed above under *Periodical Directories.*

Also useful are the following:

Editor and Publisher's *Editor and Publisher International Year Book.* New York, 1920 to date.

Contains detailed data on United States, Canadian, and for-

eign newspapers, advertising agencies, syndicates, and other
aspects of journalism.

Blum, Eleanor. *Basic Books in the Mass Media; an Annotated,
Selected Booklist Covering General Communications, Book
Publishing, Broadcasting, Film, Magazines, Newspapers,
Advertising, Indexes, and Scholarly and Professional Period-
icals.* Urbana: Univ. of Illinois Press, 1972. 252 pp.

For locating back files of newspapers, three important union
lists are available.

Brigham, Clarence S. *History and Bibliography of American
Newspapers, 1690–1820.* Worcester, Mass.: Amer. Antiquarian Soc., 1947. 2 v.

Lists 2,120 newspapers published between 1690 and 1820,
with locations.

*American Newspapers, 1821–1936; a Union List of Files Avail-
able in the United States and Canada.* New York: Wilson,
1937. 791 pp.

Locates files of papers in about 5,700 libraries and other
locations.

U.S. Library of Congress, Union Catalog Division. *Newspapers
on Microfilm,* 6th ed. Washington, D.C.: Library of Congress,
1967. 487 pp.

Lists about 21,700 titles, divided between 17,100 American
and 4,640 foreign newspapers, with locations of files.

Indexes to newspapers are considerably fewer in number than
for periodicals, but equally useful. The principal current examples are these:

New York Times Index. New York: The Times, 1913 to date.
Semimonthly and annual.

A detailed index to daily issues of the *New York Times.*

Times, London. *Index to the Times,* 1906 to date. London:
Times, 1907 to date. Bimonthly.

Palmer's Index to the Times Newspapers, 1790–June, 1941.   London: Palmer, 1868–1943. Quarterly.

Less detailed than the official *Index to the Times,* but covering a longer period.

Newspaper Index.   Wooster, Ohio: Newspaper Indexing Center,

Bell & Howell, 1972 to date. Monthly with annual cumulations.

Covers the *Chicago Tribune, Los Angeles Times, New Orleans Times-Picayune,* and *Washington Post,* with keyword subject and personal name indexes.

Subject Index of the Christian Science Monitor. Boston, Mass.: Christian Science Monitor, 1960 to date. Monthly with semiannual and annual cumulations.

Indexes eastern, western, and midwestern editions.

Wall Street Journal Index. New York: Dow Jones, 1958 to date. Monthly with annual cumulations.

6
The Nonbook World

The principal types of material acquired by libraries are separately printed books, periodicals, and government publications, plus large collections of manuscripts and archives in some institutions. A variety of other records, however, are being regularly accumulated. The modern library makes liberal provision for such nonbook materials as maps, slides, documentary motion picture films, music, speech and other sound recordings, magnetic tapes, prints, and similar classes.

MICROFORMS

One of the most useful devices that twentieth-century technology has given libraries is microform reproduction. The use of microfilm in roll form came into general use in libraries in the 1930s. Subsequently there developed a variety of other forms: microcards, microprint, microfiche, and most recently ultra-microfiche. During the past forty years, microreproduction projects have proliferated, miniaturizing large bodies of newspapers, manuscripts, archives, rare and early printed books, periodical files, government publications, bibliographical works, and other types of specialized research materials. By using a high rate of reduction, these techniques manage to place a large number of pages on a very small surface. The ultra-microfiche method, for example, can contain as many as 1,200 pages on a card two inches square.

The principal general listing of microforms is an annual publication, recording books, journals, and other materials. The latest edition, covering the productions of 108 publishers, is:

Guide to Microforms in Print. Washington, D.C: Microcard Editions Books, 1974. 185 pp.

Other useful guides are the following:

Microfilm Reference Volume. Santa Monica, Calif.: UpData Publications, 1974. 163 pp.

Lists titles, chiefly serial publications, issued by thirty publishers; alphabetical arrangement, with subject index.

Serials in Microform, 1973–74. Ann Arbor, Mich.: Xerox University Microfilms, 1973. 683 pp.

Lists periodicals, documents, newspapers, and other serial literature, alphabetical by title, with separate subject listing.

Readex Microprint Publications 1972–73. New York: Readex Microprint Corp., 1972. 65 pp.

The Readex Company claims 1,500,000 titles available in microprint, consisting of 6 × 9 cards on paper card stock, each card containing an average of about 100 pages.

Under other headings in the present work are listed guides to two specialized types of material in microform:

Dissertation Abstracts International. Ann Arbor, Mich.: Xerox University Microfilms, 1969 to date. Monthly. Records dissertations produced in nearly all major American universities; copies available in microfilm. Published under various titles since 1935.

U.S. Library of Congress, Union Catalog Division. *Newspapers on Microfilm*, 6th ed. Washington, D.C.: Library of Congress, 1967. 487 pp.

Lists about 21,000 titles of American and foreign newspapers, with locations of files.

Reproduction of library material in full size is another major development in recent years, with publication usually in near-print form by xerox and photo-offset. Since the coming of these processes, no book should be considered out of print, providing that somewhere a copy is available for reproduction. Titles available in reprint may be found through the following catalog:

Guide to Reprints, 1974. Washington, D.C.: Microcard Editions
    Books, 1974. 468 pp.
    An annual publication, listing the offerings of about 350
    publishers; books, journals, and other material available in
    reprint form.

RECORDED SOUND

Sound recordings are of several principal types. The oldest and
most popular are records of all varieties of music. The best
sources for current records are two trade catalogs:

Schwann Record & Tape Guide. Boston, Mass.: W. Schwann,
    1949 to date. Monthly.
    Lists more than 45,000 items by composers and collections.
Harrison Catalog of Stereophonic Tapes. New York: M. & N.
    Harrison, 1955 to date. Bimonthly.
    Listings for cassettes, eight-track cartridges, and open-reel
    tapes.

Another extensive listing is contained in the following title,
recording material received by the Library of Congress of "permanent value":

Library of Congress Catalog: Music and Phonorecords. Wash-
    ington, D.C.: Library of Congress, 1953 to date. Semiannual.

A more selective listing is *Records in Review* (New York:
Scribner, 1955 to date), the "High Fidelity Annual"; reviews of
currently issued records, arranged alphabetically by composers.

Special categories of music recordings are covered in the following works:

Malone, Bill C. *Country Music, U.S.A.: A Fifty-Year History.*
    Austin: Univ. of Texas Press, 1968. 422 pp.
Rust, Brian. *Jazz Records, A-Z, 1897–1931,* 2d ed. Hatch End,
    Middlesex, England, 1962. 736 pp. Also Rust, *Jazz Records,
    A-Z, 1932–1945,* Hatch End, 1965. 680 pp.
U.S. Library of Congress. *Folk Music; a Catalog of Folk Songs,
    Ballads, Dances, Instrumental Pieces, and Folk Tales of the
    United States and Latin America on Phonograph Records.*
    Washington D.C.: Library of Congress, 1958. 107 pp.

Another type of sound recording deals with literary material.

Two useful sources of information about available recordings are:

Roach, Helen. *Spoken Records*, 3d ed. Metuchen, N.J.: Scarecrow Press, 1970. 288 pp.

Grouped by types: authors' readings, documentaries, plays, poetry, etc.

U.S. Library of Congress. *Literary Recordings; a Checklist of the Archive of Recorded Poetry and Literature in the Library of Congress.* Washington, D.C.: Library of Congress, 1966. 190 pp.

Since 1948, when Columbia University began its Oral History Project, the importance of oral recordings for historical purposes has become increasingly recognized. The usual form is taped interviews with prominent personalities relating to their participation in events of historical significance. Various guides to the field exist:

Columbia University Oral History Research Office. *The Oral History Collection of Columbia University,* ed. by Elizabeth B. Mason and Louis M. Starr. New York: The Office, 1973. 460 pp.

A catalog describing "the largest hoard of unpublished reminiscence in the world."

Oral History Association. *Oral History in the United States, a Directory,* comp. by Gary L. Shumway. New York: The Association, 1971. 120 pp.

Arranged by states; descriptions of 230 collections under names of institutions.

Oral History Association. *A Bibliography on Oral History,* by Donald J. Schippers and Adelaide Tusler. Los Angeles, Calif.: The Association, 1968. 18 pp.

Association for Recorded Sound Collections. *A Preliminary Directory of Sound Recordings Collections in the United States and Canada.* New York: New York Public Library, 1967. 157 pp.

Includes all types of recordings; lists more than 1,700 collections.

Oral History Collections, by Alan Meckler and Ruth McMullin. New York: Bowker, 1974. 368 pp.

"Trends in Archival and Reference Collections of Recorded Sound." *Library Trends,* 21 (July, 1972), 155 pp. (whole issue).
Contains eight articles on all aspects of recorded sound from copyright to oral history, including listing of bibliographical sources for American and foreign recordings.

MOVING PICTURE FILMS

Works relating to the motion-picture world are described under the heading "Moving Pictures" in the section devoted to "Specialized Subject Reference Books." The titles listed there are primarily concerned with American and foreign commercial films, produced for entertainment.

For documentary and other films intended for educational purposes, the *Educational Film Guide* (New York: Wilson, 1936–62) records more than 6,000 titles; it is now mainly of historical interest. More recent guides are:

National Information Center for Educational Media. *Index to 16mm Educational Films.* New York: McGraw-Hill, 1967. 955 pp.
Resource guide to films recorded since 1958 in the Master Data Bank at the University of Southern California.

National Information Center for Educational Media. *Index to 35mm Educational Filmstrips,* 2d ed. New York: Bowker, 1970. 872 pp.

A comprehensive listing of all types of films may be found in the *Library of Congress Catalog: Motion Pictures and Filmstrips,* issued periodically from 1948 to date, arranged by authors and subjects.

Other important bibliographies of educational films are the following:

National Audiovisual Center. *U.S. Government Films.* Washington, D.C.: National Archives and Records Service, 1969——. Supplements issued periodically. "A catalog of motion pictures and filmstrips for rent and sale by the National Audiovisual Center."

National Medical Audiovisual Center. *Mental Health Film Guide.* Atlanta, Ga., 1969. 69 pp.

Many universities and public libraries maintain film libraries for rental purposes to schools, clubs, and other organizations, and publish catalogs. Examples are the following:

Arizona, University of, Bureau of Audiovisual Services. *16mm Educational Motion Pictures.*

Boston University School of Education. *Instructional Films Available from Kranker Memorial Film Library.*

Cleveland Public Library. *Film Catalog.*

California, University of, Extension Media Center (Berkeley). *16mm Films.*

Illinois, University of, Visual Aids Service. *Educational Films.* Reputed to be largest existing collection.

Indiana University, Audio-Visual Center. *Educational Motion Pictures.*

Michigan, University of, Audio-Visual Education Center. *Educational Films.*

Minnesota, University of, Dept. of Audio-Visual Extension. *Descriptive Catalog of 16mm Films with Subject Index.*

Mountain Plains Educational Media Council. *Joint Film Catalog.* Covers collections held by universities of Colorado, Nevada, Utah, and Wyoming.

New York University Film Library. *General Catalogue.*

Southern Illinois University, Learning Resources Service. *Instructional Films Catalog.*

These and similar catalogs issued by other institutions are frequently updated.

The most complete and up-to-date guide to film collections is Joan Clark's *Directory of Film Libraries in North America* (New York: Film Library Information Council), listing 1,800 such libraries in North America.

7
Books about Words

Books about words are as varied in nature as the purposes they are designed to serve. Such works may be used as guides to meaning, proper spelling, pronunciation, linguistic study, etymology, current usage, searching for antonyms, synonyms, and rhymes, standard abbreviations, or simply, according to a well-known series of advertisements, by people who like to read dictionaries. Some of the major categories follow:

ENGLISH LANGUAGE DICTIONARIES

Murray, James A. H. *New English Dictionary on Historical Principles.* Oxford: Clarendon Press, 1888–1933. 13 v.

Also known as the *Oxford English Dictionary.* A monumental scholarly achievement, presenting the history of every word introduced into the English language since 1150, with copious quotations to show usage. Now being updated by: Burchfield, R. W., ed. *A Supplement to the Oxford English Dictionary.* Oxford: Clarendon Press, 1972———. In progress, to be completed in three volumes.

Webster's Third New International Dictionary of the English Language. Springfield, Mass.: Merriam, 1961. 2,662 pp.

Unabridged dictionary of 450,000 words, emphasizing modern usage, and with special strength in science and technology. A controversial work because of its acceptance of popular usages frowned upon by scholars; for that reason, many users prefer the second edition: Springfield, Mass.: Merriam, 1950. 3,214 pp., which contain 150,000 more words or terms.

The American Heritage Dictionary of the English Language. Boston, Mass.: American Heritage/Houghton, 1969. 1,550 pp. Defines 155,000 terms. Unique feature is emphasis on usages as established by a panel of scholars. Indo-European origin of the English language is also stressed.

Random House Dictionary of the English Language. New York: Random House, 1966. 2,059 pp.

About 260,000 entries; emphasis is on current usage. Includes proper names, place names, titles of literary works, etc.

Funk and Wagnalls Standard Dictionary of the English Language, international ed. New York: Funk & Wagnalls, 1969. 2 v.

Unabridged dictionary; emphasizes present-day meaning, spelling, and pronunciation.

Craigie, William A., and Hulbert, James R. *Dictionary of American English on Historical Principles.* Chicago: Univ. of Chicago Press, 1936–44. 4 v.

Traces history of words "by which the English of the American colonies and the United States is distinguished" from other English-speaking peoples. A highly regarded work in the same field is Henry L. Mencken's *The American Language; an Inquiry into the Development of English in the United States,* 4th ed. New York: Knopf, 1936. 769 pp., with two supplementary volumes, 1945–48. Also note: Mathews, Mitford M. *A Dictionary of Americanisms on Historical Principles.* Chicago: Univ. of Chicago Press, 1951. 2 v.

LANGUAGE USAGE

Bernstein, Theodore M. *Miss Thistlebottom's Hobgoblins: The Careful Writer's Guide to the Taboos, Bugbears and Outmoded Rules of English Usage.* New York: Farrar, 1971. 280 pp.

Identifies erroneous and overly pedantic rules in four sections: words, syntax, idioms, and style.

Copperud, Roy H. *American Usage: The Consensus*. New York: Van Nostrand Reinhold, 1970. 292 pp.

Brings together opinions of authorities in current dictionaries of usage and regular dictionaries on disputed points of usage. By the same author is: *A Dictionary of Usage and Style*. New York: Hawthorn, 1964. 452 pp. Provides readable and practical comments on modern-day use of words and phrases.

Evans, Bergen and Cornelia. *A Dictionary of Contemporary American Usage*. New York: Random House, 1957. 567 pp. Alphabetically arranged, brief articles explain grammar and syntax, word usage, style, phrases, idioms, figures of speech, etc.

Follett, Wilson. *Modern American Usage; a Guide*. New York: Hill & Wang, 1966. 436 pp.

Guide to contemporary American English usage. Also includes appendixes on the use of shall and will, and on the conventions of punctuation.

Fowler, Henry W. *Dictionary of Modern English Usage*, 2d ed. Oxford: Clarendon Press, 1965. 725 pp.

Famous guide to usage of the English language. Alphabetically arranged with brief essays on grammar, syntax, word choice, etc. Also covers spelling, formation of plurals, pronunciation, and punctuation.

Strunk, William. *The Elements of Style*, ed. by E. B. White. New York: Macmillan, 1959. 71 pp.

Briefly outlines common errors in style and ways to avoid them. Includes essay by E. B. White on various elements of style.

BILINGUAL DICTIONARIES

FRENCH: *The New Cassell's French-English, English-French Dictionary*. New York: Funk & Wagnalls, 1965. 762 pp., 655 pp. *Gasc's Dictionary of the French and English Languages*. London: Bell, 1953. 956 pp. *Heath's Standard French and*

English Dictionary. New York: Heath, 1947–48. 2 v. *Harrap's New Standard French and English Dictionary*. New York: Scribner, 1973. 2 v.

GERMAN: *Cassell's German and English Dictionary*, 8th ed. London: Cassell, 1963. 629 pp., 619 pp. *Muret-Sanders Encyclopedic Dictionary, German and English*. New York: Ungar, 1944. 2 v. Wildhagen, Karl, and Heraucourt, Will. *The New Wildhagen German Dictionary; German-English, English-German*. Chicago: Follett, 1965. 1,296 pp., 1,061 pp.

ITALIAN: *Cassell's Italian-English, English-Italian Dictionary*, 7th ed. London: Cassell, 1967. 1,096 pp. Hoare, Alfred. *Short Italian Dictionary*. Cambridge: Cambridge Univ. Press, 1925. 906 pp. Reynolds, Barbara. *The Cambridge Italian Dictionary*. Cambridge: Cambridge Univ. Press, v. 1, 1962, v. 2 in preparation.

LATIN: *Cassell's New Latin Dictionary; Latin-English, English-Latin*, rev. ed. New York: Funk & Wagnalls, 1968. 883 pp. Levine, Edwin B., and others. *Follett World-Wide Latin Dictionary; Latin-English, English-Latin*. Chicago: Follett, 1967. 767 pp.

RUSSIAN: Müller, Vladimir K. *English-Russian Dictionary*, 7th ed. New York: Dutton, 1965. 1,192 pp. Segal, Louis. *Russian-English, English-Russian Dictionary*. New York: Praeger, 1959. 2 v. Smirnitskii, Aleksandr I. *Russian-English Dictionary*, 7th ed. New York: Dutton, 1966. 766 pp. Wheeler, Marcus. *The Oxford Russian-English Dictionary*. New York: Oxford Univ. Press, 1972. 918 pp.

SPANISH: *Cassell's Spanish-English, English-Spanish Dictionary*, 5th ed. London: Cassell, 1967. 1,477 pp. Amador, Emilio M. Martinez. *Standard English-Spanish and Spanish-English Dictionary*. Boston, Mass.: Heath, 1958. 2,130 pp. Velazquez de la Cadena, Mariano. *New Revised Velazquez Spanish and English Dictionary*. Chicago: Follett, 1967. 698 pp., 778 pp. *Crowell's Spanish-English and English-Spanish Dictionary*. New York: Crowell, 1963. 1,261 pp. *Collins Spanish-English/ English-Spanish Dictionary*. New York: Collins, 1972. 602 pp., 640 pp. Cuyas, Arturo. *Appleton's New Cuyas English-Spanish and Spanish-English Dictionary,* 5th ed. New York: Appleton, 1966. 698 pp., 589 pp.

The preceding list of bilingual dictionaries for French, German, Italian, Latin, Russian, and Spanish are recent editions of standard works. Many other languages are also covered by English bilingual dictionaries, for example: Afrikaans, Albanian, Arabic, Armenian, Bengali, Bulgarian, Burmese, Chinese, Cornish, Croatian, Czech, Danish, Dutch, Finnish, Gaelic, Georgian, Greek, Hawaiian, Hebrew, Hindi, Hindustani, Hungarian, Icelandic, Indonesian, Irish, Japanese, Korean, Latvian, Lithuanian, Malay, Mongolian, Norwegian, Pali, Persian, Polish, Portuguese, Rumanian, Sanskrit, Slovenian, Swedish, Tamil, Thai, Tibetan, Tongan, Turkish, Ukrainian, Vietnamese, Welsh, Yiddish, and Zulu.

SLANG DICTIONARIES

Dictionaries of slang exist for all the major languages. In the American and English area, the following titles are among the most comprehensive:

Berrey, Lester V., and Van den Bark, Melvin. *American Thesaurus of Slang,* 2nd ed. New York: Crowell, 1953. 1,272 pp. "A complete reference book of colloquial speech," including slang of particular classes and occupations.

Partridge, Eric. *A Dictionary of Slang and Unconventional English: Colloquialisms and Catch-Phrases, Solecisms and Catachreses, Nicknames, Vulgarisms, and Such Americanisms as Have Been Naturalized,* 7th ed. New York: Macmillan, 1970. 2 v. in 1.

Emphasis on English slang, but extremely comprehensive, including a high proportion of historical slang since about 1600.

Wentworth, Harold, and Flexner, Stuart B. *Dictionary of American Slang.* New York: Crowell, 1967. 718 pp.

A full listing of current American slang, with many taboo words and expressions.

SYNONYMS AND ANTONYMS

Dictionaries of synonyms and antonyms are indispensable tools for the writer, amateur or professional. Among the best are:

Allen, F. Sturges. *Synonyms and Antonyms*. New York: Harper, 1938. 427 pp.

  About 10,000 main entries, including colloquial, vulgar, technical, and specialized terms.

Hayakawa, Samuel I., and others. *Funk and Wagnalls Modern Guide to Synonyms and Related Words; Lists of Antonyms, Copious Cross References, a Complete and Legible Index.* New York: Funk & Wagnalls, 1968. 726 pp.

  Terms are defined, compared, and contrasted in textual essays.

March, Francis A. *March's Thesaurus and Dictionary of the English Langauge.* Garden City, N.Y.: Doubleday, 1968. 1,240 pp.

Roget's International Thesaurus, 3d ed. New York: Crowell, 1962. 1,258 pp.

  Contains 240,000 entries with words grouped according to their ideas; modern edition of work first published in 1852. Comparable is: Roget, Peter M. *The Original Roget's Thesaurus of English Words and Phrases*, rev. ed. New York: St. Martin's, 1965. 1,405 pp.

Webster's New Dictionary of Synonyms; a Dictionary of Discriminated Synonyms, with Antonyms and Analogous and Contrasted Words, 2d ed. Springfield, Mass.: Merriam, 1968. 909 pp.

RHYMING DICTIONARIES

For the poet still concerned with rhymes and rhythm, rather than with "free verse," several standard rhyming dictionaries are available for guidance.

Johnson, Burges. *New Rhyming Dictionary and Poets' Handbook.* New York: Harper, 1957. 464 pp.

  In three parts: one-syllable, two-syllable, and three-syllable rhymes.

Stillman, Frances. *The Poet's Manual and Rhyming Dictionary.* New York: Crowell, 1965. 464 pp.

  Lists about 115,000 words, grouped according to meaning and according to number of syllables.

Walker, John. *Rhyming Dictionary of the English Language.* New York: Dutton, 1924. 549 pp.

A standard work since 1775; 54,000 entries arranged according to final vowel sounds.

ABBREVIATIONS

Long before the coming of the New Deal, abbreviations were common, for example in medieval manuscripts, but under the pressure of modern life the number is growing rapidly. Several compilations of abbreviations in current use have been published.

Allen, Edward F. *Allen's Dictionary of Abbreviations and Symbols; Over 6,000 Abbreviations and Symbols Commonly Used in Literature, Science, Art, Education, Business, Politics, Religion, Engineering, Industry, War.* New York: Coward-McCann, 1946. 189 pp.

De Sola, Ralph. *Abbreviations Dictionary,* rev. ed. New York: Meredith, 1967. 298 pp.

International coverage; defines abbreviations, acronyms, contractions, signs and symbols, etc.

Gale Research Co. *Acronyms and Initialisms Dictionary: A Guide to Alphabetic Designations, Contractions, Acronyms, Initialisms, and Similar Condensed Appellations,* 4th ed. Detroit, Mich.: Gale Research Co., 1973. 635 pp.

Alphabetically arranged by acronym; contains 103,000 entries. Annual supplements, *New Acronyms and Initialisms,* planned for 1974 and 1975. Complemented by *Reverse Acronyms and Initialisms Dictionary.* Detroit, Mich.: Gale Research Co., 1972. 485 pp. Gives acronyms for 80,000 terms or phrases.

Matthews, Cecily C. *A Dictionary of Abbreviations, Comprising All Standard Forms in Commercial, Social, Legal, Political, Naval and Military, and General Use.* London: Routledge, 1947. 232 pp.

Pugh, Eric. *A Dictionary of Acronyms and Abbreviations; Some Abbreviations in Management, Technology and Information Science,* 2d ed. Hamden. Conn.: Archon, 1970. 389 pp.

About 10,000 entries; subject index.

Schwartz, Robert J. *The Complete Dictionary of Abbreviations.*
   New York: Crowell, 1955. 211 pp.
   About 25,000 general and specialized abbreviations, including
   science and technology.
Shankle, George E. *Current Abbreviations.* New York: Wilson,
   1945. 207 pp.
   A very comprehensive list.
Stephenson, Herbert J. *Abbrevs.* New York: Macmillan, 1943.
   126 pp.
   Special lists for Bible, Shakespeare, legal literature, Christian
   names, geography, railroads, chemical elements, monetary
   units, government agencies, etc.

8
Books about Places

Geographical reference books are of three principal types: atlases, gazetteers, and guidebooks, each coming in a variety of forms, and on occasion combining all three in one work.

ATLASES

The leading examples of American and British atlases are the following titles:

Bartholomew, John. *The Advanced Atlas of Modern Geography,* 3d ed. New York: McGraw-Hill, 1956. 159 pp.
> Basic collection of world maps, extensively indexed.

Espenshade, Edward B. *Goode's World Atlas,* 13th ed. Chicago: Rand McNally, 1970. 315 pp.
> Good for subject maps; index includes pronunciations and altitudes and longitudes.

Hammond's Ambassador World Atlas, new census ed. Maplewood, N.J.: Hammond, 1971. 480 pp.
> Contains 170 plates of maps, gazetteer data on major cities of the world, and maps of city centers.

Hammond Medallion World Atlas. Maplewood, N.J.: Hammond, 1971. 655 pp.
> Over 600 maps: political, topographic, and thematic. 1970 census figures used.

Life Pictorial Atlas of the World. New York: Time, Inc., 1961. 600 pp.

Combination of photography and mapmaking, including global views, terrain maps, selected photographs, diagrams, and charts; gazetteer-index lists 75,000 places.

The National Atlas of the United States of America. Arlington, Va.: U.S. Dept. of the Interior, Geological Survey, 1970. 417 pp.

The official national atlas of the United States; 765 maps show physical, economic, social, and historical features. Index identifies 41,000 place names.

National Geographic Atlas of the Fifty United States. Washington, D.C.: National Geographic Society, 1960. 72 pp.

Detailed general and regional maps, with index of 30,000 names.

National Geographic Atlas of the World, 3d ed. Washington, D.C.: National Geographic Society, 1970. 331 pp.

Regional arrangement; lists 139,000 names, with brief gazetteer information.

Rand McNally Commercial Atlas and Marketing Guide. Chicago: Rand McNally, 1911 to date. Annual.

Chiefly an American atlas, emphasizing commercial aspects; lists 125,000 places.

Rand McNally Cosmopolitan World Atlas. Chicago: Rand McNally, 1971. 428 pp.

Emphasis on North America and Europe in basic political-physical maps. Four special map series: ocean world, global views, physical world, and metropolitan area maps.

Times Atlas of the World. London: Times Pub. Co., 1955–60. 5 v.

An international atlas, comprehensive in scope and of first importance. Reflecting more recent changes (political boundaries, names, etc.) is *The Times Atlas of the World: Comprehensive Edition,* 2d ed. Boston, Mass.: Houghton, 1971. 518 pp.

Includes thematic maps of the world's food, mineral, and energy resources.

GAZETTEERS

Geographical dictionaries or gazetteers, usually alphabetically arranged by names of places, are helpful for location purposes and for providing minimum essential data. Four important titles, all worldwide in scope, are these:

Columbia-Lippincott Gazetteer of the World. New York: Columbia Univ. Press, 1962. 2,148 pp.

A very complete and modern geographical dictionary, listing 130,000 names with basic information; the most comprehensive gazetteer in the English language.

Macmillan World Gazetteer and Geographical Dictionary. New York: Macmillan, 1957. 793 pp.

American edition of *Chamber's World Gazetteer.* Contains about 12,000 entries, emphasizing British interests.

The Times Index Gazetteer of the World. Boston, Mass.: Houghton, 1966. 964 pp.

Place name index to about 345,000 geographical locations. Based on *The Times Atlas of the World;* gives longitude and latitude coordinates.

Webster's New Geographical Dictionary. Springfield, Mass.: Merriam, 1972. 1,370 pp.

Identifies about 47,000 countries, regions, cities, and natural features of the world; 1970 census figures used.

Three more specialized works limit themselves to particular geographic features of the earth's surface:

Gresswell, R. Kay, and Huxley, Anthony. *Standard Encyclopedia of the World's Rivers and Lakes.* New York: Putnam, 1966. 384 pp.

Huxley, Anthony. *Standard Encyclopedia of the World's Mountains.* New York: Putnam, 1962. 383 pp.

Contains 1,500 articles, with maps, photographs, and basic facts.

Huxley, Anthony. *Standard Encyclopedia of the World's Oceans and Islands.* New York: Putnam, 1962. 383 pp.

About 2,000 articles, containing maps, photographs, and essential information.

GUIDEBOOKS

Since Americans have become the greatest of world travelers, the popularity and need for reliable, up-to-date guidebooks have grown. Publishers have responded to the demand by issuing travel guides to practically every area of the globe. Many appear in series and new editions are brought out frequently to keep up with changing conditions. Among recommended series and individual titles are the following:

Alsberg, Henry G. *The American Guide*. New York: Hastings House, 1949. 1,348 pp.

Covers whole of United States, arranged by regions.

American Guide Series, 1937–49. Various publishers.

More than 100 volumes, compiled by Federal Writers' Project, on individual states, cities, and regions.

Clark, Sydney. *"All the Best" Travel Books*. New York: Dodd, 1956–65. Frequently revised guides to European, Latin American, Oriental, and South Pacific travel.

Encyclopedia of World Travel. Garden City, N.Y.: Doubleday, 1961. 4 v.

Guide to international travel, with concise general and tourist information arranged by countries.

Fodor's Modern Guides. New York: McKay, 33 v. revised annually.

Mainly European, but includes also Caribbean, South America, India, Japan, and East Asia.

Hanson, Earl P., and others. *The New World Guides to the Latin American Republics*, 3d ed. New York: Duell, 1950. 3 v.

V. 1, Mexico, Central America, and the West Indies; v. 2, Andes and West Coast countries; v. 3, East Coast countries.

Mobil Travel Guides. New York: Simon and Schuster, 1960 to date. Seven regional volumes for the United States, containing road maps and information on hotels, motels, restaurants, resorts, and points of interest. In the same field: American Automobile Association. *Tour Guides: What to See and Where to Stay, Where to Dine—a Catalog of Complete Travel*

Information. Washington, D.C.: Amer. Auto. Assoc., 1971 to date. Annual. Issued in twelve regional series for the United States.

Muirhead's Blue Guides. Chicago: Rand McNally, 1958–72. 18 v.
Confined to European countries and cities.

Nagel's Travel Guides. New York: Taplinger, 1949–62. 40 v.
Chiefly European countries and cities.

Neal, Jack A., comp. *Reference Guide for Travelers.* New York: Bowker, 1969. 674 pp.
Geographically arranged annotated list of English-language guidebooks and background readings for the traveler; over 1,200 entries cover the United States and seventy other countries.

New Horizons World Guide. New York: Simon and Schuster, 1954 to date. Annual.
Sponsored by Pan American World Airways; worldwide scope. Supplemented by individual guidebooks for eight European countries.

Regions of America. New York: Harper, 1959–68. 11 v.
Series in progress. Thus far relates mainly to north and south Atlantic states, the midwest, and the Rocky Mountains.

Rivers of America. New York: Holt, 1938–63. 53 v.
Gives history and folklore of the area through which each river flows.

World Travel Directory; Official Guide to the Worldwide Travel Industry. New York: Ziff-Davis, 1973. 626 pp.

GENERAL

Alexander, Gerard L. *Guide to Atlases: World, Regional, National, Thematic; an International Listing of Atlases Published since 1950.* Metuchen, N.J.: Scarecrow Press, 1971. 671 pp.
Lists 5,556 atlases, with indexes to publishers, language, and authors, cartographers, and editors.

American Geographical Society of New York, Map Dept. *Index to Maps in Books and Periodicals.* Boston, Mass.: G. K. Hall, 1968. 10 v.

Photoreproduction of card catalog maintained by Map Department. Arranged alphabetically by subject and geographical-political division.

Geographical Abstracts A-F. Norwich, England: Geo Abstracts, Univ. of East Anglia, 1966 to date. Bimonthly.

Subject arrangement in six sections: geomorphology; biogeography and climatology; economic geography; social geography and cartography; sedimentology; regional and community planning. Section and comprehensive annual author-subject indexes.

Larousse Encyclopedia of World Geography (Europe). New York: Putnam, 1961. 440 pp.

Lock, C. B. Muriel. *Geography; a Reference Handbook,* 2d ed. Hamden, Conn.: Shoe String Press, 1972. 529 pp.

Covers geographical works, scholars, organizations, publishers, and national bibliographies. Author, subject, and title index.

Stamp, Sir Laurence D., ed. *Longmans Dictionary of Geography.* London: Longmans, 1966, 492 pp.

Defines geographical terms, gives brief biographies of leading geographers and descriptions of many countries and cities. Refers to sources of additional information.

Walsh, S. Padraig, ed. *General World Atlases in Print; a Comparative Analysis,* 4th ed. New York: Bowker, 1973. 208 pp.

Provides guidelines for selection; title index and directory of publishers.

Wright, John K., and Platt, Elizabeth T. *Aids to Geographical Research,* 2d ed. New York: Columbia Univ. Press, 1947. 331 pp.

Comprehensive listing and descriptions of bibliographies, periodicals, atlases, gazetteers, and other reference books.

9
Books about People

Following Alexander Pope's dictum that "The proper study of mankind is man," biographical reference books have proliferated, ranging from those which attempt to cover all the world in every era to specialized works relating to particular localities or professions. Major categories of biographical dictionaries and similar compilations in the field are these:

GENERAL BIOGRAPHY

Slocum, Robert B. *Biographical Dictionaries and Related Works.* Detroit, Mich.: Gale Research Co., 1967. 1,056 pp. *Supplement.* Detroit, Mich.: Gale Research Co., 1972. 852 pp.
International bibliography of biographical works. With supplement, over 8,000 titles are listed.

Chamber's Biographical Dictionary: The Great of All Nations and All Times, rev. ed.   New York: St. Martin's, 1969. 1,432 pp.
Includes about 10,000 sketches of historically famous persons.

Hyamson, Albert M.   *A Dictionary of Universal Biography of All Ages and of All Peoples,* 2d ed. New York: Dutton, 1951. 679 pp.
An index of over 100,000 names, from all countries and all times, appearing in twenty-four standard biographical dictionaries.

The McGraw-Hill Encyclopedia of World Biography. New York: McGraw-Hill, 1973. 12 v.

Student-oriented (junior high school through college) compilation of 5,000 biographies. Individuals of historical prominence in all fields of endeavor are included, with annotated bibliographies for each. Classified index.

New Century Cyclopedia of Names, rev. ed.   New York: Appleton, 1954. 3 v.

Contains more than 100,000 proper names of persons, places, literary characters, fictional works, etc.

The New York Times Obituaries Index, 1858–1968.   New York: New York Times, 1970. 1,136 pp.

Alphabetical cumulation of over 353,000 names listed in the *New York Times* obituary columns from September, 1858, through December, 1968.

Thomas, Joseph. *Universal Pronouncing Dictionary of Biography and Mythology.* Philadelphia, Pa.: Lippincott, 1930. 2,550 pp.

Brief accounts of about 50,000 persons of all nations and periods.

Webster's Biographical Dictionary.   Springfield, Mass.: Merriam, 1971. 1,697 pp.

A universal biographical compilation of some 40,000 names, living and dead.

Biography Index.   New York: Wilson, 1947 to date. Quarterly with annual and triennial cumulations.

Index to biographical material in books and magazines in English wherever published.

GENERAL BIOGRAPHY: CURRENT

Blue Book; Leaders of the English-Speaking World, 1971–72. New York: St. Martin's, 1972. 1,429 pp.

Covers arts, sciences, business, and the professions; about 15,000 individuals are listed.

Current Biography.   New York: Wilson, 1940 to date. Monthly and annual.

Contains several hundred sketches, written in informal, popular style, each year of persons prominent in the news, na-

tional and international. Annual editions indexed by names
and professions.

International Who's Who. London: Europa Pub., 1935 to date.
Annual.
Sketches of internationally prominent individuals in various
countries.

Who's Who in the World. Chicago: Marquis, 1970 to date. Biennial.
First edition contains about 25,000 biographies of individuals
from 150 countries whose "position or achievement makes
them noteworthy."

World Biography, 5th ed. Farmingdale, N.Y.: Inst. for Research
in Biography, 1954. 1,215 pp.
Contains *Who's Who* type sketches of about 40,000 persons
from sixty countries.

AMERICAN BIOGRAPHY

Appleton's Cyclopaedia of American Biography. New York: Ap-
pleton, 1887–1900. 7 v.
Long articles, many illustrated with portraits and facsimiles
of autographs. Includes prominent individuals from Canada,
Mexico, and South America as well as United States citizens.
Analytical index.

Dictionary of American Biography. New York: Scribner, 1928–
37. 20 v. Supplements 1–3. New York: Scribner, 1944–73. 3 v.
The leading scholarly American biographical dictionary; excludes living persons. There is an abbreviated edition: *Concise Dictionary of American Biography.* New York: Scribner,
1964. 1,273 pp.

James, Edward T. and Janet W., eds. *Notable American
Women, 1607–1950.* Cambridge, Mass.: Belknap Press of
Harvard Univ., 1972. 3 v.
Evaluative articles on 1,359 American women influential in
all fields of endeavor.

National Cyclopaedia of American Biography. New York: White,
1892 to date. 53 v.
More complete but less selective than the *Dictionary of
American Biography.* New volume added annually.

AMERICAN BIOGRAPHY: CURRENT

Who's Who in America. Chicago: Marquis, 1899 to date. Biennial.

"A biographical dictionary of notable living men and women." Supplemented by *Who's Who in the East, Who's Who in the Midwest, Who's Who in the South and Southwest,* and *Who's Who in the West,* issued by the same publisher.

Who Was Who in America. Chicago: Marquis, 1942–68. 4 v.

Sketches removed from *Who's Who in America* because of death, 1897–1968. Supplemented by *Who Was Who in America; Historical Volume, 1607–1896.* Chicago: Marquis, 1963. 672 pp. Contains 13,300 biographies of prominent Americans who died prior to 1896.

Who's Who of American Women. Chicago: Marquis, 1958 to date. Biennial.

"A biographical dictionary of notable living American women."

BRITISH BIOGRAPHY

Dictionary of National Biography. London: Smith, Elder, 1908–9. 22 v. Supplements 1–7. London: Oxford Univ. Press, 1912–71. 7 v. Condensed edition: *The Concise Dictionary of National Biography from the Beginnings to 1950.* London: Oxford Univ. Press, 1948–61. 2 v.

The outstanding collection of British biography, containing more than 30,000 accounts of deceased persons.

Who's Who. London: Black, 1849 to date. Annual.

Biographical sketches of living persons, mainly British.

Who Was Who, 1897–1970. London: Black, 1929–72. 6 v.

"A companion to *Who's Who;* containing the biographies of those who died during the period."

NATIONAL BIOGRAPHY: CURRENT

In addition to the American and British current biographical compilations, many other countries have who's who publications, the major ones in English. Examples are the following:

Asia Who's Who
Who's Who in Australia
Who's Who in Austria
Who's Who in Belgium
Who's Who in Canada
Who's Who in China
Who's Who in France
Who's Who in Germany
Who's Who in Italy
Japan Biographical Encyclopedia and Who's Who
Who's Who in the Netherlands
Who's Who in New Zealand
Who's Who in Southern Africa
Who's Who in Spain
Who's Who in Switzerland
Who's Who in Turkey
Who's Who in the U.A.R. and the Near East
Prominent Personalities in the USSR

BIOGRAPHICAL GUIDES IN SPECIAL FIELDS

American Architects Directory, 3d ed.   New York: Bowker, 1970.
   1,126 pp.
   Biographical and professional data on 23,000 United States
   architects.
American Men of Medicine, 3d ed.   Farmingdale, N.Y.: Inst. for
   Research in Biography, 1961. 768 pp.
American Men and Women of Science, 12th ed.   New York:
   Bowker, 1971–73. 8 v.
   Who's who of living scientists: v. 1–6, physical and biological
   sciences; v. 1–2, social and behavioral sciences. Similar works
   are the *Directory of British Scientists* and *Who's Who in
   Soviet Science and Technology.*
American Political Science Association.   *Biographical Directory,*
   4th ed. Washington, D.C.: The Association, 1961. 355 pp.
Asimov, Isaac.   *Asimov's Biographical Encyclopedia of Science
   and Technology: The Lives and Achievements of 1195 Great
   Scientists from Ancient Times to the Present, Chronologically*

Arranged, rev. ed. Garden City, N.Y.: Doubleday, 1972. 805 pp.

Biographical Directory of the American Psychiatric Association, 6th ed. New York: Bowker, 1973.

Biographical sketches include information on training, experience, special areas of certification, publications, etc.

A Biographical Directory of Librarians in the United States and Canada, 5th ed. Chicago: Amer. Library Assoc., 1970. 1,250 pp.

Dictionary of Scientific Biography. New York: Scribner, 1970————. In progress, to be completed in twelve volumes.

Over 4,500 scientists from all areas and periods will be included.

Directory of American Scholars, 5th ed. New York: Bowker, 1969. 4 v. New edition: 1974.

Intended as a companion to *American Men and Women of Science.* Contents: v. 1, history; v. 2, English, speech, and drama; v. 3, foreign languages, linguistics, and philology; v. 4, philosophy, religion, and law. Name index.

Friedman, Leon, and Israel, Fred L., eds. *The Justices of the United States Supreme Court, 1789–1969; Their Lives and Major Opinions.* New York: Chelsea House/Bowker, 1969. 4 v.

Biographical sketches by scholars; includes select bibliographies, texts of representative opinions.

International Businessmen's Who's Who. London: Burke's Peerage, 1967. 562 pp.

Leaders in Education, 4th ed. New York: Jacques Cattell/Bowker, 1971. 1,097 pp.

Includes 15,000 leading educators in the United States and Canada.

National Faculty Directory. Detroit, Mich.: Gale Research Co., 1970 to date. Annual.

Includes faculty members at United States junior colleges, colleges, and universities.

Who's Who in Advertising. New York: Who's Who in Advertising, 1963. 1,275 pp.

Who's Who in American Art, 11th ed.   New York: Bowker, 1973. 895 pp. Triennial.

In the same field is *Who's Who in Art*. London: Art Trade Press, 1927 to date. Biennial.

Who's Who in American College and University Administration. New York: Crowell-Collier Educational Corp., 1970 to date. Successor to *Presidents and Deans of American Colleges and Universities*, 8th ed., 1965.

Who's Who in American Education; an Illustrated Biographical Dictionary of Eminent Living Educators of the United States and Canada.   Nashville, Tenn.: Who's Who in Amer. Education, 1928 to date.
Biennial.

Who's Who in American Politics; a Biographical Directory of United States Political Leaders.   New York: Bowker, 1967 to date. Biennial.

Includes politicians at the local, state, and national levels.

Who's Who in Atoms; an International Reference Book, 5th ed. New York: International Publications Service, 1969.

Who's Who in Engineering, 9th ed.   New York: Lewis Historical Pub. Co., 1964. 2,198 pp.

Who's Who in Finance and Industry, 1974–1975, 18th ed.   Chicago: Marquis, 1973.

Who's Who in Government, 1972–1973.   Chicago: Marquis, 1972. 785 pp. Over 16,000 entries; emphasis on United States federal government.

Who's Who in Graphic Art.   Zurich: Amstutz & Herdeg, 1962. 586 pp.

Who's Who in Insurance.   New York: Underwriter Printing and Pub. Co., 1948 to date. Annual.

Who's Who in Music and Musicians' International Directory, 6th ed.   New York: Hafner, 1972. 498 pp.

Who's Who in Science in Europe; a New Reference Guide to West European Scientists.   Guernsey: F. Hodgson, 1967. 3 v.

Who's Who in Soviet Social Sciences, Humanities, Art and Government. New York: Telberg Book Co., 1961. 147 pp.

Who's Who in the Theatre; a Biographical Record of the Contemporary Stage, 15th ed. New York: Pitman, 1972.

World Who's Who in Science; a Biographical Dictionary of Notable Scientists from Antiquity to the Present. Chicago: Marquis, 1968. 1,855 pp.
Contains 30,000 biographical sketches for the physical and biological sciences.

BIOGRAPHIES OF AUTHORS

Browning, David C. *Everyman's Dictionary of Literary Biography.* New York: Dutton, 1960. 769 pp.
Brief biographical sketches of more than 2,000 English and American authors, listing principal works with dates.

Burke, William J., and Howe, Will D. *American Authors and Books, 1640 to the Present Day,* 3d ed. New York: Crown, 1972. 719 pp.
Biographical and bibliographical data for authors in all fields.

Contemporary Authors: The International Bio-Bibliographical Guide to Current Authors and Their Works. Detroit, Mich.: Gale Research Co., 1962 to date. Annual.
Each issue contains sketches of about 1,000 authors in various fields.

Kunitz, Stanley J., and Haycraft, Howard. *American Authors, 1600–1900; a Biographical Dictionary of American Literature . . . with 1,300 Biographies and 400 Portraits.* New York: Wilson, 1938. 846 pp.

Kunitz, Stanley J., and Haycraft, Howard. *British Authors before 1800; a Biographical Dictionary . . . with 650 Biographies and 220 Portraits.* New York: Wilson, 1952. 584 pp.
Popular sketches, 300 to 1,500 words in length; principal works listed.

Kunitz, Stanley J. *British Authors of the Nineteenth Century . . . with 1000 Biographies and 350 Portraits.* New York: Wilson, 1936. 677 pp.

Kunitz, Stanley J., and Colby, Vineta. *European Authors, 1000–*

1900; a Biographical Dictionary of European Literature.
New York: Wilson, 1967. 1,016 pp.

Biographical sketches for 967 continental European authors.

Kunitz, Stanley J., and Haycraft, Howard. *Twentieth Century
Authors; a Biographical Dictionary of Modern Literature . . .
with 1850 Biographies and 1700 Portraits.* New York: Wilson,
1942. 1,577 pp. *First Supplement.* New York: Wilson, 1955.
1,123 pp.

Magill, Frank N. *Cyclopedia of World Authors.* New York:
Harper, 1958. 1,198 pp.

Treats lives and works of about 750 authors included in compiler's *Masterpieces of World Literature.*

GENEALOGY AND HERALDRY

American Genealogical-Biographical Index.   Middletown, Conn.:
The Index, 1942–54. 48 v. (Series 1); 1955——, v. 1 (Series 2),
in progress.

Bibliographical guide to biographical and genealogical publications.

Doane, Gilbert H.   *Searching for Your Ancestors,* 3d ed. Minneapolis: Univ. of Minnesota Press, 1960. 198 pp.

Guide to genealogical research methods.

Filby, P. William.   *American and British Genealogy and Heraldry: a Selected List of Books.*   Chicago: Amer. Library
Assoc., 1970. 184 pp.

Lists more than 1,800 items published through 1968. Author-
subject index.

Fox-Davies, Arthur C. *Armorial Families,* 7th ed. London:
Hurst & Blackett, 1929. 2 v. (Reprinted: Rutland, Vt.: Tuttle,
1969.)

"A dictionary of gentlemen of coat-armour." Extensively illustrated.

Fox-Davies, Arthur C.   *A Complete Guide to Heraldry,* rev. ed.
London: Nelson, 1969. 513 pp.

Deals in detail with origin and history of heraldry; illustrated.

Franklyn, Julian, and Tanner, John. *An Encyclopaedic Dictionary of Heraldry.* Oxford: Pergamon, 1970. 367 pp.
Covers entire field of heraldry; illustrated.

Kaminow, Marion J. *Genealogies in the Library of Congress: A Bibliography.* Baltimore, Md.: Magna Carta Bk., 1972. 2 v.
Comprehensive listing of American and British family histories; 20,000 entries are arranged by family surname.

Parker, James. *A Glossary of Terms Used in Heraldry.* Rutland, Vt.: Tuttle, 1969. 659 pp.

Pine, Leslie G. *American Origins.* Garden City, N.Y.: Doubleday, 1960. 357 pp.
Guide to European genealogical sources for American families.

Pine, Leslie G. *The Genealogist's Encyclopedia.* New York: Weybright and Talley, 1969. 360 pp.
Emphasizes Great Britain and continental Europe.

Reaney, Percy H. *The Origin of English Surnames.* New York: Barnes & Noble, 1967. 415 pp.
Gives development, classification, changes in pronunciation and spelling, etc., of hereditary family names.

Smith, Elsdon C. *American Surnames.* Philadelphia, Pa.: Chilton, 1969. 370 pp.
Discusses origins of the most common American family names. Index; bibliography.

Virkus, Frederick A. *The Compendium of American Genealogy.* Chicago, Ill.: Inst. of Amer. Genealogy, 1925–42. 7 v. (Reprinted: Baltimore, Md.: Genealogical Pub. Co., 1968.)
"The standard genealogical encyclopedia of the first families of America."

10
Covering the Universe

"Encyclopedias," wrote C. M. Francis, "are the barebones of all subjects and the rotundity of none." Nevertheless, along with language dictionaries, general encyclopedias are the most constantly consulted of reference books. While seldom treating any subject in exhaustive detail, a reliable encyclopedia is usually an excellent beginning point for research on practically any topic.

All major encyclopedias have abandoned the plan once in vogue to issue completely revised editions at intervals of some years. Instead, they follow a "continuous revision" policy, updating a certain proportion annually. Thus, at any given time, some articles are more abreast of current developments than are others. This fact makes desirable consultation of yearbooks and other sources for more recent information, to supplement the encyclopedias.

There is a wide range of general encyclopedias available on the market and in libraries, varying from highly condensed, one-volume compilations to such giants as the *Britannica* and the *Americana*. Critical analyses appear in the American Library Association's semimonthly *Booklist* (formerly *The Booklist and Subscription Books Bulletin*). Another useful guide is S. P. Walsh's *General Encyclopedias in Print, 1973, a Comparative Analysis,* 9th ed. (New York: Bowker, 1973), 300 pp. Among English-language encyclopedias, the following lead the field:

GENERAL ENCYCLOPEDIAS

American Peoples Encyclopedia. New York: Grolier, annual editions. 20 v.

Extensively revised, good general encyclopedia, featuring short, concise articles, excellent illustrations, atlas and index volume.

Collier's Encyclopedia. New York: Collier, annual editions. 24 v.

Excellent general encyclopedia, mainly up-to-date, well illustrated, recent maps, and an index.

Columbia Encyclopedia, 3d ed. New York: Columbia Univ. Press, 1963. 2,400 pp.

With its 75,000 articles and more than 7,000,000 words, the best and most complete of the one-volume encyclopedias.

Encyclopedia Americana. New York: Americana Corp., annual editions. 30 v.

One of the best and most dependable of general encyclopedias. Articles are generally short, except for major subjects; emphasizes modern scientific and technological developments. Has index volume.

Encyclopaedia Britannica, 15th ed. Chicago, Ill.: Encyclopaedia Britannica, 1974. 30 v.

Oldest, largest, and most famous of modern encyclopedias. Latest edition extensively revised.

Encyclopedia International. New York: Grolier, annual revisions. 20 v.

A new encyclopedia, first issued in 1964. Contains 36,000 articles, 18,500 illustrations (8,000 in color), and index; stresses up-to-dateness. Abridged version: *Grolier Universal Encyclopedia,* 10 v.

The Lincoln Library of Essential Information. Columbus, Ohio: Frontier Press. 2 v.

Revised with every printing; organized under twelve major subject divisions. Many charts, graphs, and tables; index. From the same publisher: *The Lincoln Library of the Arts,* 2 v.; *The Lincoln Library of the Language Arts,* 2 v.; *The Lincoln Library of Social Studies,* 3v.

New Standard Encyclopedia. Chicago, Ill.: Standard Education Society, annual revisions. 14 v.
Concise, well-written articles, accurate, up-to-date, and reasonably comprehensive. Excellent illustrations and maps.

ENCYCLOPEDIAS FOR CHILDREN AND YOUNG PEOPLE

Britannica Junior. Chicago, Ill.: Encyclopaedia Britannica, annual revisions. 15 v.
Designed for elementary and junior high school level. Illustrations and maps good. Index volume.
Compton's Pictured Encyclopedia. Chicago, Ill.: Compton, an-
nual revisions. 22 v.
A leading juvenile encyclopedia; reliable also for simple
reference questions at adult level. Some 21,000 illustrations,
about one-third in color.
Merit Students Encyclopedia. New York: Crowell-Collier Edu-
cational Corp., annual revisions. 20 v.
For fifth grade through high school. Curriculum-oriented
with signed articles, many illustrations. Index.
New Book of Knowledge; the Children's Encyclopedia. New
York: Grolier, annual revisions. 20 v.
Designed for children between ages of seven and fourteen.
World Book Encyclopedia. Chicago, Ill.: Field, annual revisions.
22 v.
High school and beginning college level. A modern, compre-
hensive, extensively illustrated work.

FOREIGN ENCYCLOPEDIAS

Among numerous foreign encyclopedias, the Russian, French,
German, Italian, and Spanish are outstanding:
Bol'shaia Sovetskaia Entsiklopediia. Moscow: Sovetskaia Entsik-
lopediia, 1949–60. 53 v.
Official Soviet encyclopedia; international scope.
Brockhaus' Konversations-Lexikon, 16th ed. Wiesbaden, Ger-
many: Brockhaus, 1952–58. 12 v.
Enciclopedia Italiana di Scienze, Lettere ed Arti. Rome: In-

stituto della Enciclopedia Italiana, 1929–37. 35 v. Supplements, 1938–61. 5 v.

Enciclopedia Universal Ilustrada Europeo-Americana. Barcelona, Spain: Espasa, 1905–33. 81 v. Annual supplements, 1935–58.

Encyclopaedia Universalis. Paris: Encyclopaedia Universalis France, 1968———. ———v. In progress.

A major new encyclopedia to be completed in twenty volumes.

Grand Larousse Encyclopédique. Paris: Libraire Larousse, 1960. 10 v.

YEARBOOKS

General yearbooks, usually supplementary to encyclopedias, include a variety of information relating to events, progress, and conditions during the year covered, and usually have the advantage of being more up-to-date than general encyclopedias. The principal examples are the following:

Americana Annual. New York: Americana Corp., 1923 to date.

American Yearbook, 1910–19, 1925 to date. New York: Nelson, 1929 to date. Emphasizes national and international politics and other social sciences.

Britannica Book of the Year. Chicago, Ill.: Encyclopaedia Britannica, 1938 to date.

Collier's Yearbook. New York: Collier, 1939 to date.

New International Year Book. New York: Funk & Wagnalls, 1907 to date.

World Book Year Book. Chicago, Ill.: Field, 1922 to date.

World Progress, the Standard Quarterly Review. Supplement to *New Standard Encyclopedia.*

ALMANACS

Of another type of yearbook—almanacs—there are four excellent examples, all comprehensive, generally reliable, and frequently useful compilations of miscellaneous information. The *Information Please, Reader's Digest Almanac,* and *World* almanacs emphasize the American, *Whitaker's* the British, point of view.

Information Please Almanac. New York: Macmillan, 1947 to
    date. Annual.
Reader's Digest Almanac and Yearbook. Pleasantville, N.Y.:
    Reader's Digest Assoc., 1966 to date. Annual.
Whitaker's Almanack. London: Whitaker, 1869 to date. Annual.
World Almanac and Book of Facts. New York: World-Tele-
    gram, 1868 to date. Annual.

GENERAL HANDBOOKS

Douglas, George W. *The American Book of Days,* 2d ed. New
    York: Wilson, 1948. 697 pp.
    Arranged by days of the year, gives information on holidays,
    festivals, notable anniversaries, and birthdays of famous
    Americans.
Kane, Joseph N. *Famous First Facts,* 3d ed. New York: Wilson,
    1964. 1,165 pp.
    Record of first happenings, discoveries, and inventions in the
    United States. Indexed by years, days of the month, personal
    names, and geographical locations.
McWhirter, Morris and Ross. *Guinness Book of World Records.*
    New York: Sterling Pub. Co., 1955 to date. Annual.
    Compilation of records in human endeavors and natural
    phenomena: the least, the most; the highest, the lowest, etc.

11
The Literary World

The broad field of belles lettres has attracted a host of compilers of reference works—literary dictionaries and encyclopedias, handbooks, histories, anthologies, concordances, lives of authors, bibliographies, atlases, indexes, synopses, collections of quotations, and guides to special fields, such as drama, fiction, essays, and poetry. A selection of the most useful and most frequently consulted titles in various categories follows:

GENERAL LITERATURE
Benét, William R. *The Reader's Encyclopedia,* 2d ed. New York: Crowell, 1965. 1,118 pp.
> Information on books and authors, fictional characters, literary allusions, art works, musical compositions, etc.

Cassell's Encyclopaedia of World Literature. New York: Funk & Wagnalls, 1954. 2,086 pp.
> Worldwide scope; articles on national and group literatures; 10,000 biographies of authors.

Columbia Dictionary of Modern European Literature. New York: Columbia Univ. Press, 1947. 899 pp.
> About 1,200 articles surveying literature of thirty-one European countries since 1870; mainly biographical.

Encyclopedia of World Literature in the Twentieth Century. New York: Ungar, 1967–71. 3 v.

Over 1,300 articles cover individual authors, literary movements, genres, and national literatures.

Great Books of the Western World. Chicago, Ill.: Encyclopaedia Britannica, 1952. 54 v.
Includes 443 selected works of fifty-four authors from Homer
to Freud. Comparable to the older *Harvard Classics*, reprinted 1957 in fifty-one volumes by Collier.

Grigson, Geoffrey. *The Concise Encyclopedia of Modern World
Literature*, 2d ed. London: Hutchinson, 1970. 430 pp.
Discussions of over 300 modern poets, dramatists, and novel-
ists, with illustrations.

Hackett, Alice P. *Seventy Years of Best Sellers, 1895–1965.* New
York: Bowker, 1967. 280 pp.
Over 600 books which have sold more than 750,000 copies
are analyzed, with background notes, facts, and figures. Title
and author index.

Holman, C. Hugh. *A Handbook to Literature*, 3d ed. Indianapolis, Ind.: Odyssey, 1972. 646 pp.
Over 1,360 entries cover literary terms, periods, schools, concepts. English and American literary history is outlined to
the present day.

Magill, Frank. *Cyclopedia of Literary Characters.* New York:
Harper, 1963. 1,280 pp.
Identifies 16,000 characters from 1,300 novels, dramas, etc.,
from all periods and literatures.

Myers, Robin. *A Dictionary of Literature in the English Language from Chaucer to 1940.* Oxford: Pergamon, 1970. 2 v.
Biobibliographical guide to some 3,500 authors. Geographical and chronological index to authors; title-author index.

The Penguin Companion to American Literature, 384 pp.; *The
Penguin Companion to Classical, Oriental and African Literature*, 359 pp.; *The Penguin Companion to English Literature*, 575 pp.; *The Penguin Companion to European
Literature*, 907 pp. New York: McGraw-Hill, 1969–71. 4 v.
Arranged alphabetically with emphasis on critical biographies of authors.

Reader's Companion to World Literature. New York: Dryden, 1956. 493 pp.

Articles on world literatures, biographies of authors, major literary works, literary movements, and terms.

Shaw, Harry. *Dictionary of Literary Terms.* New York: McGraw-Hill, 1972. 416 pp.

A handy guide to more than 2,000 foreign and American words and expressions.

Shipley, Joseph T. *Dictionary of World Literature,* 3d ed. Boston, Mass.: Writer, 1970. 466 pp.

About 2,000 entries on literary criticism, forms, schools, terms, etc.

Trawick, Buckner B. *World Literature.* New York: Barnes & Noble, 1953–55. 2 v.

Survey of principal world literatures, classical, medieval, and modern.

ENGLISH LITERATURE

Barnhart, Clarence L., and Halsey, William D. *The New Century Handbook of English Literature,* rev. ed. New York: Appleton, 1967. 1,167 pp.

Some 14,000 entries for literature of English and British Commonwealth nations.

Cambridge Bibliography of English Literature. Cambridge: Cambridge Univ. Press, 1941–57. 5 v. New edition in progress.

Most comprehensive bibliography in its field.

Cambridge History of English Literature. Cambridge: Cambridge Univ. Press, 1919–30. 15 v.

Most authoritative and important general history, each chapter written by a specialist. Covers from earliest times through the nineteenth century. A more recent survey based on this work is: Sampson, George. *Concise Cambridge History of English Literature,* 3d ed. Cambridge: Cambridge Univ. Press, 1970. 976 pp.

Chamber's Cyclopaedia of English Literature. Philadelphia, Pa.: Lippincott, 1922–38. 3 v.

Chronological arrangement; includes many biographies of major authors and articles on literary forms, periods, and movements.

Oxford Companion to English Literature, 4th ed. Oxford: Clarendon Press, 1967. 961 pp.
Dictionary arrangement; short articles on authors, individual books, literary characters, forms, and allusions. Also available in abridged version: Eagle, Dorothy. *Concise Oxford Dictionary of English Literature.* Oxford: Oxford Univ. Press, 1970. 628 pp.

Oxford History of English Literature. Oxford: Oxford Univ. Press, 1945————. In progress, to be completed in twelve volumes.
When completed, will be most comprehensive, up-to-date, and scholarly history of field, from beginning to present.

SHAKESPEARE, WILLIAM

Asimov, Isaac. *Asimov's Guide to Shakespeare.* Garden City, N.Y.: Doubleday, 1970. 2 v.
V. 1, Greek, Roman, and Italian plays; v. 2, English plays. Religious, historical, and technical notes accompany summaries of, and quotations from, thirty-eight plays.

Bartlett, John. *Complete Concordance . . . of Shakespeare.* New York: St. Martin's, 1953. 1,910 pp.

Campbell, Oscar J., and Quinn, Edward G., eds. *The Reader's Encyclopedia of Shakespeare.* New York: Crowell, 1966. 1,014 pp.
Contains entries for all aspects of Shakespeare study: characters, plots, critical works, related persons, places, and subjects. Selected bibliography.

Halliday, Frank E. *A Shakespeare Companion,* 1564–1964. New York: Schocken, 1964. 569 pp.
Alphabetic handbook dealing with wide variety of Shakespearean topics.

McSpadden, J. Walker. *Shakespearean Synopses; Outlines of All the Plays of Shakespeare.* New York: Crowell, 1959. 210 pp.

A similar work: Watt, Homer A. *Outlines of Shakespeare's Plays*. New York: Barnes & Noble, 1947. 219 pp.

Martin, Michael R., and Harrier, Richard C. *The Concise Encyclopedic Guide to Shakespeare*. New York: Horizon Press, 1971. 450 pp.

Plot synopses, identification of characters and quotations, etc. Appendixes include review of Shakespeare's life and theater, genealogical chart for the historical plays.

Spevack, Marvin. *A Complete and Systematic Concordance to the Works of Shakespeare*. Hildesheim, Germany: G. Olms, 1968–70. 6 v.

Accurate, computer-generated concordance to Shakespeare's comedies, tragedies, histories, and nondramatic works. Includes statistical information and index of words arranged according to frequency of occurrence.

Stevenson, Burton E. *Home Book of Shakespeare Quotations*. New York: Scribner, 1937. 2,055 pp. Reissued, 1966.

By same compiler: *The Standard Book of Shakespeare Quotations*. New York: Funk & Wagnalls, 1953. 766 pp.

Stokes, Francis G. *Dictionary of the Characters and Proper Names in the Works of Shakespeare*. Gloucester, Mass.: Peter Smith, 1949. 359 pp.

Brief accounts, in alphabetical order, of characters, names, editions, plots, and related topics.

AMERICAN LITERATURE

American Literature Abstracts; a Review of Current Scholarship in the Field of American Literature. San Jose: Dept. of English, Calif. State Univ., San Jose, 1967 to date. Semiannual.

Abstracts of periodical articles and "book review consensus" for reviews of current books in the field. Author and subject index.

Blanck, Jacob. *Bibliography of American Literature*. New Haven, Conn.: Yale Univ. Press, 1955–69. 5 v., Adams-Longfellow. In progress.

Alphabetically arranged bibliographies of about 300 American authors who died before 1930, listing first editions, important reprints, and biographical, bibliographical, and critical works.

Cambridge History of American Literature. New York: Putnam, 1917-21. 4 v. Reissued, New York: Macmillan, 1954. 3 v.

Standard history of subject, beginning with colonial and Revolutionary and continuing with early and later national literature. Interprets literature to include accounts of early travelers, explorers, and observers, newspapers and magazines, literary annuals and gift books, children's literature, and non-English writings.

Hart, James D. *The Oxford Companion to American Literature,* 4th ed. Oxford: Oxford Univ. Press, 1965. 991 pp.

Literary and social history of America, from 1000 to 1964, alphabetically arranged biographies and bibliographies of nearly 900 American authors, including summaries of novels, stories, essays, poems, and plays, and information on literary movements, magazines, and related topics.

Herzberg, Max J. *The Reader's Encyclopedia of American Literature.* New York: Crowell, 1962. 1,280 pp.

Covers American and Canadian literature, inclusive of articles on individual authors, titles, fiction characters, literary movements and groups, and periodicals.

Jones, Howard Mumford, and Ludwig, Richard M. *Guide to American Literature and Its Backgrounds since 1890,* 3d ed. Cambridge, Mass.: Harvard Univ. Press, 1964. 240 pp.

Lists background books on various aspects of American literature.

Leary, Lewis G. *Articles on American Literature, 1900–1950.* Durham, N.C.: Duke Univ. Press, 1954. 437 pp.

Supplemented by the same compiler's *Articles on American Literature, 1950–1967.* Durham, N.C.: Duke Univ. Press, 1970. 751 pp.

Nilon, Charles H. *Bibliography of Bibliographies in American Literature.* New York: Bowker, 1970. 483 pp.

Lists about 6,500 bibliographies concerned with American literature over the past 400 years. Four sections: bibliography, authors, genres, and special subjects. Author and subject indexes.

Spiller, Robert E., and others. *Literary History of the United States*, 3d ed. New York: Macmillan, 1963. 2 v.

Comprehensive history, extending and updating the *Cambridge History of American Literature*, dealing broadly with the influences that have shaped literary life of the nation from colonial times to present day. Second volume is bibliographical, containing extensive references on literature and culture, literary movements, and individual authors.

CLASSICAL LITERATURE

Avery, Catherine B. *The New Century Classical Handbook*. New York: Appleton, 1962. 1,162 pp.

Encyclopedic articles on Greek and Roman history, chiefly devoted to personal names: "the figures of myth and legend, gods and heroes, persons and places, fact and fancy."

Crowell's Handbook of Classical Literature. New York: Crowell, 1964. 448 pp.

Summaries of plays and nondramatic works of Greece and Rome, biographies of authors, notes on characters, mythological figures, etc.

Harper's Dictionary of Classical Literature and Antiquities. New York: Harper, 1897. 1,701 pp.

Articles on biography, mythology, geography, art, history, etc.

Heyden, A. A. M. van der. *Atlas of the Classical World*. New York: Nelson, 1959. 221 pp.

Photographs and maps covering cultural, religious, literary, political, and military affairs.

Oxford Classical Dictionary, 2d ed. Oxford: Clarendon Press, 1970. 1,176 pp.

Includes biography, literature, mythology, philosophy, religion, science, geography, etc.

Oxford Companion to Classical Literature. Oxford: Clarendon Press, 1937. 468 pp.

Guide to principal classical authors and their works.

Rose, H. J. *A Handbook of Greek Literature.* New York: Dutton, 1935. 454 pp.
Guide to literature from Homer to the age of Lucian.

Rose, H. J. *A Handbook of Latin Literature.* London: Methuen, 1936. 557 pp.
Guide to all aspects of Latin literature.

Seyffert, Oskar. *Dictionary of Classical Antiquities, Mythology, Religion, Literature, Art.* New York: Meridian, 1956. 716 pp.
A general handbook for classical subjects.

ESSAYS

A.L.A. Index to General Literature, 2d ed.   Chicago, Ill.: Amer. Library Assoc., 1901–14. 2 v.
Indexes books of essays and general literature dealing with biography, literary criticism, history, travel, and social sciences.

Essay and General Literature Index.   New York: Wilson, 1934 to date. Semiannual with annual and five-year cumulations.
Continuation of *A.L.A. Index to General Literature;* author-subject index to collections of essays and anthologies of all types published since 1900. A seventy-year cumulation of 9,917 titles has been published: *Essay and General Literature Index: Works Indexed 1900–1969.* New York: Wilson, 1972. 437 pp.

FICTION

Adelman, Irving, and Dworkin, Rita.   *The Contemporary Novel: A Checklist of Critical Literature on the British and American Novel since 1945.* Metuchen, N.J.: Scarecrow Press, 1972. 614 pp.
Arranged under 187 authors, then by title of work. Cites critical reviews from about 400 journals and 600 books.

Baker, Ernest A. *History of the English Novel.* New York: Barnes & Noble, 1924–39. 10 v. Reprinted 1960.
V. 11, *Yesterday and After* by Lionel Stevenson, was published in 1967. 431 pp.

Baker, Ernest A., and Packman, James. *Guide to the Best Fiction, English and American,* 3d ed. New York: Barnes & Noble, 1967. 634 pp.
Lists several thousand works, with brief descriptions. Index of authors, titles, subjects, historical names, allusions, places, and characters.

Coan, Otis W., and Lillard, R. G. *America in Fiction; an Annotated List of Novels that Interpret Aspects of Life in the United States, Canada, and Mexico,* 5th ed. Palo Alto, Calif.: Pacific Books, 1967. 232 pp.

Cook, Dorothy E., and Monro, Isabel S. *Short Story Index.* New York: Wilson, 1953. 1,553 pp. *Supplement, 1950–54* (1956); *Supplement, 1955–58* (1960); *Supplement, 1959–63* (1965); *Supplement, 1964–68* (1969).
Indexes by author, title, and frequently by subject about 60,000 stories published before 1950, in main work; supplements add over 36,000 stories.

Dickinson, A. T., Jr. *American Historical Fiction,* 3d ed. Metuchen, N.J.: Scarecrow Press, 1971. 380 pp.
In chronological groups from colonial period to 1970; brief annotations.

Fiction Catalog, 8th ed. New York: Wilson, 1971. 653 pp. Annual supplements.
Author list of 4,350 selected works of adult fiction in English, with annotations. Title and subject index.

Hagen, Ordean A. *Who Done It? An Encyclopedic Guide to Detective, Mystery and Suspense Fiction.* New York: Bowker, 1969. 834 pp.
Information on 20,000 titles published from 1841 to 1967. Includes subject guide and indexes for characters and locales.

Irwin, Leonard B. *A Guide to Historical Fiction: For the Use of Schools and Libraries and for the General Reader,* 10th ed. Philadelphia, Pa.: McKinley, 1971. 255 pp.
First nine editions compiled by Hannah Logasa under title *Historical Fiction.* Classified list with author and title indexes.

McGarry, Daniel D., and White, Sarah H. *Historical Fiction Guide: Annotated, Chronological, Geographical, and Topical*

List of Five Thousand Selected Historical Novels. Metuchen, N.J.: Scarecrow Press, 1964. 628 pp.

Lists works in English from ancient times to 1900; author and title index.

Siemon, Fred. *Ghost Story Index: An Author-Title Index to More than 2,200 Stories of Ghosts, Horrors, and the Macabre Appearing in 190 Books and Anthologies.* San Jose, Calif.: Library Research Assoc., 1967. 141 pp.

POETRY

Granger's Index to Poetry, 5th ed.   New York: Columbia Univ. Press, 1962. 2,123 pp. *Supplement,* 1967. 416 pp.

Indexes 574 anthologies of poetry, with indexes to titles, first lines, authors, and subjects. Supplement adds ninety-seven anthologies.

Preminger, Alex, and others.   *Princeton Encyclopedia of Poetry and Poetics.* Princeton, N.J.: Princeton Univ. Press, 1972. 906 pp.

About 1,000 articles by 215 scholars on history of poetry, techniques of poetry, poetics and criticism, and poetry's relationship to other fields of interest.

Stevenson, Burton E.   *The Home Book of Modern Verse,* 2d ed. New York: Holt, 1953, 1,124 pp.

Selection of English and American twentieth-century poetry.

Stevenson, Burton E.   *The Home Book of Verse, American and English,* 9th ed. New York: Holt, 1953. 2 v.

Includes poems from 1580 to 1922, arranged by subjects, with author, title, and first line indexes.

QUOTATIONS

Bartlett, John.   *Familiar Quotations; a Collection of Passages, Phrases and Proverbs Traced to Their Sources in Ancient and Modern Literature,* 14th ed. Boston, Mass.: Little, Brown, 1968. 1,750 pp.

Arranged chronologically by author with author and word indexes.

Hoyt's New Cyclopedia of Practical Quotations, 3d ed. New
York: Funk & Wagnalls, 1940. 1,343 pp.
Arranged by subjects with full index.
Magill, Frank N. *Magill's Quotations in Context.* New York:
Harper, 1966. 1,230 pp.
Gives background and surrounding passages for more than
2,000 quotations from all periods of Western literature. Sup-
plemented by *Magill's Quotations in Context: Second Series.*
New York: Harper, 1969. 1,350 pp.; adds 1,500 quotations.
Mencken, Henry L. *A New Dictionary of Quotations on Histori-
cal Principles from Ancient and Modern Sources.* New York:
Knopf, 1942. 1,347 pp.
Includes many proverbs, foreign and literary quotations, ar-
ranged by subjects; no index.
Oxford Dictionary of Quotations, 2d ed. Oxford: Oxford Univ.
Press, 1953. 1,003 pp.
Arranged alphabetically by authors, with index of key words.
Stevenson, Burton E. *The Home Book of Proverbs, Maxims, and
Familiar Phrases.* New York: Macmillan, 1948. 2,957 pp.
Collection of about 73,000 sayings from many languages and
periods, with index of key words. Reprinted in 1965 under
title *The Macmillan Book of Proverbs, Maxims, and Famous
Phrases.*
Stevenson, Burton E. *Home Book of Quotations, Classical and
Modern,* 10th ed. New York: Dodd, 1967. 2,816 pp.
About 100,000 quotations from authors of all periods and
countries, arranged by subjects with full index. Two similar
compilations are: Bohle, Bruce. *Home Book of American
Quotations.* New York: Dodd, 1967. 512 pp. Evans, Bergen.
Dictionary of Quotations. New York: Delacorte, 1968.
2,029 pp.
Tripp, Rhoda T. *The International Thesaurus of Quotations.*
New York: Crowell, 1970. 1,088 pp.
Some 16,000 quotations are arranged under key concepts
with references from author, source, and key word indexes.

SYNOPSES

Haydn, Hiram, and Fuller, Edmund. *Thesaurus of Book Digests: Digests of the World's Permanent Writings from the Ancient Classics to Current Literature.* New York: Crown, 1949. 831 pp. Digests of standard works of all periods.

Keller, Helen R. *The Reader's Digest of Books.* New York: Macmillan, 1936. 1,447 pp.
   Outlines of standard works of world literature, fiction and nonfiction, of all periods.

Lovell, John. *Digests of Great American Plays.* New York: Crowell, 1961. 452 pp.
   Summaries of more than 100 plays, 1776 to date.

Magill, Frank N. *Masterpieces of World Literature in Digest Form.* New York: Harper, 1952–69. 4 v.
   Summaries of plots and other details of novels, plays, and major poems.

Magill, Frank N. *Masterplots.* New York: Salem Press, 1960. 6 v.
   Contains 1,510 plot stories and essay reviews.

Shipley, Joseph T. *Guide to Great Plays.* Washington, D.C.: Public Affairs Press, 1956. 867 pp.
   Covers about 600 plays of all periods, including plot highlights.

JUVENILE LITERATURE

Brewton, John E. and Sara W. *Index to Children's Poetry.* New York: Wilson, 1942. 966 pp. *First Supplement,* 1954, 405 pp.; *Second Supplement,* 1965, 453 pp.
   Indexes by author, title, subject, and first line a total of 30,000 poems by 5,200 authors in 281 collections. Extended by same authors' *Index to Poetry for Children and Young People: 1964–1969.* New York: Wilson, 1972. 574 pp.; indexes 11,000 poems by 2,000 authors in 117 collections.

Children's Catalog, 12th ed.   New York: Wilson, 1971. 1,156 pp. Annual supplements.
   Annotated list of 5,119 selected books for children; author, title and subject index.

Cushing, Helen G. *Children's Song Index.* New York: Wilson, 1936. 798 pp.

Indexes some 22,000 songs by titles, first lines, authors, composers, and subjects.

Eastman, Mary H. *Index to Fairy Tales, Myths, and Legends,* 2d ed. Boston, Mass.: Faxon, 1926–52. 3 v.

Title index to fairy tales and legends in numerous collections.

Kunitz, Stanley J. *Junior Book of Authors,* 2d ed. New York: Wilson, 1951. 309 pp.

"The lives of writers and illustrators for younger readers, from Lewis Carroll and Louisa Alcott to the present day." Supplemented by: Fuller, Muriel. *More Junior Authors.* New York: Wilson, 1963. 235 pp. Montreville, Doris de, and Hill, Donna. *Third Book of Junior Authors.* New York: Wilson, 1972. 320 pp.

Macpherson, Maud R. *Children's Poetry Index.* Boston, Mass.: Faxon, 1938. 453 pp.

Indexes more than 12,000 poems under author, title, and subject.

Oxford Dictionary of Nursery Rhymes. Oxford: Clarendon Press, 1951. 467 pp.

Anthology of 550 English nursery rhymes, alphabetically arranged by catchword or first line; includes illustrations.

Sell, Violet, and others. *Subject Index to Poetry for Children and Young People.* Chicago, Ill.: Amer. Library Assoc., 1957. 582 pp.

Indexes 157 collections.

Subject Index to Children's Plays. Chicago, Ill.: Amer. Library Assoc., 1940. 277 pp.

Guide to 202 collections of plays, indexed under 793 subjects.

12
The Historical View

Since Herodotus, Thucydides, and Xenophon changed history from mythology and legend to a reasonable facsimile of factual reality, historians have flourished in every era. The mazes of historical literature, in turn, have encouraged the creation of various types of guides—bibliographies, dictionaries, encyclopedic treatments, atlases, chronologies, and so forth. Reference librarians place extensive reliance upon the following works.

GENERAL HISTORY

Annual Register of World Events; a Review of the Year, 1758 to date.   New York: St. Martin's. Annual.
Published for over two centuries. Includes text of selected documents and abstracts of important speeches.

Baldwin, Hanson W., ed.   *The Great Battles of History Series.* Philadelphia, Pa.: Lippincott, 1962——. In progress.
Thirteen volumes by various authors published, 1962–66.

Bengtson, Hermann.   *Introduction to Ancient History.* Berkeley: Univ. of California Press, 1970. 213 pp.
Translation of *Einfuhrung in die alte Geschichte* by R. I. Frank and Frank D. Gilliard. Carefully selected bibliographies for main areas of ancient history and allied fields. Most titles are recent and are in English.

Cambridge Ancient History.   New York: Macmillan, 1922–39.

12 v., and 5 v. of illustrative plates. 3d edition in progress, 1970——.

Chronological and regional arrangement.

Cambridge Mediaeval History. New York: Macmillan, 1911–36. 8 v.

Deals mainly with Western Europe from end of Roman Empire through Middle Ages. 2d edition in progress, 1966——.

Cottrell, Leonard. *The Concise Encyclopedia of Archaeology,* 2d ed. New York: Hawthorn, 1971. 430 pp.

Deals with recent archeological discoveries and techniques.

Facts on File, a Weekly World News Digest with Cumulative Index. New York: Facts on File, 1940 to date. Weekly with annual cumulations.

Classified digest of general news events with emphasis on the United States and international developments affecting the United States. A similar service with a British perspective is *Keesing's Contemporary Archives; Weekly Diary of World Events with Index Continually Kept Up-to-Date.* London: Keesing's, 1931 to date.

Historical Abstracts; Bibliography of the World's Periodical Literature, 1775 to Present. Santa Barbara, Calif.: American Bibliographical Center, Clio Press, 1955 to date. Quarterly.

Includes articles relating to world history in some 2,200 periodicals. Classified arrangement with annual and five-year subject and author indexes. In two parts: Part A, modern history abstracts, 1775–1914; Part B, twentieth-century abstracts, 1914 to the present.

Howe, George F., and others. *The American Historical Association's Guide to Historical Literature.* New York: Macmillan, 1961. 962 pp.

Listing of most significant printed materials relating to world history of various eras, selected by 230 specialists.

Keller, Helen R. *Dictionary of Dates.* New York: Macmillan, 1934. 2 v. Reprinted, New York: Hafner, 1971.

Records events of world history by dates from ancient times to 1930; arranged chronologically under countries.

Langer, William L. *An Encyclopedia of World History*, 5th ed. Boston, Mass.: Houghton, 1972. 1,569 pp.
From prehistoric times to 1970; in form of outlines chronologically arranged, with detailed index.

Larned, Josephus N. *New Larned History for Ready References.* Springfield, Mass.: Nichols, 1922–24. 12 v.
Alphabetical dictionary of world history, based on quoted articles from authoritative writers.

Larousse Encyclopedia of Ancient and Medieval History. New York: Harper, 1963. 413 pp.

Larousse Encyclopedia of Modern History: From 1500 to the Present Day. New York: Harper, 1964. 405 pp.
Richly illustrated and comprehensive treatment.

Mirkin, Stanford M. *What Happened When; a Noted Researcher's Almanac of Yesterdays,* rev. ed. New York: Washburn, 1966. 442 pp.
Dictionary of dates of important events in world history, arranged chronologically under days of the year.

Morris, Richard B., and Irwin, Graham W., eds. *Harper Encyclopedia of the Modern World; a Concise Reference History from 1760 to the Present.* New York: Harper, 1970. 1,271 pp.
Summary of most significant facts of world history in two parts: chronology by area of political, military, and diplomatic history; topical treatment of social, cultural, technological, and economic developments. Detailed index.

The New Cambridge Modern History. Cambridge: Cambridge Univ. Press, 1957–70. 14 v.
Covers modern history from the Renaissance through 1945. Final volume is an atlas. Supplemented by: Roach, John P. C., ed. *A Bibliography of Modern History*. Cambridge: Cambridge Univ. Press, 1968. 388 pp.

Palmer, Alan W. *A Dictionary of Modern History, 1789–1945.* London: Cresset, 1962. 314 pp.
About 1,000 entries on people, places, historical events, and movements.

Palmer, Robert R. *Atlas of World History,* rev. ed. Chicago, Ill.: Rand McNally, 1970. 216 pp.

Historical maps, some in color, with background text.

Poulton, Helen J. *The Historian's Handbook; a Descriptive Guide to Reference Works.* Norman: Univ. of Oklahoma Press, 1972. 304 pp.

Annotated guide to 940 reference works on history and closely allied fields, emphasizing English language sources.

Putnam, George P. and George H. *Dictionary of Events; a Handbook of Universal History.* New York: Grosset, 1936. 565 pp.

Chronological tables of important historical events from earliest times through 1935. Subject index and genealogical tables.

Shepherd, William R. *Historical Atlas,* 9th ed. New York: Barnes & Noble, 1964. 353 pp.

Covers world history from 1450 B.C. to 1964.

Williams, Neville. *Chronology of the Modern World: 1763 to the Present Time.* New York: McKay, 1967. 923 pp.

Precise dates are given for political and international news events and for events in the fields of arts and sciences. Detailed index. A companion volume is the same author's *Chronology of the Expanding World, 1492–1762.* New York: McKay, 1969. 700 pp.

Wright, Esmond, and Stampp, Kenneth M. *The McGraw-Hill Illustrated World History.* New York: McGraw-Hill, 1964. 529 pp.

Lavishly illustrated work, from prehistoric era to present.

AMERICAN HISTORY

Adams, James T. *Album of American History.* New York: Scribner, 1969. 6 v.

A pictorial history of the United States through 1968, starting with the colonial period, illustrating persons, places, events, customs, etc.

Adams, James T. *The Dictionary of American History.* New York: Scribner, 1942–61. 7 v. Abridged edition: *Concise Dictionary of American History.* New York: Scribner, 1962. 1,156 pp.

Short articles, written by more than a thousand historians, dealing with political, economic, social, industrial, and cultural aspects of American history, omitting biography.

America: History and Life; a Guide to Periodical Literature. Santa Barbara, Calif.: American Bibliographical Center, Clio Press, 1964 to date. Quarterly.

Abstracts articles from some 800 American and Canadian and 1,400 foreign periodicals concerned with United States and Canadian history and life. Classified arrangement; annual subject and personal name indexes.

American Heritage Book of Great Historic Places. New York: American Heritage Pub. Co., 1957. 376 pp.

Geographically arranged; illustrations, many in color, and text cover almost 3,000 historical sites.

The American Heritage Pictorial Atlas of United States History. New York: American Heritage Pub. Co., 1966. 424 pp.

Beautifully reproduced maps in color with accompanying text. Good coverage on United States operations in World War II and more recent conditions.

The Annals of America. Chicago, Ill.: Encyclopaedia Britannica, 1968–71. 21 v.

"Collection of 2,202 original source readings drawn from America's past" organized in chronological order by subject. Two-volume conspectus provides topical approach to eighteen text volumes. Index volume: proper names.

Carruth, Gorton. *The Encyclopedia of American Facts and Dates,* 6th ed. New York: Crowell, 1972. 922 pp.

Chronological arrangement, 986 to date, on wide range of topics.

Commager, Henry S. *Documents of American History,* 8th ed. New York: Appleton, 1968. 634 pp., 746 pp.

Famous documents relating to American history, 1492–1967.

Handlin, Oscar, and others. *Harvard Guide to American History.* Cambridge, Mass.: Belknap Press, 1954. 689 pp.

Guide to historical literature and sources.

Johnson, Thomas H. *The Oxford Companion to American History.* Oxford: Oxford Univ. Press, 1966. 906 pp.

Alphabetically arranged, 4,710 brief articles summarize significant periods, events, and places. Biographies of 1,800 individuals influential in American history are included.

Kane, Joseph N. *Famous First Facts: A Record of First Happenings, Discoveries and Inventions in the United States,* 3d ed. New York: Wilson, 1964. 1,165 pp.

Lord, Clifford L. and Elizabeth H. *Historical Atlas of the United States.* New York: Holt, 1953. 238 pp. Reprinted, 1969.

Maps cover political and economic history, military campaigns, population, transportation, education, agriculture, natural resources, labor, manufacturing, etc.

Morris, Richard B. *Encyclopedia of American History.* 3d ed. New York: Harper, 1970. 850 pp.

Three parts: basic chronology, listing major events in American history to 1970; topical, listing events under a variety of subjects; and biographies of 400 notable Americans.

Pageant of America, a Political History of the United States. New Haven, Conn.: Yale Univ. Press, 1925–29. 15 v.

Pictures of events and personages relating to the development of America in all periods; covers political and military history, sports, art, literature, education, etc.

Putnam, George P. and George H. *Dictionary of Events; a Handbook of Universal History.* New York: Grosset & Dunlap, 1936. 565 pp.

Chronological tables of historical events from ancient times to 1935. Subject index and genealogical tables.

Shankle, George E. *State Names, Flags, Seals, Birds, Flowers, and Other Symbols; a Study Based on Original Documents.* New York: Wilson, 1938. 522 pp. Reprinted, 1971.

U.S. Library of Congress, Reference Division. *A Guide to the Study of the United States of America.* Washington, D.C.: G.P.O., 1960. 1,193 pp.

"Representative books reflecting the development of American life and thought."

Van Doren, Charles, and others. *Webster's Guide to American History; a Chronological, Geographical, and Biographical*

Survey and Compendium. Springfield, Mass.: Merriam, 1971. 1,428 pp.

Three parts: chronology of important American events from 1492–1969; historical maps and tables; biographical information for about 1,000 prominent Americans.

Writings on American History; a Bibliography of Books and Articles on United States History. Various places and publishers, 1902 to date.

An excellent annual bibliography, though behind schedule in publication.

13
Specialized Subject Reference Books

There is scarcely any field of knowledge for which specialized reference works have not been provided. Because of the constantly expanding nature of information, experimentation, and research in many areas, as well as different approaches to available data, old reference books are frequently being superseded by new ones, or at least by revised editions.

For the convenience of the user, grouped alphabetically by subject, some of the most useful reference books relating to special subjects follow.

ACCOUNTING

Accountants' Handbook, 5th ed.   New York: Ronald Press, 1970. Various pagings.

A standard work, written by various authorities, covering all major divisions of accounting.

Davidson, Sidney, ed.   *Handbook of Modern Accounting.* New York: McGraw-Hill, 1970. 1,280 pp.

Comprehensive coverage in forty-four articles written by experts.

Includes new concepts and techniques as well as established theories and procedures.

Demarest, Rosemary R.   *Accounting: Information Sources.* Detroit, Mich.: Gale Research Co., 1971. 420 pp.

Annotated guide covers wide variety of accounting information resources; also recommends basic accounting library. Author, title, and subject indexes.

Encyclopedia of Accounting Forms and Reports. Englewood Cliffs, N.J.: Prentice-Hall, 1964. 3 v.

Forms and reports used in accounting practice, accounting systems, and in specific industries.

Kohler, Eric L. *A Dictionary for Accountants,* 4th ed. Englewood Cliffs, N.J.: Prentice-Hall, 1970. 456 pp.

Defines and explains over 2,800 accounting terms and terms in related fields.

Lasser, Jacob K. *Standard Handbook for Accountants; a Modern Encyclopedia of Auditing, Cost Control, Management, Systems Design, Forecasting, Operation of the Accounting Office, and Other Phases of Business Planning; Prepared by Sixty-two Specialists.* New York: McGraw-Hill, 1956. 1,056 pp. By the same author: *Handbook of Accounting Methods,* 3d ed. New York: Van Nostrand, 1964. 970 pp. Covers accounting problems in more than sixty industries.

Prentice-Hall, Inc. *Accountant's Encyclopedia.* Englewood Cliffs, N.J.: Prentice-Hall, 1962. 4 v.

Articles by various authorities, grouped under ten main areas of accounting practice; detailed index.

Williams, Robert I., and Dorris, Lillian. *Encyclopedia of Accounting Systems.* Englewood Cliffs, N.J.: Prentice-Hall, 1956–57. 5 v.

"Describes and illustrates accounting systems for diversified industries, businesses, and professions."

ADVERTISING

Aspley, John C. *The Sales Promotion Handbook,* 5th ed. Chicago, Ill.: Dartnell, 1966. 1,000 pp.

Deals with sales promotional activities, tools, and devices.

Barton, Roger, ed. *Handbook of Advertising Management.* New York: McGraw-Hill, 1970. Various pagings.

Covers organizing, marketing, planning, copy, media, research, legal aspects, advertising's role in society, etc.; glossary and index.

Graham, Irvin. *Encyclopedia of Advertising*, 2d ed. New York: Fairchild, 1969. 494 pp.

About 1,100 entries relating to advertising, marketing, publishing, law, research, public relations, publicity, and graphic arts.

Melcher, Daniel, and Larrick, Nancy. *Printing and Promotion Handbook; How to Plan, Produce, and Use Printing, Advertising, and Direct Mail*, 3d ed. New York: McGraw-Hill, 1966.   451 pp.

AFRICA

Africa Annual Review 1972.   New York: Africana Pub. Corp., 1972. 188 pp.

Survey of the African economies: development, place in the world economy, and country-by-country analysis.

Africa South of the Sahara.   London: Europa Pub., 1971 to date. Annual.

Economic, political, social, and educational data in four parts: background to the continent; regional organizations; country surveys; other reference material.

Junod, Violaine I., and Resnick, Idrian N. *The Handbook of Africa.* New York: New York Univ. Press, 1963. 472 pp.

Factual information on each of the more than fifty political units of Africa, stressing social, political, and economic data.

Legum, Colin. *Africa: A Handbook to the Continent,* rev. ed. New York: Praeger, 1966. 558 pp.

Deals with history, economics, and "basic information" on individual countries, biographies of leaders, and essays on Africa's sociology, culture, religions, international relations, press, and trade unionism.

Legum, Colin, and Drysdale, John, eds. *Africa Contemporary Record: Annual Survey and Documents.* London: Africa Research Ltd., 1969 to date. Annual.

"Survey of major economic, social and political developments" in three sections: essays dealing with major issues facing African nations; country-by-country review of events; reprinting of pertinent documents.

Lystad, Robert A. *The African World*. New York: Praeger, 1965. 575 pp.
> General handbook, with excellent bibliographies.

Morrison, Donald G., and others. *Black Africa; a Comparative Handbook*. New York: Free Press, 1972. 483 pp.
> Quantitative and comparative data showing social, economic, political development, etc., for thirty-two independent African nations.

Rosenthal, Eric, ed. *Encyclopaedia of Southern Africa*, 5th ed. New York: Warne, 1970. 653 pp.
> Alphabetical work treating history, biography, literature, geography, geology, natural history, social life and customs, etc., of southern African nations.

West Africa Annual. London: James Clarke, 1962 to date. Annual.
> Arranged by countries, under each providing a variety of statistics and general information.

The Year Book and Guide to East Africa. London: R. Hale, 1950 to date. Annual.
> Up-to-date social and economic information, including maps and photographs, for Kenya, Uganda, Tanganyika, Zanzibar, Portuguese East Africa, etc.

The Year Book and Guide to Southern Africa. London: R. Hale, 1901 to date. Annual.
> Current social and economic data, supplemented by maps and photographs, for South Africa, South West Africa, Rhodesia, Zambia, Malawi, etc.

AGRICULTURE

Agricultural Index, 1916–64. New York: Wilson, 1919–64.
> Alphabetical subject index to large number of agricultural periodicals and reports, bulletins, and circulars of agricultural departments and experiment stations. Title changed, October, 1964, to date, to *Biological and Agricultural Index; a Cumulative Subject Index to Periodicals in the Fields of Biology, Agriculture, and Related Sciences*. Monthly except August with annual cumulations.

Bailey, Liberty H. *Hortus Second; a Concise Dictionary of Gardening, General Horticulture, and Cultivated Plants in North America.* New York: Macmillan, 1941. 778 pp.

Bibliography of Agriculture. New York: CCM Information Corp., 1942 to date. Monthly.

Comprehensive index to over 8,000 foreign and domestic agricultural and related periodicals received in the National Agricultural Library. Arranged by broad subject categories, then alphabetically by journal citation. Subject index cumulates annually.

Blanchard, J. Richard, and Ostvold, Harald. *Literature of Agricultural Research.* Berkeley: Univ. of California Press, 1958. 231 pp.

Classified, annotated guide to reference materials, from both American and foreign sources, for agriculture in general, plant sciences, animal sciences, physical sciences, food and nutrition, and social sciences. Detailed subject and author index.

Brown, Mary Ruth, and others. *Agricultural Education in a Technical Society; an Annotated Bibliography of Resources.* Chicago, Ill.: Amer. Library Assoc., 1973. 228 pp.

Graf, Alfred Byrd. *Exotica, Series 3; Pictorial Cyclopedia of Exotic Plants from Tropical and Near-Tropical Regions,* 6th ed. E. Rutherford, N.J.: Roehrs Co., 1973. 1,834 pp.

International Association of Agricultural Economists. *World Atlas of Agriculture.* Novara, Italy: Instituto Geografico de Agostini, 1969. 3 v.

Arranged by countries.

Midwest Farm Handbook, 7th ed. Ames: Iowa State Univ. Press, 1969. 505 pp.

General handbook for farmers, not limited to midwest.

Richey, C. B. *Agricultural Engineers' Handbook.* New York: McGraw-Hill, 1961. 880 pp.

Deals with crop production equipment, soil and water conservation, farmstead structures and equipment, and basic agricultural data.

Schlebecker, John T., ed. *Bibliography of Books and Pamphlets* on the History of Agriculture in the United States, 1607–1967. Santa Barbara, Calif.: American Bibliographical Center, Clio Press, 1969. 183 pp.

Over 2,000 publications are arranged alphabetically by authors; subject and title index.

U.S. Dept. of Agriculture. *Agricultural Statistics.* Washington, D.C.: G.P.O., 1936 to date. Annual.

Covers production, foreign trade, farm capital and income, conservation, etc.

U.S. Dept. of Agriculture. *Yearbook of Agriculture,* 1894 to date. Washington, D.C.: G.P.O., 1895 to date. Annual.

Since 1936 each *Yearbook* has been devoted to a particular subject: food, water, climate, grass, trees, etc.

Van Royen, William. *Atlas of the World's Resources.* New York: Prentice-Hall, 1952–54. 2 v.

Contents: v. 1, agricultural resources of the world; v. 2, mineral resources of the world.

Wilcox, Earley V. *Modern Farmers' Cyclopedia of Agriculture.* New York: Orange Judd, 1952. 543 pp.

Deals with field crops, garden crops, fruits and nuts, beef cattle and dairying, other livestock, poultry, drainage, fertilizers, irrigation, soils, etc. Illustrated.

Winburne, John N. *A Dictionary of Agricultural and Allied Terminology.* East Lansing: Michigan State Univ. Press, 1962. 905 pp.

Brief definitions of thousands of terms used in agriculture.

ANECDOTES

Braude, Jacob M. *Second Encyclopedia of Stories, Quotations, and Anecdotes; 2,842 Stories, Quips, Anecdotes, Poems, Proverbs.* Englewood Cliffs, N.J.: Prentice-Hall, 1957. 468 pp.

Supplemented by the same compiler's *Speaker's and Toastmaster's Handbook of Anecdotes by and about Famous Personalities.* Englewood Cliffs, N.J.: Prentice-Hall, 1971. 303 pp.

Braude, Jacob M. *Speaker's Encyclopedia of Stories, Quota-*

tions, and Anecdotes.   Englewood Cliffs, N.J.: Prentice-Hall, 1955. 476 pp.

A collection of 2,961 stories, jokes, proverbs, and other material for public speakers.

Fanning, Clara E., and Williams, Harold W. *Toaster's Handbook: Jokes, Stories, and Quotations,* 3d ed. New York: Wilson, 1955. 483 pp.

Friedman, Edward L. *Toastmaster's Treasury.* New York: Harper, 1960. 366 pp.

About 3,000 anecdotes, jokes, similes, and introductions.

Williams, Leewin B. *Encyclopedia of Wit, Humor and Wisdom.* New York: Abingdon, 1949. 576 pp.

Includes 4,118 jokes, toasts, and stories.

ANIMALS

American Kennel Club. *The Complete Dog Book,* rev. ed. Garden City, N.Y.: Doubleday, 1969. 580 pp.

History, breeds, training, feeding, and care. Related works are: Dangerfield, Stanley, and Howell, Ellsworth, eds. *The International Encyclopedia of Dogs.* New York: McGraw-Hill, 1971. 480 pp. Hamilton, Ferelith, ed. *The World Encyclopedia of Dogs.* New York: World, 1971. 672 pp.

Burton, Maurice and Robert, eds. *International Wildlife Encyclopedia.* New York: Marshall Cavendish, 1969–70. 20 v. Alphabetically arranged, profusely illustrated. Indexes for animals, subjects, and zoological classification.

Grzimek, Berhnhard, ed. *Grzimek's Animal Life Encyclopedia.* New York: Van Nostrand Reinhold, 1972–74. To be completed in thirteen volumes. Comprehensive treatment of the animal kingdom: v. 1, lower animals; v. 2, insects; v. 3, mollusks and echinoderms; v. 4–5, fishes; v. 5, amphibia; v. 6, reptiles; v. 7–9, birds; v. 10–13, mammals. Index in each volume; many illustrations.

Handbooks of American Natural History.   Ithaca, N.Y.: Comstock Pub. Co., 1943–57. 8 v.

Individual volumes deal with snakes, frogs, lizards, sala-

manders, turtles, aquatic plants, mosquitoes, and mammals
of eastern United States.

Hope, C. E. G., and Jackson, G. N. *The Encyclopedia of the
Horse.* New York: Studio-Viking, 1973. 336 pp.

Beautifully illustrated treatment of the horse in all phases.

The Larousse Encyclopedia of Animal Life. New York: McGraw-
Hill, 1967. 640 pp.

Arranged by phylum, profusely illustrated. Includes classification table, glossary, and bibliography.

*The Merck Veterinary Manual; a Handbook of Diagnosis and
Therapy for the Veterinarian,* 3d ed. Rahway, N.J.: Merck &
Co., 1967. 1,674 pp.

Current information on diagnosis, treatment, and prophylaxis
of important animal diseases. Index.

Miller, William C., and West, Geoffrey P. *Encyclopedia of
Animal Care,* 9th ed. Baltimore, Md.: Williams & Wilkins,
1970. 1,023 pp.

Includes new developments in veterinary medicine and care
of domesticated animals.

Pond, Grace, ed. *The Complete Cat Encyclopedia.* New York:
Crown, 1972. 394 pp.

Information on breeds, associations, and shows. Illustrated.

The Rand McNally Atlas of World Wildlife. Chicago, Ill.: Rand
McNally, 1973. 208 pp.

Outlines animal life in eight zoogeographical regions of the
world. Stresses interrelationships of species with each other
and the environment. Illustrated with maps, photographs,
and drawings. Glossary, bibliography, and index.

Stanek, V. J. *Pictorial Encyclopedia of the Animal Kingdom.*
New York: Crown, 1962. 614 pp.

Includes 1,000 extraordinary photographs and descriptions
of structural features, habitats, and behavior patterns of animals.

Taylor, Louis. *Harper's Encyclopedia for Horsemen; the Complete Book of the Horse.* New York: Harper, 1973. 558 pp.

Walker, Ernest P. *Mammals of the World,* 2d ed. Baltimore Md.:
Johns Hopkins Press, 1968. 3 v.

A major work in field; first two volumes arranged by tax-onomic classification, third volume comprehensive bibliography. Describes 1,044 genera with more than 1,800 photographs.

ANTIQUES

Boger, Louise A. and H. B. *The Dictionary of Antiques and the Decorative Arts*, rev. ed. New York: Scribner, 1967. 662 pp.
"A book of reference for glass, furniture, ceramics, silver, periods, styles, technical terms, etc."

Comstock, Helen. *The Concise Encyclopedia of American Antiques*. New York: Hawthorn, 1965. 864 pp.
Covers firearms, wallpaper, whaling, instruments, stoves, mirrors, etc.

Connoisseur. *Complete Encyclopedia of Antiques*. New York: Hawthorn, 1962. 1,472 pp.
Chapters on furniture, glass, enamels, silver, pewter, clocks, prints, ceramics, etc., compiled by editors of *Connoisseur* magazine.

Coysh, A. W. *The Antique Buyer's Dictionary of Names*. New York: Praeger, 1970. 278 pp.
Gives information on about 1,700 European and American artists, craftsmen, designers, and firms. Illustrated; bibliographies.

Drepperd, Carl W. *Dictionary of American Antiques*. Garden City, N.Y.: Doubleday, 1952. 404 pp.

Durant, Mary B. *The American Heritage Guide to Antiques*. New York: American Heritage Pub. Co., 1970. Unpaged.
Illustrated glossary of about 800 terms. Includes furniture style charts and section on colonial crafts.

Hornung, Clarence P. *Treasury of American Design*. New York: Abrams, 1972. 2 v.

The International Antiques Yearbook. London: Antiques Yearbooks Ltd., 1972. 1,058 pp. Annual.
Selective guide to approximately 6,000 antique dealers, art galleries, and antiquarian booksellers in Great Britain,

Europe, and North America. Arranged alphabetically by countries. Index to dealers and subject index.

Ramsey, L. G. G.   *The Complete Encyclopedia of Antiques*. New York: Hawthorn, 1962. 1,472 pp.
Chapters on furniture, glass, enamels, silver, pewter, clocks, prints, ceramics, etc.; many illustrations. Includes list of major museums in Europe, Great Britain, and the United States.

Savage, George.   *Dictionary of Antiques*.   New York: Praeger, 1970. 534 pp.
Illustrated articles on principal European and American styles and craftsmen of past 500 years. Extensive subject-arranged bibliography; appendix of "marks."

Schwartz, Marvin D., and Wade, Betsy.   *The New York Times Book of Antiques*. New York: Quadrangle Books, 1972. 344 pp.
Illustrated guide for the collector; includes bibliography.

ARCHITECTURE AND BUILDING

Briggs, Martin S.   *Everyman's Concise Encyclopedia of Architecture*. New York: Dutton, 1959. 372 pp.
Dictionary of architectural terms and biography, illustrated with drawings and plates.

Columbia University Avery Architectural Library.   *Avery Index to Architectural Periodicals*. Boston, Mass.: G. K. Hall, 1963. 12 v. Annual supplements, 1963 to date.
Indexes articles on architecture and related fields from major architectural periodicals found in the Avery Architectural Library.

Fleming, John, and others.   *The Penguin Dictionary of Architecture*, 2d ed. Baltimore, Md.: Penguin Books, 1972. 315 pp.
Emphasizes history of architecture; also covers styles, trends, terms, and architects.

Fletcher, Banister F.   *A History of Architecture on the Comparative Method*, 17th ed. New York: Scribner, 1961. 1,366 pp.
Treats styles of architecture, chief characteristics of each style, and influences that produced them; 652 pages of illustrations.

Giedion, Sigfried.   *Space, Time and Architecture; the Growth of a New Tradition*, 5th ed. Cambridge, Mass.: Harvard Univ. Press, 1967. 897 pp.

"The architect's bible."

Hatje, Gerd. *Encyclopedia of Modern Architecture*. New York: Abrams, 1963. 336 pp.

Includes biographies and summaries of movements.

Jordan, R. Furneaux. *European Architecture in Color from the Greeks to the Nineteenth Century*. London: Thames & Hudson, 1961. 460 pp.

Includes 112 full-page color plates with descriptions of famous architectural structures from the sixth century B.C. to 1878.

Ware, Dora and Betty. *A Short Dictionary of Architecture, Including Some Common Building Terms*, 3d ed. London: Allen & Unwin, 1953. 136 pp.

Waugh, Herbert R., and Burbank, Nelson L. *Handbook of Building Terms and Definitions*. New York: Simmons-Boardman, 1954. 421 pp.

Whiffen, Marcus. *American Architecture since 1780; a Guide to the Styles*. Cambridge, Mass.: M.I.T. Press, 1969. 313 pp.

Chronological grouping of forty styles with descriptions and history given for each.

World Architecture; an Illustrated History.   New York: McGraw-Hill, 1963. 348 pp.

Broad in scope and well illustrated.

ART

American Art Directory.   New York: Bowker, 1899 to date. Triennial.

Contains variety of information about museums, associations, and other organizations in the United States and Canada.

Art Index; a Cumulative Author and Subject Index to a Selected List of Fine Arts Periodicals and Museum Bulletins.   New York: Wilson, 1929 to date. Quarterly with annual cumulations.

Indexes American and foreign publications in archaeology,

architecture, art history, arts and crafts, fine arts, graphic
arts, industrial design, interior design, landscape design,
photography and films, and related subjects.

Britannica Encyclopedia of American Art. New York: Simon
and Schuster, 1973. 669 pp.
Includes more than 1,100 entries and 800 reproduced illustrations.

Bryan, Michael. *Dictionary of Painters and Engravers.* London:
G. Bell, 1925–27. 5 v.
Standard biographical dictionary for older artists.

Chamberlin, Mary W. *Guide to Art Reference Books.* Chicago:
Amer. Library Assoc., 1959. 418 pp. New edition announced.
Lists more than 2,000 titles by subjects, with annotations. Re-
lated works are: Carrick, Neville. *How to Find Out about the
Arts: A Guide to Sources of Information.* Oxford: Pergamon,
1965. 164 pp. Lucas, Edna L. *Art Books; a Basic Bibliog-
raphy on the Fine Arts.* Greenwich, Conn.: New York Graphic
Society, 1968. 245 pp.

Clapp, Jane. *Sculpture Index.* Metuchen, N.J.: Scarecrow Press,
1970. 2 v. in 3 pts.

Cummings, Paul. *A Dictionary of Contemporary American
Artists,* 2d ed. New York: St. Martin's, 1971. 368 pp.
Concise biographies of 787 American artists, with good
coverage of collections owning works; bibliographies.

Encyclopedia of World Art. New York: McGraw-Hill, 1959–68.
15 v.
Articles on architecture, sculpture, painting, and other arts
by specialists from many countries; about one-half of each
volume consists of illustrative plates. A monumental and
authoritative work.

Fielding, Mantle. *Dictionary of American Painters, Sculptors,
and Engravers. With an Addendum Containing Corrections
and Additional Material on the Original Entries,* comp. by
James F. Carr. New York: J. F. Carr, 1965. 529 pp.

Gardner, Helen. *Art through the Ages,* 5th ed. New York: Harcourt, 1970. 801 pp.
Survey of Western art for all periods; ninety-six color plates.

Excludes the arts of Asia and the Americas and primitive art.

Gaunt, William. *Everyman's Dictionary of Pictorial Art.* New York: Dutton, 1962. 2 v.

Biographies of about 1,200 artists and articles on main periods and schools of art, galleries and museums, and famous paintings.

Haftmann, Werner. *Painting in the Twentieth Century,* rev. ed. New York: Praeger, 1965. 2 v.

Standard work on modern art; second volume consists of illustrations.

Harper's Dictionary of the Graphic Arts. New York: Harper, 1963. 295 pp.

Defines 6,500 basic terms, with information on methods and processes.

Janson, Horst W. and Dora Jane. *History of Art; a Survey of the Major Visual Arts from the Dawn of History to the Present Day,* rev ed. Englewood Cliffs, N.J.: Prentice-Hall and Abrams, 1969. 616 pp.

Kaltenbach, Gustave Emile. *Dictionary of Pronunciation of Artists' Names with Their Schools and Dates.* Chicago, Ill.: Art Institute of Chicago, 1934. 73 pp.

Larousse Encyclopedia of Byzantine and Medieval Art. New York: Prometheus Press, 1963. 416 pp.

More than 1,000 pictures, including color plates.

Larousse Encyclopedia of Modern Art, from 1800 to the Present Day. New York: Putnam, 1965. 444 pp.

Larousse Encyclopedia of Prehistoric and Ancient Art. New York: Prometheus Press, 1962. 414 pp.

Larousse Encyclopedia of Renaissance and Baroque Art. New York: Prometheus Press, 1964. 444 pp.

Covers 400-year period.

Mayer, Ralph. *A Dictionary of Art Terms and Techniques.* New York: Crowell, 1969. 447 pp.

Gives definitions and historical background for over 3,200 terms "encountered in the study and practice of the visual arts and in their literature." Excludes architecture.

Monro, Isabel S. and Kate M. *Index to Reproductions of American Paintings.* New York: Wilson, 1948. 731 pp. *First Supplement.* New York: Wilson, 1964. 480 pp.
Reproductions in a total of 820 books and catalogs are indexed by name of artist, title of painting, and subject. By the same compilers: *Index to Reproductions of European Paintings.* New York: Wilson, 1956. 668 pp. Indexes reproductions in 328 books.

Myers, Bernard S., ed. *Encyclopedia of Painting: Painters and Painting of the World from Prehistoric Times to the Present Day.* New York: Crown, 1955. 511 pp.
Profusely illustrated with brief articles on painters, schools, styles, and techniques. Special section on Chinese, Japanese, Indian, and Persian painters.

Myers, Bernard S., ed. *McGraw-Hill Dictionary of Art.* New York: McGraw-Hill, 1969. 5 v.
Comprehensive coverage of artists, styles, periods, museums, terminology, etc., with 15,000 entries, 2,300 illustrations. Many cross-references; bibliographies.

Osborne, Harold, ed. *The Oxford Companion to Art.* Oxford: Clarendon Press, 1970. 1,277 pp.
Introduction to the visual arts for the nonspecialist, excluding practical arts and handicrafts. Selective bibliography of 3,000 items.

Pelican History of Art. Baltimore, Md.: Penguin Books, 1953
———. In progress, to be completed in fifty volumes.
Individual volumes treat all major aspects of art and architecture, ancient, medieval, and modern.

The Praeger Encyclopedia of Art. New York: Praeger, 1971. 5 v.
Entries for artists, art periods, styles, schools, and movements; with bibliographies. About 5,000 illustrations, one-third in color. Index.

Stevenson, George A. *Graphic Arts Encyclopedia.* New York: McGraw-Hill, 1968. 402 pp.
Defines terms, describes processes, tools, and materials in the graphic arts. Index.

ASTRONOMY AND SPACE

Astronomy and Astrophysics Abstracts. New York: Springer-Verlag, 1969 to date. Semiannual.

Classified arrangement with subject-author indexes. Covers the literature relating to all fields of astronomy and astrophysics.

Fairbridge, Rhodes W. *The Encyclopedia of Atmospheric Sciences and Astrogeology.* New York: Reinhold, 1967. 1,200 pp.

Dictionary arrangement with signed articles; illustrated with charts and diagrams. Bibliographies and analytical index.

Flammarion, Camille. *The Flammarion Book of Astronomy.* New York: Simon and Schuster, 1964. 670 pp.

Revised and updated edition of the nineteenth-century French classic, *Astronomie Populaire.* In eight parts: the earth; the moon; the sun; the planets; comets, meteorites, and meteors; the sidereal universe; the instruments of astronomy; and space vehicles. Beautifully illustrated.

Howard, Neale E. *The Telescope Handbook and Star Atlas.* New York: Crowell, 1967. 226 pp.

For the amateur astronomer; describes celestial phenomena, astronomical instruments. Star atlas and celestial gazetteer; many photographs and diagrams.

Kemp, D. A. *Astronomy and Astrophysics; a Bibliographical Guide.* Hamden, Conn.: Archon, 1970. 584 pp.

Selective coverage of all branches of astronomy; 3,600 entries include general references and specialized materials. Author and subject indexes.

Larousse Encyclopedia of Astronomy, 2d ed. New York: Prometheus Press, 1959. 506 pp.

Extensively illustrated guide to science of space and astronomy.

Lowman, Paul D., Jr. *Space Panorama.* Zurich, Switzerland: Weltflugbild, 1968. Unpaged.

Contains sixty-nine spectacular photographs of the earth from outer space, with description of each photograph.

The McGraw-Hill Encyclopedia of Space. New York: McGraw-Hill, 1968. 831 pp.
Written for the layman; articles cover such topics as rockets, satellites, space navigation, and electronics. Many illustrations.

Menzel, Donald H. *A Field Guide to the Stars and Planets, Including the Moon, Satellites, Comets, and Other Features of the Universe.* Boston, Mass.: Houghton Mifflin, 1964. 397 pp.
Handbook for the amateur astronomer. Well illustrated with charts, maps, photographs, drawings, and astronomical tables.

Monthly Evening Sky Map. Brooklyn, N.Y.: Celestial Map Pub. Co., 1906 to date.
"A journal for the amateur—northern and southern hemispheres—also a star, constellation, and planet finder map, arranged for the current month."

Moore, Patrick. *The Atlas of the Universe.* Chicago: Rand McNally, 1970. 272 pp.
Compilation of 1,500 maps and photographs, many in color, of the earth as seen from space, the moon, solar system, stars, and common constellations. Accompanied by textual commentary. Glossary of astronomical terms; catalog of stellar objects. Detailed index.

Moore, Patrick. *A Handbook of Practical Amateur Astronomy.* New York: Norton, 1964. 254 pp.
"An observational guide for the serious amateur astronomer."

Olcott, William T., and others. *Field Book of the Skies,* 4th ed. New York: Putnam, 1954. 482 pp.
Excellent handbook for amateur astronomer, useful in locating stars and constellations.

Sidgwick, John B. *Amateur Astronomer's Handbook,* 2d ed. New York: Macmillan, 1961. 580 pp.
Comprehensive guide to astronomical study, including telescopes, films, oculars, observatories, atmosphere, spectroscopy, etc.

U.S. National Aeronautics and Space Administration. *Scientific and Technical Aerospace Reports.* Washington, D.C.: Supt. of Documents, 1963 to date. Semimonthly.

Abstracting service. Note also: *International Aerospace Abstracts.* New York: American Institute of Aeronautics and Astronautics, Technical Information Service, 1961 to date.

AUSTRALIA

Australian Dictionary of Biography. Melbourne: Melborne Univ. Press, 1966———. In progress, to be completed in twelve volumes.

Chronological treatment; will contain about 6,000 entries for prominent Australians.

Australian Encyclopaedia. East Lansing: Michigan State Univ. Press, 1958. 10 v.

Signed articles cover all aspects of Australian life, culture, and history. Index.

Learmonth, Andrew T. A. and Agnes M. *Encyclopaedia of Australia.* London and New York: Warne, 1968. 606 pp.

Includes biography, natural history, literature, the arts, etc.; updates the *Australian Encyclopaedia.*

AUTOMOBILES

Auto 19———. New York: Tudor Pub. Co., 1953 to date. Annual. Guide to new automobiles, stock and sport cars, United States and foreign; many illustrations.

Automobile Facts and Figures. New York: Automobile Manufacturers Assoc., 1920 to date.

Annual compilation of information on all types of automobiles, trucks, and buses made in the United States.

Automobile Quarterly Editors. *The American Car since 1775.* New York: Dutton, 1971. 504 pp.

Historical information on automotive developments and manufacturers.

Chilton's Auto Repair Manual 1973; American Cars from 1966 to 1973. Philadelphia, Pa.: Chilton, 1972. 976 pp., 508 pp.

Revised annually; repair information for car models of American manufacturers. From the same publisher: *Chilton's*

Foreign Car Repair Manual. V. 1, *German, Swedish, Italian Cars;* v. 2, *French, British, Japanese Cars.*

Georgano, G. N., ed. *The Complete Encyclopedia of Motorcars, 1885–1968.* New York: Dutton, 1968. 640 pp.

Car models and companies in over twenty countries are described. Illustrated with photographs.

Georgano, G. N., ed. *The Encyclopedia of Motor Sport.* New York: Studio/Viking, 1971. 656 pp.

Guide to auto racing and other events: cars, drivers, racing formulas, clubs, etc. Many photographs, glossary, and index.

Motor Service's Automotive Encyclopedia. South Holland, Ill.: Goodheart-Wilcox, 1970. 768 pp.

Frequently revised; information on specific models from the previous ten to fifteen years, and on general principles of automobile mechanics. Many illustrations.

Motor's Auto Repair Manual. New York: Hearst Books, 1938 to date. Annual.

Guide to repair of American automobiles; arranged by make of car. From the same publisher: *Motor's Truck and Tractor Repair Manual.* 1943 to date. Annual. Guide to repair and maintenance of all makes of American trucks and tractors.

SAE Handbook. New York: Society of Automotive Engineers, 1926 to date. Annual.

A standard handbook on automotive engineering.

AVIATION

Aerospace Year Book. Washington, D.C.: American Aviation Pub., 1919 to date. Annual.

Data on development and manufacture of aircraft; fully illustrated.

AOPA Airport Directory. Washington, D.C.: Aircraft Owners and Pilots Assoc., 1961 to date. Annual.

Alphabetical listing by states of over 11,500 aircraft landing places (airports, heliports, and seaplane bases) available to civil aircraft in the United States and its territories.

Gentle, Ernest J., and Reithmaier, Larry, eds. *Aviation and Space Dictionary,* 5th ed. Fallbrook, Calif.: Aero Publishers, 1973.

Definitions of terms used in aerospace sciences, with numerous illustrations.

Jane's All the World's Aircraft. New York: McGraw-Hill, 1909 to date. Annual.
Authoritative guide to each year's civil and military aircraft, wherever made.

Official Airline Guide. Washington, D.C.: American Aviation Pub., 1943 to date. Monthly.
Air schedules for established commercial flights, domestic and foreign.

Ralfe, Douglas. *Airplanes of the World, 1490–1969,* rev. ed. New York: Simon and Schuster, 1969. 440 pp.
Historical survey, with descriptions and illustrations for civil and military airplanes.

Taylor, John W. R., and Munson, Kenneth. *History of Aviation.* New York: Crown, 1972. 511 pp.
History of human flight from earliest attempts through supersonic transports and manned space vehicles. Illustrated with photographs; index.

World Aviation Directory. Washington, D.C.: American Aviation Pub., 1940 to date. Semiannual.
Detailed listing of companies and organizations concerned with the aircraft industry.

BIBLE

The Cambridge History of the Bible. Cambridge: Cambridge Univ. Press, 1963–70. 3 v.
V. 1: From the beginnings to Jerome; v. 2: The West, from the fathers to the Reformation; v. 3: The West, from the Reformation to the present day. Articles by scholars represent current biblical scholarship and thought.

Cornfeld, Gaalyahu. *Pictorial Biblical Encyclopedia; a Visual Guide to the Old and New Testaments.* New York: Macmillan, 1965. 712 pp.
Numerous photographs and maps illustrating text.

Douglas, J. D. *The New Bible Dictionary.* Grand Rapids, Mich.: Eerdmans, 1962. 1,375 pp.

Includes 2,300 articles written by specialists, supplemented by drawings, illustrations, and maps.

Gehman, Henry S., ed. *The New Westminster Dictionary of the Bible,* rev. ed. Philadelphia, Pa.: Westminster, 1970. 1,027 pp.

Covers events, places, persons, fauna, and flora of biblical times, including recent archaeological discoveries.

Hartman, Louis F. *Encyclopedic Dictionary of the Bible.* New York: McGraw-Hill, 1963. 2,634 columns.

A scholarly Catholic Bible dictionary.

Hastings, James. *Dictionary of the Bible,* new ed. New York: Scribner, 1963. 1,059 pp.

Long a standard work, dealing with language, literature, and contents of Bible and biblical theology.

Interpreter's Bible: The Holy Scriptures in the King James and Revised Standard Versions with General Articles and Introduction, Exegesis, Exposition for Each Book of the Bible. New York: Abingdon, 1951–57. 12 v.

A guide and commentary on the Bible, by 146 specialists.

Interpreter's Dictionary of the Bible; an Illustrated Encyclopedia Identifying and Explaining All Proper Names and Significant Terms and Subjects in the Holy Scriptures, Including the Apocrypha. New York: Abingdon, 1962. 4 v.

Layman, Charles M., ed. *Interpreter's One Volume Commentary on the Bible.* New York: Abingdon, 1971. 1,368 pp.

Deals with historical background, scope and significance of each book of the Bible and the books of the Apocrypha; forty-three general articles discuss aspects of biblical scholarship. Index.

Miller, Madeleine S. and J. L. *Encyclopedia of Bible Life.* New York: Harper, 1955. 493 pp.

Covers all aspects of life in biblical times: agriculture, apparel, homes, arts and crafts, etc. Includes bibliographical references. In the same field is: Corswant, Willy. *A Dictionary of Life in Bible Times.* Oxford: Oxford Univ. Press, 1960. 308 pp.

Nelson's Complete Concordance of the Revised Standard Version

of the Bible. Camden, N.J.: Thomas Nelson, 1957. 2,157 pp.
Computer-produced; lists context and location for all significant words.

Stevenson, Burton E. *The Home Book of Bible Quotations.*
New York: Harper, 1949. 645 pp.
Based on King James Version; 20,000 quotations arranged by subjects and indexed.

Strong, James. *The Exhaustive Concordance of the Bible.* New York: Abingdon, 1963. 1,340 pp., 262 pp., 127 pp., 79 pp.
Most complete concordance to authorized and revised English versions; includes also Hebrew, Chaldee, and Greek dictionaries of Bible. Note also: Young, Robert. *Analytical Concordance to the Bible.* New York: Funk & Wagnalls, 1955. 1,280 pp. Thompson, Newton W. *Complete Concordance to the Bible (Douay Version).* St. Louis, Mo.: Herder, 1945. 1,914 pp.

Wright, George E., and Filson, Floyd V. *The Westminster Historical Atlas of the Bible.* Philadelphia, Pa.: Westminster, 1956. 130 pp.
Includes maps, illustrations, and historical commentary. Other atlases: Baly, Denis, and Tushingham, A. D. *Atlas of the Biblical World.* Cleveland, Ohio: World, 1971. 208 pp. Freitag, Anton. *The Twentieth Century Atlas of the Christian World.* New York: Hawthorn, 1963. 199 pp. Grollenberg, Lucas H. *Nelson's Atlas of the Christian World.* New York: Nelson, 1956. 165 pp. Kraeling, Emil G. *Rand McNally Bible Atlas,* 3d ed. Chicago, Ill.: Rand McNally, 1966. 487 pp. May, Herbert G. *Oxford Bible Atlas.* Oxford: Oxford Univ. Press, 1962. 144 pp. Meer, F. van der. *Atlas of the Early Christian World.* New York: Nelson, 1958. 216 pp.

BIOLOGY

Altman, Philip L., and Dittmer, Dorothy S., eds. *Biology Data Book.* Washington, D.C.: Federation of American Societies for Experimental Biology, 1972. 3 v.
Tables, charts, and diagrams provide quantitative and de-

scriptive data for the biological sciences. References are
given for further investigation.

Biological Abstracts.   Philadelphia, Pa.: BioSciences Information
Service, 1926 to date. Semimonthly.

About 140,000 abstracts a year from approximately 8,000
worldwide journals, books, government reports, and sym-
posia proceedings. Indexes in each issue cumulate annually:
B.A.S.I.C. (Biological Abstracts Subjects in Context), author,
systematic, and cross-indexes. Supplemented by *BioResearch
Index*. Philadelphia, Pa.: BioSciences Information Service,
1967 to date. Monthly. Provides access to research papers.

*Biological and Agricultural Index; a Cumulative Subject Index to
Periodicals in the Fields of Biology, Agriculture, and Related
Sciences.*   New York: Wilson, 1964 to date. Monthly except
August, with annual cumulations.

Indexes approximately 189 English language periodicals.

Bottle, Robert T., and Wyatt, H. V.   *The Use of Biological Literature*, 2d ed. Hamden, Conn.: Archon, 1971. 379 pp.

Guide to reference materials and research in the biological
sciences.

Chinery, Michael.   *A Science Dictionary of the Animal World:
An Illustrated Demonstration of Terms Used in Animal Biology.* 288 pp.; *A Science Dictionary of the Plant World: An
Illustrated Demonstration of Terms Used in Plant Biology.*
264 pp. New York: Franklin Watts, 1969.

Companion volumes provide concise, accurate definitions of
botanical and zoological terms.

Emerson, William K.   *Shells.* New York: Viking, 1972. 295 pp.

Beautifully illustrated with full-page color and black and
white photographs by Andreas Feininger. Chapters on
shapes, structures, colors, textures, and design of shells.
"Catalog of marine shells" identifies shells by classes. Index.

Foundations of Modern Biology, 2d ed.   Englewood Cliffs, N.J.:
Prentice-Hall, 1964. 12 v.

A scholarly series with a volume devoted to each of the following: chemical background for the biological sciences, the
cell, cell physiology and biochemistry, heredity, adaptation,

growth and development, animal physiology, animal diversity, animal behavior, life of the green plant, plant kingdom, and man in nature.

Gray, Asa. *Gray's Manual of Botany*, 8th ed. New York: American Book Co., 1950. 1,632 pp.

"A handbook of the flowering plants and ferns of the central and northeastern United States and adjacent Canada." First issued in 1848.

Gray, Peter. *The Dictionary of the Biological Sciences*. New York: Reinhold, 1967. 602 pp.

Authoritative definitions for more than 40,000 terms relating to the biological sciences.

Gray, Peter, ed. *The Encyclopedia of the Biological Sciences*, 2d ed. New York: Van Nostrand Reinhold, 1970. 1,027 pp.

Approximataely 800 authoritative, signed articles with bibliographies.

Kingsbury, John M. *Poisonous Plants of the United States and Canada*. Englewood Cliffs, N.J.: Prentice-Hall, 1964. 626 pp. Information on all plants known to be toxic to man or animals.

Laskin, Allen I. *Handbook of Microbiology*. Cleveland, Ohio: CRC Press, Chemical Rubber Company, 1973. 4 v.

Leftwich, A. W. *A Dictionary of Zoology*, 3d ed. London: Constable, 1973. 478 pp.

Museum of Natural History. *The Illustrated Library of the Natural Sciences*. New York: Simon and Schuster, 1958. 4 v. Sound basic information, edited and sponsored by American Museum of Natural History, N.Y.

Pennak, Robert W. *Collegiate Dictionary of Zoology*. New York: Ronald Press, 1964. 583 pp.

Comprehensive work defining about 19,000 terms.

Smith, Roger C., and Painter, Reginald H. *Guide to the Literature of the Life Sciences*, 8th ed. Minneapolis, Minn.: Burgess, 1972. 166 pp.

Annotated bibliography of important reference works in zoological sciences.

BIRDS

Alexander, Wilfrid B. *Birds of the Ocean,* 2d ed. New York: Putnam, 1963. 306 pp.
"A handbook for voyagers containing descriptions of all the sea-birds of the world, with notes on their habits and guides to their identification."

American Ornithologists' Union. *Check-List of North American Birds,* 5th ed. Ithaca, N.Y.: The Union, 1957. 691 pp.

Fisher, James, and Peterson, Roger T. *The World of Birds.* Garden City, N.Y.: Doubleday, 1964. 288 pp.
General treatise; includes hundreds of paintings and distribution atlas in color.

Grossman, Mary L., and Hamlet, John. *Birds of Prey of the World.* New York: Potter, 1964. 496 pp.
Photographs in color and text describe the principal species of predatory birds.

Hvass, Hans. *Birds of the World in Color.* New York: Dutton, 1964. 210 pp. Describes 1,100 species; 110 pictures in color.

Palmer, Ralph S. *Handbook of North American Birds.* New Haven, Conn.: Yale Univ. Press, 1962. 567 pp.
Includes charts, maps, and illustrations of identifying characteristics.

Peterson, Roger T. *Birds over America.* New York: Dodd, 1964. 342 pp.
Studies of birds in all parts of the United States; 105 photographs. By same author: *How to Know the Birds,* 2d ed. Boston, Mass.: Houghton, 1962. 168 pp. An "introduction to bird recognition," containing seventy-two color illustrations and 400 line drawings; *A Field Guide to the Birds: Giving Field Marks of All Species Found East of the Rockies,* 2d ed. Boston, Mass.: Houghton, 1947. 290 pp. *A Field Guide to Western Birds,* 2d ed. Boston, Mass.: Houghton, 1961. 366 pp., which includes birds of western Canada, Alaska, and Hawaii.

Reed, Chester A. *Bird Guide; Land Birds East of the Rockies.* Garden City, N.Y.: Doubleday, 1964. 238 pp.
Contains 300 color illustrations of 222 species.

Ridgway, Robert. *Birds of North and Middle America*. Washington, D.C.: G.P.O., 1901–50. 11 v.

For the professional ornithologist; "a descriptive catalogue of the higher groups, genera, species, and subspecies of birds known to occur in North America from the Arctic lands to the Isthmus of Panama, the West Indies and other islands of the Caribbean sea and the Galapagos archipelago"; many plates.

Rutgers, A., and Norris, K. A. *Encyclopaedia of Aviculture*. London: Blandford Press, 1970. 3 v.

Scientific descriptions by orders and suborders, with illustrations.

Thomson, A. Landsborough. *A New Dictionary of Birds*. New York: McGraw-Hill, 1964. 928 pp.

Encyclopedic work on all aspects of bird life.

Wetmore, Alexander. *Song and Garden Birds of North America*. Washington, D.C.: National Geographic Society, 1964. 400 pp.

Includes section on bird songs with accompanying sound recordings.

BLACKS IN AMERICA

Baskin, Wade, and Runes, Richard N. *Dictionary of Black Culture*. New York: Philosophical Library, 1973. 493 pp.

Includes important black individuals, publications, historical events, and issue controversies.

Bergman, Peter M. *The Chronological History of the Negro in America*. New York: Harper, 1969. 698 pp.

Year-by-year presentation of facts and miscellaneous information. Index.

Black List: The Concise Reference Guide to Publications and Broadcasting Media of Black America, Africa, and the Caribbean. New York: Panther House, 1971. 289 pp.

Davis, John P., ed. *The American Negro Reference Book*. Englewood Cliffs, N.J.: Prentice-Hall, 1966. 969 pp.

Summary of information on main aspects of Negro life in America, including historical background material. Index.

Ebony.   *The Negro Handbook*. Chicago: Johnson Pub. Co., 1966. 535 pp.
  General directory and statistical information plus other data compiled by the editors of *Ebony* magazine.

Index to Periodical Articles by and about Negroes.   Boston, Mass.: G. K. Hall, 1950 to date. Annual.
  Formerly titled *Index to Selected Periodicals*. Includes articles relating to all aspects of Negro life from about twenty periodicals, with entries for authors and subjects. Cumulations available: 1950–59; 1960–70.

International Library of Negro Life and History.   New York: Publishers Co., Inc., 1967–68. 10 v.
  Designed to "treat in detail the cultural and historical backgrounds of Negro Americans."

Krash, Ronald, and others.   *Black America: A Research Bibliography*. St. Louis, Mo.: St. Louis Univ., Pius XII Library, 1972. 113 pp. (Bibliographic series, no. 6.)

McPherson, James M., and others.   *Blacks in America; Bibliographical Essays*. Garden City, N.Y.: Doubleday, 1971. 430 pp.
  Aspects of the Afro-American experience from 1500 to the present are treated in 100 bibliographical essays.

Miller, Elizabeth W., comp.   *The Negro in America: A Bibliography*, 2d ed. Cambridge, Mass.: Harvard Univ. Press, 1970. 351 pp.
  Selective listing of 6,500 topically arranged entries; author index. Coverage is from 1954 to February, 1970.

Ploski, Harry A., and Kaiser, Ernest.   *The Negro Almanac*, 2d ed. New York: Bellwether, 1971. 1,110 pp.
  Covers many aspects of black American life, history, and culture; includes current events and organizations. Illustrated; bibliography.

Porter, Dorothy B., comp.   *The Negro in the United States; a Selected Bibliography*. Washington, D.C.: Library of Congress, 1969. 313 pp.
  Selected list of recent monographs in the Library of Con-

gress and eleven other research libraries. Author and subject index.

Race Relations Information Center. *Directory of Afro-American Resources.* New York: Bowker, 1970. 512 pp.

Arranged by states, lists 2,108 resource centers and 4,500 collections of resource materials. Detailed index.

Reference Library of Black America. New York: Bellwether, 1971. 5 v.

Expanded version of the *Negro Almanac.* Treats wide range of subjects under broad headings.

Sanders, Charles L., and McLean, Linda, comps. *Directory: National Black Organizations.* New York: Afram, 1972. 109 pp.

Lists 239 organizations under eight broad subject groups: educational, religious, etc.

Sloan, Irving J., ed. *Blacks in America, 1492–1970: A Chronology and Fact Book.* Dobbs Ferry, N.Y.: Oceana, 1971. 149 pp.

Historical chronology plus data on publications and associations; bibliography of books and audiovisual materials.

Welsch, Erwin K. *The Negro in the United States: A Research Guide.* Bloomington: Indiana Univ. Press, 1965. 160 pp.

Analyzes books and periodical references dealing with historical and sociological aspects, civil rights issues, and the Negro in the arts.

BOATS

Brindze, Ruth. *The Experts' Book of Boating.* Englewood Cliffs, N.J.: Prentice-Hall, 1959. 291 pp.

Articles by experts on yachts, sails, inboard and outboard motors, piloting, etc.

Chapman, Charles F. *Piloting, Seamanship and Small Boat Handling.* New York: Motor Boating, 1922 to date. Biennial.

Compendium of boating information: equipment, rules and regulations, boat handling, charts, aids to navigation, etc. Many illustrations; index.

Hutchinson, James. *All about Boats.* Chicago: Popular Mechanics Press, 1958. 156 pp.

Deals with boat selection and upkeep of boats and motors;
appendixes contain directory of manufacturers, dictionary of
nautical terms, and regulations on boating.

One-Design and Offshore Yachtsman Editors. *Encyclopedia of
Sailing*. New York: Harper, 1971. 468 pp.
Comprehensive guide to sailing and sailboats: history, rules
and techniques, racing tactics, equipment. Includes catalog
of sailboat classes and glossary of sailing terms.

Sports Illustrated Book of Better Boating. Philadelphia, Pa.:
Lippincott, 1963. 86 pp.
Articles by specialists on outboarding, racing class boats,
deep-sea fishing, and sailboats.

Weeks, Morris, Jr. *The Complete Boating Encyclopedia*. New
York: Golden Press, 1964. 560 pp.
Over 2,500 entries covering all aspects of pleasure boating;
500 drawings and photographs.

Zadig, Ernest A. *The Complete Book of Boating; an Owner's
Guide to Design, Construction, Piloting, Operation and
Maintenance*. Englewood Cliffs, N.J.: Prentice-Hall, 1972.
640 pp.

CAMPS AND CAMPING

American Camping Association. *National Directory of Accredited Camps for Boys and Girls*. Martinsville, Ind.: The Association, 1933 to date. Annual.
Gives pertinent information, arranged by state, then alphabetically by name.

Bier, James A., and Raup, Henry A. *Campground Atlas of the
United States and Canada*. Champaign, Ill.: Alpine Geographical Press, 1964. 188 pp.

Duncan, S. Blackwell. *Camping Today; Backpacking, Tenting
and Trailering*. Chicago, Ill.: Rand McNally, 1973. 192 pp.
Guide to camping: equipment, modes of travel, regulations,
etc. Index.

Guide to Summer Camps and Summer Schools, 17th ed. Boston,
Mass.: Sargent Porter, 1971. Annual.
Geographical listing of camps, classified by types.

MacFall, Russell P. *Family Fun Outdoors.* New York: Crowell, 1965. 212 pp.

Rand McNally Campground and Trailer Park Guide. Chicago, Ill.: Rand McNally, 1958 to date. Annual.
Selective listing of about 20,000 campgrounds and trailer parks open to the public in the United States, Mexico, and Canada.

Sunset Western Campsite Directory, 2d ed. Menlo Park, Calif.: Lane Book Co., 1961. 81 pp.
Lists about 34,000 campsites in 1,800 locations in far western states and British Columbia.

Wells, George S. *The Fun of Family Camping, a Practical Guide.* Indianapolis, Ind.: Bobbs-Merrill, 1962. 320 pp.

Wells, George S. and Iris. *The Handbook of Auto Camping, and Motorist's Guide to Public Campgrounds.* New York: Harper, 1958. 274 pp.
Guide to public campgrounds in the United States, arranged by states; includes list of national and state parks in which living accommodations are available.

Woodall's Trailering Parks and Campgrounds. Highland Park, Ill.: Woodall Pub. Co., 1967 to date. Annual.
Selective listing, based on annual ratings, of public and private trailer parks and campgrounds in the United States; sixty-four-page map section locates parks by area. Name index.

CANADA

Canada Year Book. Ottawa: Bureau of Statistics, 1905 to date.
Comprehensive annual covering Canadian history, government, institutions, population, business, industry, etc.

Canadian Almanac and Directory. Toronto: Copp Clark Co., 1847 to date.
Annual guide to legal, commercial, institutional, governmental, educational, and general information on Canada.

Dictionary of Canadian Biography. Toronto: Univ. of Toronto Press, 1966———. In progress, to be completed in twenty volumes.

Biographical essays and bibliographies for significant individuals in Canadian history; chronologically arranged.

Encyclopedia Canadiana, centennial ed. Toronto: Grolier of Canada, 1966. 10 v.
Excellent general encyclopedia, inclusive of all phases of Canadian affairs, historical and current; numerous illustrations, good atlas, and index.

Encyclopedia of Canada. Toronto: Univ. Associates of Canada, 1935–37. 6 v.
An older general Canadian encyclopedia, with special strength for history, biography, and geography.

McGraw-Hill Directory and Almanac of Canada. Toronto: McGraw-Hill, 1966 to date. Annual.
Yearbook of general information, including legal, commercial, financial, educational data, etc.

Story, Norah. *The Oxford Companion to Canadian History and Literature.* Oxford: Oxford Univ. Press, 1967. 935 pp.
Includes bibliographies, biographies, places, periodicals, and societies of Canada. Cross-references and alphabetical list of titles referred to in text.

CHEMISTRY

Beilstein, Friedrich. *Handbuch der organischen Chemie,* 4th ed. Berlin: Springer, 1918——. In progress.
Of first importance in the field of organic chemistry.

Bottle, Robert T. *The Use of Chemical Literature,* 2d ed. Hamden, Conn.: Archon, 1969. 294 pp.
Survey of the literature in all branches of chemistry.

Chemical Abstracts. Columbus: Chemical Abstracts Service, Ohio State Univ., 1907 to date. Weekly on a biweekly cycle.
Most comprehensive guide to chemical literature worldwide; includes about 330,000 abstracts a year. Indexes to authors, subjects, formulas, patent numbers, ring systems. Semiannual and five-year cumulative indexes.

Clark, George L., ed. *The Encyclopedia of Chemistry,* 2d ed. New York: Reinhold, 1966. 1,144 pp.

Survey of chemical knowledge, including new topics and developments.

Condensed Chemical Dictionary, 8th ed.   New York: Van Nostrand Reinhold, 1971. 1,044 pp.

Data on chemicals and other substances used in manufacturing and research; terms used in chemistry and process industries.

Crane, Evan Jay, and others. *A Guide to the Literature of Chemistry,* 2d ed. New York: Wiley, 1957. 397 pp.

Describes methods for literature searching.

Encyclopedia of Chemical Technology, 2d ed. New York: Wiley, 1963–72. 25 v., supplement and index.

Arranged by broad subjects; signed articles by specialists.

Florkin, Marcel, and Stotz, Elmer H.   *Comprehensive Biochemistry.* New York: Elsevier, 1962———. In progress.

Grant, Julius, ed.   *Hackh's Chemical Dictionary,* 4th ed. New York: McGraw-Hill, 1969. 738 pp.

American and British usage; defines about 55,000 terms in chemistry and related fields drawn from the recent chemical literature.

Hampel, Clifford A., ed.   *Encyclopedia of the Chemical Elements.* New York: Reinhold, 1968. 849 pp.

Information on the nature, properties, and behavior of the 103 elements plus topics of related interest. Subject index.

Handbook of Chemistry and Physics, 52d ed.   Cleveland, Ohio: Chemical Rubber Co., 1971. Various pagings.

"A ready-reference book of chemical and physical data, 1971–72." Frequently revised.

Heilbron, Ian, and Bunbury, H. M., eds.   *Dictionary of Organic Compounds; the Constitution and Physical, Chemical and Other Properties of the Principal Carbon Compounds and Their Derivatives, Together with Relevant Literature References,* 4th ed. Oxford: Oxford Univ. Press, 1965. 5 v. and supplements 5 (summary of 1 through 5), 6, and 7.

International Encyclopedia of Chemical Science.   New York: Van Nostrand, 1964. 1,331 pp.

Comprehensive coverage for chemists, chemical engineers, teachers, and students.

Jacobson, Carl A. *Encyclopedia of Chemical Reactions.* New York: Reinhold, 1946–59. 8 v.

Kolthoff, I. M., and Elving, Philip J. *Treatise on Analytical Chemistry: A Comprehensive Account.* New York: Wiley, 1959———.
In progress.

Lange, Norbert Adolph, and Forker, Gordon M. *Handbook of Chemistry,* 10th ed. New York: McGraw-Hill, 1967. 2,001 pp. Concerned with chemical and physical data used in laboratory work and manufacturing.

Mark, Herman F., and others. *Encyclopedia of Polymer Science and Technology: Plastics, Resins, Rubbers, Fibers.* New York: Wiley, 1964———. In progress.
To be definitive reference work in polymer field; international coverage.

Mellon, Melvin G. *Chemical Publications, Their Use and Nature,* 4th ed. New York: McGraw-Hill, 1965. 324 pp.
Reviews various types of chemical literature and their uses.

Mellor, Joseph W. *A Comprehensive Treatise on Inorganic and Theoretical Chemistry.* New York: Wiley, 1922–37. 16 v. Supplements, 1956———.
In progress.

Merck Index of Chemicals and Drugs; an Encyclopedia for Chemists, Pharmacists, Physicians and Members of Allied Professions, 8th ed. Rahway, N.J.: Merck and Co., Inc., 1968. 1,713 pp.
Describes some 10,000 chemical substances: structure, properties, journal and patent references. Cross-index to 42,000 names of chemicals and drugs.

Thorpe, Jocelyn F., and Whiteley, M. A. *Dictionary of Applied Chemistry,* 4th ed. New York: Longmans, 1937–56. 12 v.
Standard encyclopedia for applied chemistry.

Williams, Roger J., and Lansford, Edwin M. *The Encyclopedia of Biochemistry.* New York: Reinhold, 1967. 876 pp.

Alphabetically arranged articles, most with bibliographies. Index.

COINS AND MONEY COLLECTING

Carson, R. A. G. *Coins of the World*. New York: Harper, 1962. 642 pp.

Covers last 2,500 years; photographs of 1,061 coins.

Friedberg, Robert. *Coins of the British World*. New York: Coin and Currency Institute, 1962. 210 pp.

Catalog of coinage of British Isles from A.D. 500 and the British empire from 1600.

Friedberg, Robert. *Paper Money of the United States,* 7th ed. New York: Coin and Currency Institute, 1972.

Illustrated guide to paper money of all periods.

Hobson, Burton, and Obojski, Robert. *Illustrated Encyclopedia of World Coins*. New York: Doubleday, 1970. 512 pp.

Brief entries provide useful data on both ancient and modern coins. Index.

Narbeth, Colin. *The Coin Collector's Encyclopaedia*. London: Stanley Paul, 1968. 232 pp.

Raymond, Wayte. *Coins of the World, Nineteenth Century Issues,* 2d ed. New York: Raymond, 1953. 251 pp.

Arranged geographically, with illustrations and market prices. Continued by same author's *Coins of the World, Twentieth Century Issues,* 5th ed. New York: Raymond, 1955. 326 pp.

Raymond, Wayte. *Standard Catalog of United States Coins and Tokens from 1652 to Present Day*. New York: Raymond, 1934 to date. Annual.

All types of coins included; about 1,000 illustrations.

Reed, Fred M. *Encyclopedia of United States Coins,* rev. ed. Chicago, Ill.: Regnery, 1972. 303 pp.

Descriptions and illustrations of United States coins since 1793; includes historical and technical background information. Index.

Reinfeld, Fred. *A Catalogue of the World's Most Popular Coins,* rev. ed. Garden City, N.Y.: Doubleday, 1971. 288 pp.

Coins of all periods, including descriptions, illustrations, and market values.

Taxay, Don, ed. *The Comprehensive Catalogue and Encyclopedia of United States Coins.* New York: Scott Pub. Co., 1971. 397 pp.

Comprehensive coverage of all aspects of United States coins. Includes price quotations; photographs of coins.

Yeoman, R. S. *A Guide Book of United States Coins.* Racine, Wis.: Whitman Pub. Co., 1947 to date. Annual.

Illustrated catalog with prices, 1616 to date.

COLLEGES AND UNIVERSITIES

American Council on Education. *American Junior Colleges,* 8th ed. Washington, D.C.: The Council, 1971. 850 pp.

Directory, arranged by states, presenting basic information for each institution.

American Council on Education. *American Universities and Colleges,* 10th ed. Washington, D.C.: The Council, 1968. 1,782 pp.

A comprehensive directory of senior colleges and universities, alphabetically arranged under states, with detailed information.

American Council on Education. *Fellowships in the Arts and Sciences.* Washington, D.C.: The Council, 1957 to date. Annual.

American Council on Education. *A Guide to Graduate Study: Programs Leading to the Ph.D. Degree,* 4th ed. Washington, D.C.: The Council, 1969. 637 pp.

Alphabetical list of universities offering doctorate, containing data on programs, admission requirements, fields of study, fees, etc.

Baird, William R. *Baird's Manual of American College Fraternities,* 18th ed. Menasha, Wis.: Banta Pub. Co., 1968. 891 pp.

Most complete guide to collegiate fraternities and sororities.

Cass, James, and Birnbaum, Max. *Comparative Guide to American Colleges for Students, Parents, and Counselors,* 4th ed. New York: Harper, 1969. 837 pp.

Analyzes every accredited four-year college in the United States, with data on enrollment, entrance requirements, faculty, costs, and degrees. By the same compilers: *Comparative Guide to Junior and Two-Year Community Colleges.* New York: Harper, 1972. 397 pp.

College Blue Book, 14th ed. New York: CCM Information Corp., 1972. 4 v.

Directory and statistical information; emphasis on American two-year and four-year colleges, but includes section on study abroad.

Commonwealth Universities Yearbook. London: Assoc. of Commonwealth Univs., 1914 to date.

Directory with detailed information on universities of Great Britain and the Commonwealth nations.

Fine, Benjamin. *Barron's Profiles of American Colleges.* Woodbury, N.Y.: Barron's Educational Series, 1970. 882 pp.

Discusses over 1,350 colleges and universities accredited by regional associations.

Garraty, John A., and others. *The New Guide to Study Abroad; Summer and Full-Year Programs for High-School Students, College and University Students, and Teachers.* New York: Harper, 1969. 431 pp.

Graham, William R. *Barron's Guide to the Two-Year Colleges.* Woodbury, N.Y.: Barron's Educational Series, 1972. 2 v.

Describes 1,230 two-year colleges.

Hawes, Gene R., and Novalis, Peter N. *The New American Guide to Colleges,* 4th ed. New York: Columbia Univ. Press, 1972. 640 pp.

Arranged by type of college; includes listings in Canada and Mexico.

International Handbook of Universities and Other Institutions of Higher Education, 4th ed. Paris: International Assoc. of Univs., 1968. 1,178 pp.

Information on more than 2,000 institutions in eighty-four countries, excluding United States and British Commonwealth.

Livesey, Herbert B., and Robbins, Gene A. *Guide to American Graduate Schools.* New York: Viking, 1967. 357 pp.

Information on about 600 institutions offering graduate and professional programs in all fields of study.

Lovejoy's College Guide. New York: Simon and Schuster, 1953 to date. Biennial.

Listing of about 2,000 United States colleges and universities, arranged by states, with principal facts. Supplemented by the monthly *Lovejoy's Guidance Digest.*

The National Faculty Directory. Detroit, Mich.: Gale Research Co., 1970 to date. Annual.

"Alphabetical list, with addresses, of over 413,000 faculty members at junior colleges, colleges, and universities in the United States."

Study Abroad: International Scholarships and Courses. Paris: UNESCO, 1948 to date. Biennial.

In the 1972 edition, details are given for some 250,000 opportunities for study at the university level throughout the world. Arranged by country; indexes for international organizations and national institutions.

Wasserman, Elga R., and Switzer, Ellen E. *The Random House Guide to Graduate Study in the Arts and Sciences.* New York: Random House, 1967. 361 pp.

Data arranged by subject discipline, much of it in tabular form.

World of Learning. London: Europa Pub., 1947 to date. Annual.

"A comprehensive guide to educational, scientific and cultural institutions in all parts of the world."

COLORS

Albers, Josef. *Interaction of Color.* New Haven, Conn.: Yale Univ. Press, 1963. 80 pp.

Text volume and ninety-three separate color plates demonstrate relativity and instability of color: interaction between color and color; interdependence of color with form and placement, quantity, and quality.

Maerz, Aloys J., and Paul, Morris R. *A Dictionary of Color,* 2d ed. New York: McGraw-Hill, 1950. 208 pp., fifty-six colored plates.

Names of colors and reproductions of about 7,000 different colors.

Ridgway, Robert. *Color Standards and Color Nomenclature.* Washington, D.C.: The Author, 1912. 43 pp.

Dictionary list of 1,115 named colors and mounted color photographs of 1,431 different shades.

COOKERY AND FOOD

American Heritage Cookbook and Illustrated History of American Eating and Drinking. New York: American Heritage Pub. Co., 1964. 629 pp.

American Home Economics Association. *Handbook of Food Preparation,* 6th ed. Washington, D.C.: The Association, 1971. 116 pp.

Data on ingredients, units of measure, processes, times and temperatures, etc. Includes buying guides.

Bowes, Anna De Planter. *Food Values of Portions Commonly Used,* 9th ed. Philadelphia, Pa.: Lippincott, 1963. 130 pp.

Cook's and Diner's Dictionary: A Lexicon of Food, Wine and Culinary Terms. New York: Funk and Wagnalls, 1969. 274 pp.

Defines 3,000 terms for the gourmet and cook. Illustrated.

Good Housekeeping International Cookbook. New York: Harcourt, 1964. 245 pp.

Gunderson, Frank, and others. *Food Standards and Definitions in the United States; a Guidebook.* New York: Academic Press, 1963. 269 pp.

Guide to government standards.

Hewitt, Jean. *The New York Times Heritage Cook Book.* New York: Putnam, 1972. 804 pp.

Deals with American regional cookery.

Kraus, Barbara. *Calories and Carbohydrates.* New York: Grosset and Dunlap, 1971. 322 pp.

Alphabetical arrangement for 7,500 brand names or names of

foods and beverages, giving caloric and carbohydrate content for specified portions.

Kraus, Barbara. *The Cookbook of the United Nations,* rev. ed. New York: Simon and Schuster, 1970. 128 pp.

Schoonmaker, Frank. *Encyclopedia of Wine,* rev. ed. New York: Hastings House, 1968. 442 pp.

Contains over 2,000 alphabetical entries, with illustrations and maps. In the same field is: Simon, Andre L., ed. *Wines of the World.* New York: McGraw-Hill, 1972. 719 pp. Adams, Leon D. *The Wines of America.* Boston, Mass.: Houghton Mifflin, 1973. 465 pp.

Simon, Andre L., and Howe, Robin. *Dictionary of Gastronomy,* rev. ed. New York: McGraw-Hill, 1970. 400 pp.

Defines terms relating to food, wine, and the culinary arts; well illustrated. Bibliography.

Ward, Artemas. *Encyclopedia of Food.* New York: Peter Smith, 1941. 596 pp.

Some 2,000 articles on all types of food; numerous illustrations.

Watt, Bernice K., and Merrill, Annabel L. *Composition of Foods; Raw, Processed, Prepared.* Washington, D.C.: U.S. Dept. of Agriculture, 1963. 189 pp. (Agriculture Handbook, No. 8.)

The Wise Encyclopedia of Cookery, rev. ed. New York: Grosset and Dunlap, 1971. 1,329 pp.

Encyclopedic treatment, in alphabetic order, of foods and drinks. Contains 5,100 recipes; over 500 illustrations, charts, and diagrams.

Woman's Day Encyclopedia of Cookery. New York: Fawcett Pub., 1966. 12 v.

Includes recipes for foreign cookery.

COSTUME AND DRESS

Bradley, Carolyn G. *Western World Costume, an Outline History.* New York: Appleton, 1954. 451 pp.

Braun-Ronsdorf, Margarete. *Mirror of Fashion; a History of*

European Costume, 1789–1929. New York: McGraw-Hill, 1964. 270 pp.

Cunnington, Cecil W., and others. *A Dictionary of English Costume.* London: Black, 1960. 281 pp.
Definitions of costume terms, many line drawings, descriptions of wearing apparel, etc., 900–1900.

Cunnington, Cecil W. and Phyllis. *A Picture History of English Costume.* New York: Macmillan, 1960. 160 pp.
Illustrations showing costume development from Middle Ages to modern times.

D'Assailly, Gisele. *Ages of Elegance; Five Thousand Years of Fashion and Frivolity.* Greenwich, Conn.: New York Graphic Society, 1969. 251 pp.

Davenport, Millia. *The Book of Costume.* New York: Crown, 1948. 2 v. (Reissued. New York: Crown, 1964. 480 pp.)
History of dress to about 1850; contains 3,000 illustrations.

Monro, Isabel S., and Cook, Dorothy E. *Costume Index; a Subject Index to Plates and Illustrated Text.* New York: Wilson, 1937. 338 pp. *Supplement,* 1957. 210 pp.
Listing about 950 books.

Payne, Blanche. *History of Costume from the Ancient Egyptians to the Twentieth Century.* New York: Harper, 1965. 607 pp.

Wilcox, Ruth T. *The Dictionary of Costume.* New York: Scribner, 1969. 406 pp.
Contains more than 3,200 entries relating to dress worldwide and for all periods of history. Numerous illustrations.

Wilcox, Ruth T. *Five Centuries of American Costume.* New York: Scribner, 1963. 207 pp.
Dress of men, women, and children; illustrated by 500 individual drawings.

DANCE

Balanchine, George. *Balanchine's New Complete Stories of the Great Ballets.* Garden City, N.Y.: Doubleday, 1968. 626 pp.
Plots and other facts on classical and modern ballets.

Beaumont, Cyril W. *Complete Book of Ballets.* New York: Putnam, 1938. 900 pp. Supplements, 1942–55. 3 v.

Guide to principal nineteenth- and twentieth-century ballets, including synopses.

Chujoy, Anatole, and Manchester, P. W. *The Dance Encyclopedia*, rev. ed. New York: Simon and Schuster, 1967. 992 pp. Articles on various forms of dance, biography, ballets, and definitions of dance terms.

Grant, Gail. *Technical Manual and Dictionary of Classical Ballet*, 2d ed. New York: Dover, 1967. 127 pp. Clear definitions of ballet terms with pronunciation guide; bibliography.

Martin, John J. *Book of the Dance*. New York: Tudor Pub. Co., 1963. 192 pp. Deals with history of dance, chief modern artists, ballet, etc.

Raffe, W. G. *Dictionary of the Dance*. New York: A. S. Barnes, 1964. 583 pp.

DEBATING

Kruger, Arthur N. *A Classified Bibliography of Argumentation and Debate*. Metuchen, N.J.: Scarecrow Press, 1964. 400 pp. Comprehensive list of books and articles in English covering all phases of debating.

Reference Shelf. New York: Wilson, 1922 to date. Each of five or six annual issues deals with a controversial question, presenting affirmative and negative arguments.

University Debaters' Annual. New York: Wilson, 1915–51. 37 v. Reports of actual college debates, with briefs and bibliographies.

DIRECTORIES—BUSINESS

Goodman, Steven E. *Financial Market Place; a Directory of Major Corporations, Institutions, Services, and Publications.* New York: Bowker, 1972. 363 pp. Comprehensive coverage of financial institutions and associations, educational programs, reference and professional services, financial libraries. Index and glossary of investing terms.

Klein, Bernard, ed. *Guide to American Directories: A Guide to the Major Business Directories of the United States, Covering All Industrial, Professional and Mercantile Categories,* 8th ed. New York: Klein, 1971. 465 pp.

Extensive list arranged under several hundred categories; separate section lists foreign directories.

MacRae's Blue Book. Chicago, Ill.: MacRae's Blue Book Co., 1895? to date. Annual.

"America's greatest buying guide."

Poor's Register of Corporations, Directors and Executives. New York: Standard and Poor's Corp., 1928 to date. Annual.

Covers the United States and Canada. In three parts: list of about 33,000 companies of all kinds; list of 75,000 business executives, with brief biographies; and list of industrial products, with companies selling them.

Sweet's Catalog Service. *Sweet's Catalog File.* New York: Sweet's Catalog Division, F. W. Dodge, 1914 to date. Annual.

Bound files of manufacturers' catalogs for architecture, engineering, process industries, mechanical industries, power plants, product designers.

Thomas' Register of American Manufacturers. New York: Thomas Pub. Co., 1905 to date. Annual.

Most complete directory of United States manufacturers; includes list of manufacturers classified by products, geographically arranged, and catalogs of manufacturers.

DIRECTORIES—SOCIETIES

Annual Register of Grant Support. Los Angeles, Calif.: Academic Media, 1969 to date. Annual.

"A guide to grant support programs of government agencies, foundations, and business and professional organizations." Lists general programs and those in humanities, social sciences, and sciences. Subject, organizational, and geographic indexes.

Directory of National Trade and Professional Associations of the United States. Washington, D.C.: Potomac Books, 1966 to date. Annual.

Provides data on some 3,500 associations.

Encyclopedia of Associations, 7th ed.   Detroit, Mich: Gale Research Co., 1972. 3 v. Quarterly supplements.

V. 1, lists about 16,650 national associations of the United States: business, governmental, scientific, educational, labor, religious, etc., by classification; v. 2, geographic-executive index; v. 3, new associations and projects.

The Foundation Directory, 4th ed.   New York: Foundation Library Center (dist. by Columbia), 1971. 642 pp.

Arranged geographically by states. Gives information on 5,454 nonprofit, nongovernmental foundations in the United States: fields of interest, assets, expenditures, personnel, etc. Supplemented by *Foundation News.* New York: Foundation Library Center, 1960 to date. Bimonthly. *Foundation Grants Index, 1970–1971; a Two-Year Cumulative Listing of Foundation Grants.* New York: Foundation Library Center, 1972. 292 pp.

Research Centers Directory, 4th ed.   Detroit, Mich.: Gale Research Co., 1972. 1,033 pp.

Lists permanent university-sponsored and other nonprofit research organizations carrying on continuing research programs. Supplemented by *New Research Centers.* Detroit, Mich: Gale Research Co., 1965 to date. Quarterly.

ECOLOGY AND THE ENVIRONMENT

Air Pollution Abstracts.   Research Triangle Park, N.C.: Air Pollution Technical Information Center of the Environmental Protection Agency, 1970 to date. Quarterly.

Abstracts from periodicals, books, conference proceedings, technical reports, patents, etc. Classified arrangement; includes sections on emission sources, control and measurement methods, air quality standards, legislation, etc.

Bond, Richard G., and Straub, Conrad P.   *Handbook of Environmental Control.* Cleveland, Ohio: CRC Press, 1972. 2 v.

V. 1, air pollution; v. 2, solid waste.

Clepper, Henry.   *Leaders of American Conservation.* New York: Ronald Press, 1971. 353 pp.

Biographies of 360 leaders of the movement to conserve wild-life and natural resources in the United States during the past 100 years.

The Earth and Man: A Rand McNally World Atlas. Chicago, Ill.: Rand McNally, 1972. 439 pp.

Combines maps, text, diagrams, and tables in presentation which emphasizes ecology and preservation of the environment.

Color photographs; subject and geographical indexes.

Environment Film Review; a Critical Guide to Ecology Films. New York: Environment Information Center, 1972. 155 pp. Critical reviews of 627 16mm. sound films on twenty-one environmental topics. Subject and sponsor index.

Environment Information Access. New York: Environment Information Center, 1971 to date. Monthly.

Indexes and abstracts information from periodicals, conference proceedings, research reports, congressional hearings, and newspapers. Entries arranged by accession numbers under twenty-one subject categories. Subject, industry, author, and accession number indexes cumulate annually in the *Environment Index,* 1972 to date.

Fisher, James, and others. *Wildlife in Danger.* New York: Viking, 1969. 368 pp.

Information on characteristics, history, and present status of endangered species. Covers mammals, birds, reptiles, amphibians, fish, and plants. Many illustrations; detailed index.

Landau, Norman J., and Rheingold, Paul D. *The Environmental Law Handbook.* New York: Ballantine/Friends of the Earth, 1971. 496 pp.

Step-by-step guide to controlling or eliminating pollution-causing activities; summarizes existing laws and regulations. Glossary and bibliography.

Mitchell, John G., and Stallings, Constance L., eds. *Ecotactics: The Sierra Club Handbook for Environmental Activists.* New York: Pocket Books, 1970. 288 pp.

Describes methods and approaches for activities to protect

the environment. Includes listing of major source material in ecology, professional groups and societies, pertinent government agencies.

Pitts, James N., Jr., and Metcalf, Robert L., eds. *Advances in Environmental Sciences and Technology.* New York: Interscience, 1969. 356 pp.

Signed articles by experts cover such subjects as air pollution, water pollution, pesticides, ecology, and environment. Many bibliographical references.

Pollution Abstracts. La Jolla, Calif.: Oceanic Library and Information Center, 1970 to date. Bimonthly with annual cumulations.

Abstracts materials dealing with all forms of environmental pollution: air, fresh water, marine, land, noise, etc. Includes feature articles from organizations active in pollution prevention and control. Permuted subject and author indexes.

Water Pollution Abstracts. London: H.M.S.O., 1927 to date. Monthly.

International coverage of the literature relating to all aspects of water pollution. Annual author-subject index.

Winton, Harry N. M. *Man and the Environment; a Bibliography of Selected Publications of the United Nations System, 1946–1971.* New York: Bowker, 1972. 305 pp.

Annotated entries for 1,200 United Nations publications "which treat of man, the resources available to him, the environment, and the population problem." Indexes: author, series and serials, title, and subject.

ECONOMICS AND BUSINESS

Business Periodicals Index. New York: Wilson, 1958 to date. Monthly except August with annual cumulations.

Subject index to about 170 periodicals in business and related fields.

Coman, Edwin T. *Sources of Business Information,* 2d ed. Berkeley: Univ. of California Press, 1964. 330 pp.

Economic Almanac. New York: National Industrial Conference Board, 1940 to date. Biennial.

Statistics on prices, banking, finance, national income, resources, manufacturing, communications, transportation, industries, agriculture, labor, foreign trade, etc.

Handbook of Basic Economic Statistics. Washington, D.C.:
Govt. Statistics Bureau, 1947 to date. Annual.
"A manual of basic economic data on industry, commerce,
labor, and agriculture in the United States."

*McGraw-Hill Dictionary of Modern Economics; a Handbook of
Terms and Organizations.* New York: McGraw-Hill, 1965.
697 pp.
Defines about 1,300 modern economic and related terms; lists
and describes 200 organizations concerned with economics
and marketing.

Oxford Economic Atlas of the World, 4th ed. Oxford: Oxford
Univ. Press, 1972. 239 pp.
Maps show world distribution patterns, major trade flows;
supplemented by statistical tables, notes, and economic commentary. Gazetteer includes 8,000 names for urban areas and
economically important places.

*Rand McNally International Bankers Directory; the Bankers Blue
Book.* Chicago, Ill.: Rand McNally, 1872 to date. Semiannual with monthly supplements.
Directory of United States and foreign banks; arranged by
states and nations.

Sloan, Harold S., and Zurcher, Arnold J. *Dictionary of Economics,* 5th ed. New York: Barnes & Noble, 1971. 520 pp.
Defines about 2,500 economic, business, and commercial
terms, with many tables and charts.

Wasserman, Paul, ed. *Encyclopedia of Business Information
Sources.* Detroit, Mich.: Gale Research Co., 1970. 2 v.
Lists primary and secondary sources in an alphabetical ar-
rangement: v. 1, general subjects; v. 2, geographical subjects.

EDUCATION

Blishen, Edward. *Encyclopedia of Education.* New York: Philosophical Library, 1970. 882 pp.
Compendium of information on all aspects of education:

administration, teaching aids, legislation and reports, history and philosophy, etc. British emphasis.

Burke, Arvid J. and Mary A. *Documentation in Education.* New York: Teachers College, 1967. 413 pp.

Guide to sources of educational information and data.

Current Index to Journals in Education. New York: CCM Information Corp., 1969 to date. Monthly with semiannual and annual cumulations.

Classified arrangement with subject and author indexes; covers more than 200 journal titles. Produced in cooperation with the United States Office of Education's Educational Resources Information Center (ERIC), the index complements ERIC's *Research in Education.* Washington, D.C.: U.S. Dept. of Health, Education, and Welfare, 1966 to date. Monthly with semiannual and annual cumulated indexes. Covers the report literature.

Directory for Exceptional Children, 7th ed.   Boston, Mass.: Porter Sargent, 1971. 1,248 pp.

Describes schools, homes, clinics, hospitals, and services.

Education Index, 1929 to date.   New York: Wilson, 1932 to date. Monthly except July and August with annual cumulations.

Author and subject index to about 240 education periodicals, proceedings, yearbooks, bulletins, and monographic series.

Educator's World; the Standard Guide to American-Canadian Educational Associations, Publications, Conventions, Research Centers, Foundations. Englewood, Colo.: Fisher Pub. Co., 1971. 685 pp.

Emphasis on state, regional, and national educational associations.

Ellingson, Careth, and Cass, James. *Directory of Facilities for the Learning-Disabled and Handicapped.* New York: Harper, 1972. 624 pp.

Describes diagnostic facilities, remedial, therapeutic, and developmental programs in United States and Canada. Arranged alphabetically by state or province; facilities index.

The Encyclopedia of Education. New York: Macmillan and Free Press, 1971. 10 v.

Comprehensive survey of education with American emphasis. Signed articles include bibliographies. Separate index volume.

Encyclopedia of Educational Research, 4th ed.   New York: Macmillan, 1969. 1,522 pp.

Review of the literature of educational research, arranged alphabetically by subjects.

Good, Carter V.   *Dictionary of Education.* New York: McGraw-Hill, 1959. 676 pp.

Definitions of thousands of educational terms, including related words from psychology, sociology, and philosophy.

Handbook of Private Schools.   Boston, Mass.: Porter Sargent, 1915 to date. Annual.

Lists of schools arranged by states and localities; classification of schools by types, and pertinent data on individual schools.

International Yearbook of Education.   Paris: UNESCO, 1948 to date. Annual.

Information on educational conditions and developments in countries throughout the world during preceding year.

LaCrosse, E. Robert, Jr.   *Early Childhood Education Directory; a Selected Guide to 2,000 Preschool Educational Centers.* New York: Bowker, 1971. 455 pp.

Arranged alphabetically by state, then city.

Patterson's American Education.   Mount Prospect, Ill.: Educational Directories, 1904 to date. Annual.

Provides data on state departments of education, public and private schools, colleges and universities, special schools, associations, etc. Arranged by state, then by community.

Richmond, W. Kenneth.   *The Literature of Education; a Critical Bibliography, 1945–1970.* London: Methuen, 1972. 206 pp. Titles grouped under ten areas relating to education: philosophy, theory, curriculum, psychology, history, sociology, administration, comparative studies, economics, and technology.

Standard Education Almanac.   Los Angeles, Calif.: Academic Media, 1968 to date.

Statistical data and directory information on a variety of
educational subjects.

Teacher's Encyclopedia. Englewood Cliffs, N.J.: Prentice-Hall,
1966. 1,116 pp.

Discussions by specialists on practical learning situations and
teaching experiences. Bibliographies; subject index.

U.S. Office of Education. *Educational Directory.* Washington,
D.C.: G.P.O., 1912 to date. Annual.

Covers educational officers, county and municipal schools,
colleges and universities, and educational organizations.

ENGINEERING

Applied Science and Technology Index. New York: Wilson,
1958 to date. Monthly except July with annual cumulations.

Cumulative subject index to periodicals in the fields of aeronautics and space science, automation, chemistry, construction, earth science, electricity and electronics, engineering,
industrial and mechanical arts, machinery, materials, mathematics, metallurgy, petroleum, physics, telecommunications,
transportation, and related subjects.

Baumeister, Theodore, and Marks, Lionel S., eds. *Standard
Handbook for Mechanical Engineers,* 7th ed. New York:
McGraw-Hill, 1967. Various pagings.

Covers new developments in computers, nuclear power, aero-
dynamics, jet propulsion, etc.

Clauser, H. R. *Encyclopedia of Engineering Materials and Processes.* New York: Reinhold, 1963. 787 pp.

Concise description of thousands of materials and processes
used in modern industry and technology.

Comrie, J. *Civil Engineering Reference Book,* 2d ed. London:
Butterworth, 1961. 4 v.

Extensive coverage of all aspects of civil engineering field.

Engineering Index, 1884 to date. New York: Engineering Index,
Inc., 1934 to date. Annual.

Indexes more than 1,000 technical journals and other publications relating to engineering subjects. Supplemented by
Engineering Index Monthly, 1962 to date.

Fink, Donald G., and Carroll, John M., eds. *Standard Hand-book for Electrical Engineers*, 10th ed. New York: McGraw-Hill, 1968. Various pagings.
Comprehensive work, including recent advances in nuclear power, electronic computers, digital data transmission, etc.

Gaylord, Edwin H. and Charles N. *Structural Engineering Handbook*. New York: McGraw-Hill, 1968. Various pagings.
Treats planning, design, and construction of a variety of engineering structures.

Graf, Rudolf F. *Modern Dictionary of Electronics*, 3d ed. Indianapolis, Ind.: Howard W. Sams, 1968. 593 pp.
Defines more than 16,000 terms: illustrated with line drawings and schematic diagrams.

Handbook of Electronic Engineering, 3d ed. Cleveland, Ohio: CRC Press, 1967. 1,532 pp.

Handbook of Ocean and Underwater Engineering. New York: McGraw-Hill, 1969. Various pagings.
Deals broadly with oceanography, marine biology, underwater geology, and chemistry of the oceans.

Hartman, W., and others. *Management Information Systems Handbook; Analysis, Requirements Determination, Design and Development, Implementation and Evaluation*. New York: McGraw-Hill, 1968. Various pagings.

Henney, Keith. *Radio Engineering Handbook*, 5th ed. New York: McGraw-Hill, 1959. Various pagings.
Treats aircraft radio, television, radio broadcasting, and other areas of interest to communication engineers.

Hicks, Tyler Gregory. *Standard Handbook of Engineering Calculations*. New York: McGraw-Hill, 1972. Various pagings.

Highway Engineering Handbook. New York: McGraw-Hill, 1960. Various pagings.
Deals with "essential features of operations, design, and construction of highways."

Hughes, L. E. C., and others. *Dictionary of Electronics and Nucleonics*. New York: Barnes & Noble, 1970. 443 pp.
Defines about 9,000 terms in electronics, nuclear and atomic

physics and technology, radio, television, computing machinery, etc.

Hyslop, Marjorie R. *A Brief Guide to Sources of Metals Information.* Washington, D.C.: Information Resources Press, 1973. 180 pp.

Ireson, W. Grant, and Grant, Eugene L. *Handbook of Industrial Engineering and Management,* 2d ed. Englewood Cliffs, N.J.: Prentice-Hall, 1971. 907 pp.
Treats industrial systems and organizations, computers and data processing, etc.

Jones, Franklin D., and Schubert, Paul B. *Engineering Encyclopedia,* 3d ed. New York: Industrial Press, 1963. 1,431 pp.
"A condensed encyclopedia and dictionary for engineers, mechanics, technical schools, industrial plants, and public libraries, giving the most essential facts about 4,500 important engineering subjects."

Klerer, Melvin, and Korn, Granino A. *Digital Computer User's Handbook.* New York: McGraw-Hill, 1967. Various pagings.

Liebers, Arthur. *The Engineer's Handbook.* New York: Key Pub. Co., 1968. 319 pp.
Topical arrangement; textual material reinforced with drawings and diagrams. Bibliographies; glossaries.

Machol, Robert E. *System Engineering Handbook.* New York: McGraw-Hill, 1965. Various pagings.

Markus, John. *Electronics and Nucleonics Dictionary,* 3d ed. New York: McGraw-Hill, 1966. 743 pp.
Definitions of 16,338 terms used in television, radio, medical electronics, military electronics, avionics, radar, nuclear science, and nuclear engineering.

Maynard, H. B. *Handbook of Modern Manufacturing Management.* New York: McGraw-Hill, 1970. Various pagings.

Merritt, Frederick S., ed. *Standard Handbook for Civil Engineers.* New York: McGraw-Hill, 1968. Various pagings.
Deals with photogrammetric surveying; railway, highway, and airport engineering; hydraulics, stresses, concrete foundations, sewerage, water supply, etc.

Metals Reference and Encyclopedia. New York: Atlas Pub. Co., 1968. 379 pp. Compilation of information concerning "metals and minerals essential to industrial progress and to national security."

Oberg, Erik, and Jones, Franklin D. *Machinery's Handbook; a Reference Book for the Mechanical Engineer, Draftsman, Toolmaker and Machinist,* 19th ed. New York: Industrial Press, 1971. 2,420 pp.

Orr, William I. *Radio Handbook,* 18th ed. New Augusta, Ind.: Editors and Engineers, 1970. 896 pp.

Perry, Robert H. *Engineering Manual; a Practical Reference of Data and Methods in Architectural, Chemical, Civil, Electrical, Mechanical, and Nuclear Engineering,* 2d ed. New York: McGraw-Hill, 1967. Various pagings.

Presents commonly used formulas, methods, and tables for the various engineering fields. Indexes.

Phillips, Arthur L. *Welding Handbook,* 6th ed. New York: American Welding Society, 1968. Various pagings.

Deals with welding processes, metals, applications of welding, etc.

Polon, David D. *Encyclopedia of Engineering Signs and Symbols.* New York: Odyssey Press, 1965. 412 pp.

Potter, James H., ed. *Handbook of the Engineering Sciences.* Princeton, N.J.: Van Nostrand, 1967. 2 v.

V. 1, basic sciences; v. 2, applied sciences.

Covers all aspects of engineering in sections by specialists. Extensive bibliographies.

Pritchard, Alan. *A Guide to Computer Literature; an Introductory Survey of the Sources of Information,* 2d ed. London: Linnet Books & Clive Bingley, 1972. 194 pp.

Reference Data for Radio Engineers, 5th ed. Indianapolis, Ind.: Howard W. Sams, 1968. Various pagings.

Richter, H. P. *Practical Electrical Wiring, Residential, Farm, and Industrial.* New York: McGraw-Hill, 1970. 664 pp.

Sarbacher, Robert I. *Encyclopedic Dictionary of Electronics and Nuclear Engineering.* Englewood Cliffs, N.J.: Prentice-Hall, 1959. 1,417 pp.

Covers field broadly; large number of articles vary from brief definitions to extensive explorations of major topics.

Simonds, Herbert R., and Church, James M. *The Encyclopedia of Basic Materials for Plastics*. New York: Reinhold, 1967. 500 pp.
Concerns different types of plastics and materials from which they are made.

Susskind, Charles. *The Encyclopedia of Electronics*. New York: Reinhold, 1962. 974 pp.
Over 500 articles covering entire field.

Watt, John H., ed. *American Electricians' Handbook; a Reference Book for the Practical Electrical Man*, 9th ed. New York: McGraw-Hill, 1970. Various pagings.

ETIQUETTE

Miller, Llewellyn. *The Encyclopedia of Etiquette: A Guide to Good Manners in Today's World*. New York: Crown, 1967. 640 pp.
A practical guide to contemporary social usage. Alphabetical arrangement; index.

Post, Emily. *Etiquette,* 12th ed. New York: Funk & Wagnalls, 1969. 721 pp.
Most frequently cited guide to etiquette, emphasizing traditional and formal behavior.

Raymond, Louise. *Good Housekeeping's Book of Today's Etiquette*. New York: Harper, 1965. 470 pp.

Vanderbilt, Amy. *Amy Vanderbilt's Etiquette,* rev. ed. Garden City, N.Y.: Doubleday, 1972. 929 pp.
Covers practically all questions on behavior in modern American society.

Vogue's Book of Etiquette and Good Manners. New York: Simon and Schuster/Conde Nast Pub., 1969. 749 pp.
Stresses attitude as well as rules for correct social behavior in a variety of contemporary situations.

FIRST AID

American National Red Cross. *Standard First Aid and Personal Safety*. Garden City, N.Y.: Doubleday, 1973. 268 pp.

Official text of Red Cross first aid program; covers knowledge and skills needed in emergency first aid care, personal safety, and accident prevention. Well illustrated; index.

Henderson, John. *Emergency Medical Guide*, 3d ed. New York: McGraw-Hill, 1973. 566 pp.

Treats first aid for poisoning, emergency obstetrics, home nursing, fractures, bruises, etc.

FISH AND FISHING

Eddy, Samuel. *How to Know the Freshwater Fishes*, 2d ed. Dubuque, Iowa: W. C. Brown, 1969. 286 pp.

Taxonomic keys to fresh-water fish of the United States, including Alaska and Hawaii. Illustrated; bibliography.

Gabrielson, Ira N. *The Fisherman's Encyclopedia*, 2d ed. Harrisburg, Pa.: Stackpole, 1963. 759 pp.

Deals with game fish; fishing equipment and methods; boats; where, when, and how to fish, etc.

Herald, Earl S. *Fishes of North America*. Garden City, N.Y.: Doubleday, 1972. 254 pp.

Survey for the nonspecialist in three main categories: jawless fish, cartilaginous fish, and bony fish. Illustrated; index. By the same author: *Living Fishes of the World*. Garden City, N.Y.: Doubleday, 1961. 303 pp.

Hoar, William Stewart. *Fish Physiology*. New York: Academic Press, 1969–71. 6 v.

LaGorce, John O. *Book of Fishes*. Washington, D.C.: National Geographic Society, 1952. 339 pp.

Guide to North American salt and fresh-water fish; extensively illustrated.

McClane's Standard Fishing Encyclopedia and International Angling Guide. New York: Holt, 1965. 1,033 pp.

Schrenkeisen, Raymond M. *Field Book of Fresh-Water Fishes of North America North of Mexico*. New York: Putnam, 1963. 312 pp.

For each fish, gives common and scientific name, description, habits, and distribution.

FLAGS

Barraclough, E. M. C. *Flags of the World,* rev ed. New York: Warne, 1965. 325 pp.
> Descriptions of historical and modern flags, with color plates and drawings.

Eggenberger, David. *Flags of the U.S.A.* New York: Crowell, 1964. 222 pp.
> Popular, well-illustrated guide.

Great Britain Admiralty. *Flags of All Nations.* London: H.M.S.O., 1955–58. 2 v.
> Covers national flags and ensigns, standards of rulers and heads of state, military and naval flags, etc.

Kannik, Preben. *The Flag Book.* New York: Barrows, 1960. 196 pp.
> Illustrations of about 800 official flags, geographically arranged, eighty national coats of arms, and flags of historical interest.

Pedersen, Christian F. *The International Flag Book in Color.* New York: Morrow, 1971. 237 pp.
> Geographically arranged; short historical text accompanies color illustrations of 853 national, provincial, state, and international flags, emblems, and coats of arms.

Smith, Whitney. *The Flag Book of the United States.* New York: Morrow, 1970. 306 pp.
> Includes flags of the colonial period, state flags, military flags, flags of the Indian nations, etc.; illustrated in color.

FLOWERS

Gleason, Henry A. *The New Britton and Brown Illustrated Flora of the Northeastern United States and Adjacent Canada.* New York: New York Botanical Garden, 1963. 3 v.
> Standard guide to wild plants, describing, locating, and illustrating more than 4,500 species.

Hay, Roy, and Synge, Patrick M. *The Color Dictionary of Flowers and Plants for Home and Garden.* New York: Crown, 1969. 373 pp.

Over 2,000 color photographs are followed by a dictionary section giving information on plants and flowers.

Hylander, Clarence J. *The Macmillan Wild Flower Book.* New York: Macmillan, 1954. 480 pp.

Contains 232 colored plates.

Mathews, Ferdinand S. *Field Book of American Wild Flowers.* New York: Putnam, 1955. 601 pp.

Describes character and habitats, variations in color, and insects which fertilize all types of wild flowers found in the United States.

Perry, Frances. *Flowers of the World.* New York: Crown, 1972. 320 pp.

Information on over 800 flowering plants; fully illustrated with color paintings. Glossary, bibliography, and index.

Polunin, Oleg. *Flowers of Europe: A Field Guide.* Oxford: Oxford Univ. Press, 1969. 662 pp.

Describes about 2,800 species; over 1,000 color plates.

Rickett, Harold W. *The New Field Book of American Wild Flowers.* New York: Putnam, 1963. 384 pp.

Describes over 1,000 common wild flowers in northeastern and north central United States; drawings of 700 species.

Rickett, Harold W. *Wild Flowers of the United States.* New York: McGraw-Hill, 1966–71. 5 v.

Published for the New York Botanical Garden. Beautifully illustrated with color photographs and line drawings. V. 1, northeastern states; v. 2, southeastern states; v. 3, Texas; v. 4, southwestern states; v. 5, northwestern states.

Walcott, Mary V. *Wild Flowers of America.* New York: Crown, 1953. 71 pp., 400 plates.

Based on Smithsonian Institution's *North American Wild Flowers;* contains 400 colored illustrations of flowers.

FOLKLORE AND FOLK MUSIC

Abstracts of Folklore Studies. Austin: Univ. of Texas Press, 1963 to date. Quarterly.

Signed abstracts from about 160 worldwide journals concerned with folklore studies, ethnology, ethnomusicology, and related areas. Bibliographical notes survey the nonperiodical literature. Name-subject index cumulates annually.

Botkin, Benjamin A. *Treasury of American Folklore*. New York: Crown, 1944. 932 pp.

Anthology of folk stories, songs, and other lore. By same editor: *Treasury of New England Folklore*, 1947; *Treasury of Southern Folklore*, 1949; *Treasury of Western Folklore*, 1951; *Treasury of Mississippi River Folklore*, 1955; *Treasury of Railroad Folklore*, 1953, etc.

Briggs, Katharine M. *A Dictionary of British Folktales in the English Language*. London: Routledge, 1970–71. 4 v.

In two parts: folk narratives and folk legends. Recounts or summarizes each tale with sources identified and brief explanatory notes. Indexes of tale types and story titles; lists of references cited or consulted.

Brunvand, Jan Harold. *The Study of American Folklore: An Introduction*. New York: Norton, 1968. 383 pp.

Contains useful bibliographic notes.

Dorson, Richard M. *Folklore and Folklife: An Introduction*. Chicago, Ill.: University of Chicago Press, 1972. 561 pp.

Haywood, Charles. *A Bibliography of North American Folklore and Folksong*, 2d ed. New York: Dover, 1961. 2 v.

Comprehensive index of articles, books, and records for legends, fairy tales, songs, and similar items.

Lawless, Ray M. *Folksingers and Folksongs in America; a Handbook of Biography, Bibliography and Discography*, rev ed. New York: Duell, Sloan & Pearce, 1965. 750 pp.

Biographies of singers, bibliography of folk songs, and articles on instruments, societies, and festivals.

Leach, Maria, and Fried, Jerome, eds. *Funk and Wagnalls Standard Dictionary of Folklore, Mythology, and Legend*. New York: Funk & Wagnalls, 1972. 1,236 pp.

Worldwide in scope; articles on gods, folk heroes, demons, ogres, festivals, customs, folklore of animals and plants, dances, songs, games, proverbs, etc. Index for areas, cultures, and peoples.

Lomax, John A. and Alan. *American Ballads and Folk Songs*.

New York: Macmillan, 1934. 625 pp. Continued by *Our Singing Country*, 1941. 416 pp.
Representative ballads and folk songs, with music and comment for each song.

Robbins, Rossell H. *The Encyclopedia of Witchcraft and Demonology*. New York: Crown, 1959. 571 pp.
Relates chiefly to witchcraft of period 1450–1750.

Stambler, Irwin, and Landon, Grelun. *Encyclopedia of Folk, Country, and Western Music*. New York: St. Martin's, 1969. 396 pp.
Emphasis on biographical sketches of individual performers or groups with information on major songs, performances, awards, and albums. Some coverage of instruments, events, and history.

Thompson, Stith. *Motif-Index of Folk-Literature; a Classification of Narrative Elements in Folktales, Ballads, Myths, Fables, Mediaeval Romances, Exempla, Fabliaux, Jest-Books and Local Legends*. Bloomington: Indiana Univ. Press, 1955–58. 6 v.

FORMULAS

Bennett, Harry. *Chemical Formulary; a Collection of Valuable, Timely, Practical Commercial Formulae and Recipes for Making Thousands of Products in Many Fields of Industry*. Brooklyn, N.Y.: Chemical Pub. Co., 1933–65. 12 v.

Hiscox, Gardner D. *Henley's Twentieth Century Book of Formulas, Processes and Trade Secrets*, rev. ed. New York: Books, 1957. 867 pp.
"Containing 10,000 selected household, workshop and scientific formulas, trade secrets, chemical recipes, processes and money saving ideas for both the amateur and professional worker."

Hopkins, Albert A. *The Standard American Encyclopedia of Formulas*. New York: Grosset, 1953. 1,077 pp.
Includes over 15,000 formulas for the home, factory, and workshop.

Swezey, Kenneth M. *Formulas, Methods, Tips, and Data for*

Home and Workshop. New York: Popular Science, 1969. 691 pp.

Practical information arranged by broad categories: wood finishing and preservation; paints and paint removers; adhesives and sealing compounds; stain removing; photography, etc. Detailed index.

FURNITURE AND INTERIOR DECORATION

Aronson, Joseph. *The Encyclopedia of Furniture,* 3d ed. New York: Crown, 1965. 484 pp.

Articles on furniture types, styles, periods, and terms; 1,400 photographs.

Ball, Victoria K. *The Art of Interior Design; a Text in the Esthetics of Interior Design.* New York: Macmillan, 1960. 343 pp.

Boger, Louise A. *Complete Guide to Furniture Styles,* rev. ed. New York: Scribner, 1969. 500 pp.

Information on furniture from ancient to modern times; appendix of 500 illustrations from United States and European museum collections.

Comstock, Helen. *American Furniture: A Complete Guide to Seventeenth, Eighteenth, and Early Nineteenth Century Styles.* New York: Viking, 1962. 336 pp.

Evans, Helen M. *Man the Designer.* New York: Macmillan, 1973. 390 pp.

Faulkner, Ray N. and Sarah K. *Inside Today's Home,* 3d ed. New York: Holt, 1968. 552 pp.

Nutting, Wallace. *Furniture Treasury (Mostly of American Origin).* New York: Macmillan, 1949–54. 3 v.

V. 1–2, 5,000 numbered plates with index; v. 3, records designers, clockmakers, and glossary of furniture terms, also illustrated.

Obst, Frances M. *Art and Design in Home Living.* New York: Macmillan, 1963. 332 pp.

Pegler, Martin. *Dictionary of Interior Design.* New York: Crown, 1966. 500 pp.

Defines terms; includes brief biographies of individuals prominent in the field.

Praz, Mario. *An Illustrated History of Furnishing from the Renaissance to the Twentieth Century*. New York: Braziller, 1964. 396 pp.

Contains 400 illustrations, many in color, with paintings and drawings of the period in contemporary settings.

Rogers, Kate Ellen. *The Modern House, U.S.A.: Its Design and Decoration*. New York: Harper, 1962. 292 pp.

Many illustrations.

Schmitz, Hermann. *Encyclopedia of Furniture*. New York: Praeger, 1957. 320 pp.

History of furniture design from ancient times to mid-nineteenth century; geographically arranged; 659 photographs.

Whiton, Sherill. *Elements of Interior Design and Decoration*. Philadelphia, Pa.: Lippincott, 1963. 852 pp.

Contains 417 photographs and 120 line drawings.

GAMES

Avedon, Elliott M., and Sutton-Smith, Brian. *The Study of Games*. New York: Wiley, 1971. 448 pp.

Wide-ranging survey of games research: history; role in recreation, education, psychiatric treatment, etc.; structure and function theory. Extensive bibliography.

Borst, Evelyne, and Mitchell, Elmer D. *Social Games for Recreation*, 2d ed. New York: Ronald Press, 1959. 348 pp.

Grouped by indoor, outdoor, and party games.

Donnelly, Richard J. *Active Games and Contests*, 2d ed. New York: Ronald Press, 1958. 672 pp.

Grouped by contests between individuals, between groups, team games, water and winter games, etc.

Forbush, William B., and Allen, Harry R. *The Book of Games for Home, School, and Playground*. Philadelphia, Pa.: Winston, 1954. 358 pp.

Arranged by age groups.

Foster, Robert F. *Foster's Complete Hoyle*, rev. ed. Philadelphia, Pa.: Lippincott, 1963. 697 pp.

Encyclopedia of indoor games "with suggestions for good play, illustrative hands and all official laws to date."

Frey, Richard L., and Truscott, Alan F., eds. *The Official Encyclopedia of Bridge*, rev. ed. New York: Crown, 1971. 793 pp. "To provide an official and authoritative answer to any question a reader might ask about . . . bridge and its leading players."

Hindman, Darwin A. *Complete Book of Games and Stunts.* Englewood Cliffs, N.J.: Prentice-Hall, 1956. 2 v. Guide to about 2,000 indoor and outdoor games. By the same author: *Handbook of Indoor Games and Stunts.* New York: Funk & Wagnalls, 1968. 304 pp.

Opie, Iona and Peter. *Children's Games in Street and Playground.* Oxford: Clarendon Press, 1969. 371 pp. Deals with "chasing, catching, seeking, hunting, racing, duelling, exerting, daring, acting, pretending."

Ostrow, Albert A. *The Complete Card Player.* New York: Grosset & Dunlap, 1951. 771 pp. Rules for all major types of card games.

Sunnucks, Anne. *The Encyclopedia of Chess.* New York: St. Martin's, 1970. 587 pp. Dictionary arrangement; includes technical, statistical, and directory information, biographies of prominent players. Index.

GARDENING

American Home Garden Book and Plant Encyclopedia. Philadelphia, Pa.: Lippincott, 1963. 512 pp. Practical advice on soils and types of flowers.

Baumgardt, John Philip. *How to Prune almost Everything.* New York: Barrows, 1968. 192 pp.

Bush-Brown, James and Louise. *America's Garden Book,* rev. ed. New York: Scribner, 1966. 752 pp. Ranges from planning of formal landscapes to cultivation of vegetables and selected lists of trees, shrubs, and annuals.

Coats, Peter. *Great Gardens of the Western World.* New York: Putnam, 1963. 288 pp.

Historical and artistic data on thirty-eight famous gardens; forty color plates and 350 monochromes.

Healey, B. J. *A Gardener's Guide.* New York: Scribner, 1972. 284 pp.
Primarily a dictionary of plant names, both scientific and popular.

Hyams, Edward, and MacQuitty, William. *Great Botanical Gardens of the World.* New York: Macmillan, 1969. 288 pp.
Beautifully illustrated guide to fifty of the world's botanical gardens and arboretums.

Rockwell, F. F. *10,000 Garden Questions Answered by Twenty Experts.* New York: American Garden Guild, 1959. 1,390 pp.
Questions and answers divided into ten sections.

Taylor, Norman. *Encyclopedia of Gardening; Horticulture and Landscape Design,* 4th ed. Boston, Mass.: Houghton, 1961. 1,329 pp.
Includes new techniques, varieties, and products.

Time-Life Encyclopedia of Gardening. New York: Time-Life Books, 1971———. In progress, to be completed in nineteen volumes.
Each volume devoted to specific group of plants or aspect of gardening, separately indexed. Excellent illustrations, many in color.

Uphof, Johannes C. *Dictionary of Economic Plants,* 2d ed. New York: Stechert-Hafner, 1968. 591 pp.

Wyman, Donald. *Wyman's Gardening Encyclopedia.* New York: Macmillan, 1971, 1,222 pp.
Dictionary arrangement with descriptions and nomenclature for plants considered acceptable for general cultivation.

GEMS AND JEWELS

Desautels, Paul E. *The Gem Kingdom; Special Photography by Lee Boltin.* New York: Random House, 1971. 252 pp.

Kraus, Edward H., and Slawson, Chester B. *Gems and Gem Materials,* 5th ed. New York: McGraw-Hill, 1947. 332 pp.
Guide to precious and semiprecious stones.

MacFall, Russell P. *Gem Hunter's Guide; the Complete Handbook for the Amateur Collector of Gem Minerals*, 4th ed. New York: Crowell, 1969. 279 pp.

How to find and identify precious and semiprecious stones in United States, Canada, and Mexico; directory and maps.

Pearl, Richard M. *Gems, Minerals, Crystals, and Ores; the Collector's Encyclopedia.* New York: Odyssey, 1964. 320 pp.

Shipley, Robert M. *Dictionary of Gems and Gemology*, 6th ed. Los Angeles, Calif.: Gemological Institute of America, 1971.

Definitions of about 4,000 English and foreign terms relating to gems and jewelry, and history of jewels.

Sinkankas, John. *Gemstone and Mineral Data Book; a Compilation of Data, Recipes, Formulas and Instructions for the Mineralogist, Gemologist, Lapidary, Jeweler, Craftsman and Collector.* London: Winchester, 1972. 346 pp.

Describes about 1,000 minerals; includes tables for determination, lists of lapidary equipment, etc.

Sinkankas, John. *Prospecting for Gemstones and Minerals,* rev. ed. New York: Van Nostrand Reinhold, 1970. 397 pp.

For the amateur collector. By the same author is *Gemstones of North America.* Princeton, N.J.: Van Nostrand, 1959. 675 pp.

Webster, Robert. *Gems: Their Sources, Descriptions and Identification,* rev. ed. Hamden, Conn.: Archon, 1970. 836 pp.

Excellent illustrations.

Weinstein, Michael. *World of Jewel Stones.* New York: Sheridan, 1958. 430 pp.

Identification of precious and semiprecious jewels; color illustrations and drawings.

GEOLOGY

American Geological Institute. *Glossary of Geology.* Washington, D.C.: The Institute, 1972. 805 pp., 52 pp.

Comprehensive dictionary of geological terms.

Borner, Rudolf. *Minerals, Rocks, and Gemstones.* Edinburgh: Oliver & Boyd, 1967. 250 pp.

Illustrated guide, emphasizing British localities.

Hurlbut, Cornelius S., Jr. *Dana's Manual of Mineralogy,* 18th ed. New York: Wiley-Interscience, 1971. 579 pp.
   Standard handbook for rock and mineral specialists since 1848.

MacFall, Russell P., and Wollin, Jay. *Fossils for Amateurs.* New York: Van Nostrand Reinhold, 1972. 341 pp.
   Treats collecting, classifying, cleaning, and displaying fossils; numerous illustrations.

MacKay, John W. *Sources of Information for the Literature of Geology; an Introductory Guide.* London: Geological Society, 1973. 61 pp.

Mutch, Thomas A. *Geology of the Moon, a Stratigraphic View.* Princeton, N.J.: Princeton Univ. Press, 1972. 391 pp.
   Numerous illustrations based on Apollo flights.

Nickles, John M. *Geologic Literature of North America, 1785–1918.* Washington, D.C.: G.P.O., 1923–24. 2 v.
   Continued by *Bibliography of North American Geology, 1919–59.* Washington, D.C.: G.P.O., 1931–67. 4 v., with annual supplements, 1960 to date. Decennial volumes cover ten-year periods, 1919–59. Complemented by *Abstracts of North American Geology.* Washington, D.C.: G.P.O., 1966–71. For citations to the literature of geology exclusive of North America see: *Bibliography and Index of Geology.* Boulder, Colo.: Geological Society of America, 1934 to date. Monthly with annual index.

Pough, Frederick H. *Field Guide to Rocks and Minerals,* 3d ed. Boston, Mass.: Houghton, 1960. 349 pp.
   Data on where and how to collect rocks, testing of rocks and minerals, etc.; numerous illustrations.

Rhodes, Frank H. T., and others. *Fossils, a Guide to Prehistoric Life.* New York: Golden Press, 1962. 160 pp.
   In the same field is: Ransom, Jay E. *Fossils in America: Their Nature, Origin, Identification, and Classification and a Range Guide to Collecting Sites.* New York: Harper, 1964. 402 pp.

Rhodes, Frank H. T. *Geology; Illustrated by Raymond Perlman.* New York: Golden Press, 1972. 160 pp.

Direct, brief, clear descriptions and illustrations.

Ward, Dederick C., and Wheeler, Marjorie W. *Geologic Reference Sources: A Subject and Regional Bibliography of Publications and Maps in the Geological Sciences.* Metuchen, N.J.: Scarecrow Press, 1972. 453 pp.

Briefly annotated guide to reference books, monographs, periodicals, and maps. Subject and geographic indexes.

Whitten, D. G. A., and Brooks, J. R. V. *The Penguin Dictionary of Geology.* Baltimore, Md.: Penguin Books, 1972. 495 pp., appendixes.

GOVERNMENT AND POLITICS

Barone, Michael, and others. *The Almanac of American Politics: The Senators, the Representatives—Their Records, States and Districts, 1972.* Boston, Mass.: Gambit, 1972. 1,030 pp.

Provides data for each state and district, as well as biographical and political information for senators and congressmen. Index.

Book of the States. Chicago, Ill.: Council of State Governments, 1935 to date. Biennial.

Comprehensive guide to state government activities, including directory of officials, statistical data, and general information.

Brock, Clifton. *The Literature of Political Science; a Guide for Students, Librarians, and Teachers.* New York: Bowker, 1969. 232 pp. Annotated guide to reference works and other documentary resources.

Congressional Quarterly's Guide to the Congress of the United States: Origins, History and Procedure. Washington, D.C.: Congressional Quarterly Service, 1971. Various pagings.

Bibliographies accompany each chapter. Appendixes include biographical index to members of Congress, 1789–1971, texts of basic documents, standing rules of the House and Senate.

Dexter, Byron, ed. *The Foreign Affairs Fifty-Year Bibliography: New Evaluations of Significant Books on International Relations, 1920–1970.* New York: Bowker, 1972. 936 pp.

Selective listing of 2,130 titles with annotations. In three parts: general international relations; the world since 1914; the world by regions. Author and title indexes.

Europa Year Book.   London: Europa Pub., 1959 to date. 2 v. Annual. V. 1: international organizations and Europe; v. 2: Africa, the Americas, Asia, Australia. Data on governments, finance, trade, press, religion, population, etc.

The International Yearbook and Statesmen's Who's Who.   London: Burke's Peerage, 1953 to date. Annual.
Detailed data on international organizations, countries of world, and biographies of governmental leaders.

Laqueur, Walter, and others.   *A Dictionary of Politics.* New York: Free Press, 1971. 593 pp.
Comprehensive compilation of some 3,000 terms found in current political science literature.

McCarthy, Eugene.   *The Crescent Dictionary of American Politics.* New York: Macmillan, 1962. 196 pp.
Deals with popular political jargon, brief definitions; includes charts of governmental structure.

Municipal Year Book.   Chicago, Ill.: International City Management Assoc., 1934 to date. Annual.
Compilation of data on American cities, e.g., statistics, personnel, finance, and directories of officials.

Plano, Jack C., and Greenberg, Milton.   *The American Political Dictionary,* rev. ed. New York: Holt, 1967. 401 pp.
Terms are grouped in chapters according to particular aspects of government.

Political Handbook and Atlas of the World.   New York: Council on Foreign Relations, 1927 to date. Annual.
Lists chief government officials, party programs and leaders, political events of year, and press.

Porter, Kirk H., and Johnson, Donald B., comps.   *National Party Platforms, 1840–1968,* 4th ed. Urbana: Univ. of Illinois Press, 1970. 723 pp.
Contains all platforms of major and influential minor political parties, unabridged. Quadrennial supplements.

Schlesinger, Arthur M., Jr., ed. *History of American Presidential Elections, 1789–1968*. New York: Chelsea House/McGraw-Hill, 1971. 4 v.

Explains basic campaign issues and includes pertinent documents for each election from Washington to Nixon.

Smith, Edward C., and Zurcher, Arnold J. *Dictionary of American Politics*, 2d ed. New York: Barnes & Noble, 1968. 434 pp.

Brief articles, in alphabetical order, on United States political history.

Sperber, Hans. *American Political Terms*. Detroit, Mich.: Wayne State Univ. Press, 1962. 516 pp.

Brief descriptions, relating mainly to history of terms.

Statesman's Year-Book; Statistical and Historical Annual of the States of the World. New York: St. Martin's, 1864 to date. Annual.

Manual on governments of the world, including variety of statistical and other information.

U.S. Congress. *Biographical Directory of the American Congress, 1774–1961*. Washington, D.C.: G.P.O., 1961. 1,863 pp.

Lists executive officers since 1789, and members of each Congress by states; biographies alphabetically arranged.

U.S. Congress. *Official Congressional Directory*. Washington, D.C.: G.P.O., 1809 to date. Annual.

Biographical sketches of members of current Congress and officials of executive departments, and other pertinent data.

U.S. Department of State. *United States Department of State Fact Book of the Countries of the World*. New York: Crown, 1970. 792 pp.

Information for each country on people, government, economy, relations with the United States, etc.

United States Government Organization Manual. Washington, D.C.: G.P.O., 1935 to date. Annual.

Information on organization, activities, and officials of departments, bureaus, and other divisions of the government.

Who's Who in American Politics; a Biographical Directory of United States Political Leaders. New York: Bowker, 1967 to date. Biennial.

Includes politicians at the local, state, and national levels.

Who's Who in Government, 1972–73. Chicago, Ill.: Marquis, 1972. 785 pp.

Over 16,000 entries; emphasis on United States federal government, but includes officials in local, state, and international government. Indexes: biographies listed under subject topics, and under departments, bureaus, and agencies.

Worldmark Encyclopedia of the Nations, 4th ed. New York: Worldmark Press/Harper, 1971. 5 v.

Contents: v. 1, United Nations; v. 2, Africa; v. 3, Americas; v. 4, Asia and Australasia; v. 5, Europe. Political, social, and economic information for 146 countries, the United Nations, and other world organizations.

HOME MANAGEMENT

Gilbreth, Lillian M., and others. *Management in the Home; Happier Living through Saving Time and Energy.* New York: Dodd, 1959. 293 pp.

Gladstone, Bernard. *The New York Times Complete Manual of Home Repairs.* New York: Crowell-Collier-Macmillan, 1967. 438 pp.

Practical advice for the do-it-yourself handyman. Illustrated.

Goodyear, Margaret R., and Klohr, Mildred C. *Managing for Effective Living,* 2d ed. New York: Wiley, 1965. 290 pp.

Gross, Irma H., and Crandall, Elizabeth W. *Management for Modern Families,* 2d ed. New York: Appleton, 1963. 589 pp.

Gruenberg, Sidonie M., ed. *The New Encyclopedia of Child Care and Guidance,* rev. ed. Garden City, N.Y.: Doubleday, 1971. 1,050 pp.

Two sections: ready reference to child care and guidance; basic aspects of child development.

Laas, William. *Good Housekeeping's Guide for Young Homemakers.* New York: Harper, 1967. 431 pp.

Covers decorating, home care, cleaning, and other phases of home management.

Ludwig, Amber C. *The Bissell Guide to Housekeeping for Young Homemakers.* New York: Bantam Books, 1967. 416 pp.

Nickell, Paulena, and Dorsey, Jean M. *Management in Family Living*, 4th ed. New York: Wiley, 1967. 554 pp.

Oppenheim, Irene. *Management of the Modern Home.* New York: Macmillan, 1972. 338 pp.

HOTELS—MOTELS

Hines, Duncan. *Lodging for a Night.* Ithaca, N.Y.: Adventures in Good Eating, 1938 to date. Annual.

Guide to hotels and motels in the United States (including Alaska and Hawaii), Canada, and Mexico.

Hotel and Motel Red Book. New York: Amer. Hotel Assoc. Directory Corp., 1886 to date. Annual.

Directory of members of the American Hotel and Motel Association. Lists over 8,000 hotels and motels, primarily in the United States, with limited coverage for other countries.

Leahy's Hotel-Motel Guide and Travel Atlas. Chicago, Ill.: Amer. Hotel Register Co., 1876 to date. Annual.

Most complete guide to hotels and motels in the United States, Canada, Mexico, and Puerto Rico. Includes Rand McNally road atlas of maps for states and provinces.

INDIANS (AMERICAN)

Dennis, Henry C. *The American Indian, 1492–1970: A Chronology and Fact Book.* Dobbs Ferry, N.Y.: Oceana, 1971. 137 pp.

Historical chronology plus biographies of prominent Indians and data on publications and associations; bibliography of books and audiovisual materials. Index.

Hodge, Frederick W. *Handbook of American Indians North of Mexico.* Washington, D.C.: G.P.O., 1907–10. 2 v. (Reprinted. St. Clair Shores, Mich.: Scholarly Press, 1968).

Descriptive list of stocks, confederacies, tribes, tribal divisions, and settlements, together with biographies of noted Indians, and Indian history, archeology, manners, arts, customs, and institutions.

Index to Literature on the American Indian, 1970. San Francisco, Calif.: Indian Historian Press, 1972. 177 pp.

Planned annual index to periodical and book literature dealing with Indians of North, South, and Central America.

Klein, Bernard, and Icolari, Daniel, eds. *Reference Encyclopedia of the American Indian.* New York: Klein, 1967. 536 pp.
Provides directory information for government agencies, associations, museums, libraries, reservations, tribal councils, schools, and periodicals. Annotated bibliography with subject index. Biographical sketches of prominent American Indians and others active in Indian affairs.

Steward, Julian H. *Handbook of South American Indians.* Washington, D.C.: G.P.O., 1946–50. 6 v.
Arrangement by tribes and regions, covering anthropology, linguistics, cultural geography, and other phases of tribal life.

Swanton, John R. *The Indian Tribes of North America.* Washington, D.C.: G.P.O., 1952. 726 pp.
Comprehensive guide to Indians of Central and North America and West Indies, arranged by states or regions.

Wauchope, Robert. *Handbook of Middle American Indians.* Austin: Univ. of Texas Press, 1964–72. 12 v.

INSECTS

Borror, Donald J., and White, Richard E. *A Field Guide to the Insects of America North of Mexico.* Boston, Mass.: Houghton, 1970. 404 pp.
Systematic coverage of 579 insect families; describes characteristics for identification, how to collect, preserve, and study insects.
Many illustrations.

Metcalf, Clell L. *Destructive and Useful Insects,* 4th ed. New York: McGraw-Hill, 1962. 1,087 pp.
Guide to all varieties of insect life; well indexed, numerous illustrations.

Swain, Ralph B. *Insect Guide.* Garden City, N.Y.: Doubleday, 1948. 261 pp.
Guide to principal insect groups; 450 illustrations, mainly in color.

Swan, Lester A., and Papp, Charles S. *The Common Insects of North America*. New York: Harper, 1972. 750 pp.
Descriptions of more than 2,000 species; illustrated with 2,450 line drawings. Two appendixes: geologic eras or periods: the place of insects in time, and orders and families represented in this book. Glossary; bibliography.

U.S. Department of Agriculture. *Yearbook, 1952: Insects*. Washington, D.C.: G.P.O., 1952. 780 pp.
Articles on insect pests in relation to agriculture; color plates and descriptions.

Westcott, Cynthia. *The Gardener's Bug Book*, 3d ed. Garden City, N.Y.: Doubleday, 1964. 625 pp.
Practical guide to identification and control of 1,800 insects, good and bad, affecting agriculture; color illustrations.

INSURANCE

Athearn, James L., and Toole, Cameron S. *Questions and Answers on Insurance*, 2d ed. Englewood Cliffs, N.J.: Prentice-Hall, 1960. 448 pp.
Contains definitions, questions and answers, types of insurance policies and forms, and charts of license laws.

Best's Insurance Reports: Life-Health. New York: Best, 1906 to date. Annual.
Companion volume is *Best's Key Ratings Guide: Property-Liability*. New York: Best, 1899 to date. Annual. Both compilations give detailed information on insurance companies.

Consumers Union Report on Life Insurance; a Guide to Planning and Buying the Protection You Need. Mount Vernon, N.Y.: Consumers Union, 1967. 128 pp.

Cyclopedia of Insurance in the United States. New York: Index Pub. Co., 1891 to date. Annual.
Includes directory of insurance companies and organizations, important court decisions, definitions of insurance terms, and biographies of insurance leaders.

Insurance Almanac; Who, What, When and Where in Insurance; an Annual of Insurance Facts. New York: Underwriter Printing and Pub. Co., 1912 to date. Annual.

Levy, Michael H. *A Handbook of Personal Insurance Terminology*. Lynbrook, N.Y.: Farnsworth Pub. Co., 1968. 595 pp.
Dictionary of terms used in life, health, and group insurance, and pensions.

INVENTIONS AND PATENTS

Calvert, Robert P., ed. *The Encyclopedia of Patent Practice and Invention Management*. New York: Reinhold, 1964. 860 pp.
"A comprehensive statement of the principles and procedures in solicitation, enforcement, and licensing of patents and recognition and utilization of inventions."

Fenner, Terrence W., and Everett, James L. *Inventor's Handbook*. New York: Chemical Pub., 1969. 309 pp.
Practical guide for the inventor on steps to follow from idea through patenting and marketing.

Jones, Stacy V. *The Inventor's Patent Handbook*. New York: Dial, 1966. 229 pp.
Practical information on patents: obtaining, selling, contract agreements, compensation for inventions in industry and research, etc.

U.S. Patent Office. *Official Gazette*. Washington, D.C.: G.P.O., 1872 to date. Weekly with annual indexes.
Includes brief descriptions and drawings of patents granted each week.

LABOR

Index to Labor Union Periodicals. Ann Arbor: Univ. of Michigan, Bureau of Industrial Relations, 1960 to date. Monthly with annual cumulations.
Annotated subject index to principal labor union periodicals and newspapers.

International Labor Directory and Handbook, 2d ed. New York: Praeger, 1955. 1,043 pp.
Lists national and international unions and their officers, other labor organizations, labor periodicals, etc.

International Labour Office. *Yearbook of Labour Statistics*. Montreal: The Office, 1931 to date. Biennial.

Tabulation of labor statistics for the principal countries of world.

Labor Cases.   New York: Commerce Clearing House, 1940 to date. Semiannual.

"A full-text reporter of decisions rendered by federal and state courts throughout the United States on federal and state labor problems."

Labor Research Association.   *Labor Fact Book.* New York: International Publications Service, 1931 to date. Biennial.

Surveys influence of political, economic, and social conditions on labor movement in America; name and subject index.

Peterson, Florence.   *American Labor Unions, What They Are and How They Work,* 2d ed. New York: Harper, 1963. 271 pp.

Deals with history and government of unions; definitions of labor terms; lists unions in each industry; and contains directory of international unions.

U.S. Bureau of Labor Statistics.   *Directory of National and International Labor Unions in the United States.* Washington, D.C.: G.P.O., 1955 to date. Biennial.

Gives addresses, officers, and information on membership, publications, etc.

U.S. Bureau of Labor Statistics.   *Handbook of Labor Statistics.* Washington, D.C.: G.P.O., 1971. 369 pp.

Summarizes government material and statistics on the United States labor force and related subjects.

LATIN AMERICA

Chilcote, Ronald H.   *Revolution and Structural Change in Latin America: A Bibliography on Ideology, Development, and the Radical Left (1930–1965).* Stanford, Calif.: Hoover Institution, 1970. 2 v.

Includes general references and references by country to works relevant to the study of economic, political, and social structural change in Latin America.

Dictionary of Latin American and Caribbean Biography, 2d ed. London: Melrose Press, 1971. 458 pp.

Griffin, Charles C. *Latin America; a Guide to the Historical Literature.* Austin: Univ. of Texas Press, 1971. 700 pp.
Reviews major sources; useful for beginner in field.

Handbook of Latin American Studies. Gainesville: Univ. of Florida Press, 1936 to date. Annual.
Annotated bibliography of publications relating to Latin America; inclusive of all fields except science and technology. *Author Index to Handbook of Latin American Studies,* no. 1–28, 1936–66. Gainesville: Univ. of Florida Press, 1968. 421 pp.

Herring, Hubert. *A History of Latin America, from the Beginnings to the Present,* 3d ed. New York: Knopf, 1967. 1,002 pp.
Readable and informative text, especially for the nineteenth and twentieth centuries.

Libros en Venta. New York: Bowker, 1964. 1,892 pp. *Supplement 1967–68.* 1969. 565 pp. *Supplement 1969–1970.* 1972. 524 pp. *Supplement 1971.* 1973. 269 pp.
Spanish language books in print, Spanish America and Spain.

Martin, Michael R., and Lovett, Gabriel H. *Encyclopedia of Latin-American History,* rev. ed. Indianapolis, Ind.: Bobbs-Merrill, 1968. 348 pp.
Concise entries for people, places, and events important in Latin American history.

Pan American Union Library. *Index to Latin American Periodical Literature, 1929–1960.* Boston, Mass.: G. K. Hall, 1962. 8 v. *First Supplement, 1961–1965.* Boston, Mass.: G. K. Hall, 1968. 2 v.
Continued by *Index to Latin American Periodicals.* Metuchen, N.J.: Scarecrow Press, 1961–72. Quarterly.

Sable, Martin H. *Master Directory for Latin America, Containing Ten Directories Covering Organizations, Associations, and Institutions in the Fields of Agriculture, Business-Industry-Finance, Communications, Education-Research, Government, International Cooperation, Labor Cooperatives, Publishing and Religion, and Professional, Social and Social*

Service Organizations and Associations. Los Angeles: Univ. of California, Latin American Center, 1965. 438 pp. (Reference Series No. 2.)

South American Handbook. London: Trade and Travel Pub., 1924 to date. Annual.

Geographical and travel information about each country; data also on history, natural resources, government, communications, transportation, etc.; includes Central America, Mexico, Caribbean, and West Indies.

Trask, David F., and others. *A Bibliography of United States–Latin American Relations since 1810; a Selected List of Eleven Thousand Published References.* Lincoln: Univ. of Nebraska Press, 1968. 441 pp.

References grouped under general studies, chronological survey of United States–Latin American relations, country by country survey, and specialized topics. Author index.

Veliz, Claudio, ed. *Latin America and the Caribbean: A Handbook.* New York: Praeger, 1968. 840 pp.

Current and historical data are provided for each country. Interpretive articles survey political, social, economic, and cultural conditions. Bibliographies.

Wagley, Charles. *Social Science Research on Latin America.* New York: Columbia Univ. Press, 1964. 337 pp.

Deals with geography, history, anthropology, political science, economics, sociology, and law.

Zimmerman, Irene. *A Guide to Current Latin American Periodicals: Humanities and Social Sciences.* Gainesville, Fla.: Kallman Pub. Co., 1961. 357 pp.

Annotated list of 785 titles.

LAW

American Bar Association. Committee on Business Law Libraries. *Recommended Law Books.* Chicago, Ill.: The Association, 1969. 307 pp.

Classified, annotated listing of basic law books.

American Jurisprudence Desk Book, 2d ed. Rochester, N.Y.: Lawyers Coop. Pub. Co., 1962. 659 pp. Supplement, 1973. 269 pp.

"Historical and legal documents, facts, tables, charts, and statistics."

Ballentine, James A. *Ballentine's Law Dictionary*, 3d ed. Rochester, N.Y.: Lawyers Coop. Pub. Co., 1969. 1,429 pp.
Defines English and Latin legal words, terms, and phrases; also lists abbreviations of legal literature.

Black's Law Dictionary, 4th ed.   St. Paul, Minn.: West Pub. Co., 1951. 1,882 pp.
Contains "definitions of the terms and phrases of American and English jurisprudence, ancient and modern, and including the principal terms of international, constitutional, ecclesiastical and commercial law, and medical jurisprudence," etc.

Friedman, Leon, and Israel, Fred L., eds. *The Justices of the United States Supreme Court, 1789–1969; Their Lives and Major Opinions*. New York: Chelsea House/Bowker, 1969. 4 v.
Biographical sketches by scholars; includes select bibliographies, texts of representative opinions.

Index to Legal Periodicals.   New York: Wilson, 1908 to date. Monthly except September with annual and three-year cumulations.
Indexes contents of principal legal journals, bar association reports, and judicial council reports. In three parts: subject and author index, table of cases, and book reviews.

Kling, Samuel G.   *The Complete Guide to Everyday Law*, 2d ed. Chicago, Ill.: Follett, 1970. 623 pp.
For the layman; topical arrangement covering basic legal questions. Includes sample legal forms and glossary of legal terms.

Martindale-Hubbell Law Directory.   Summit, N.J.: Martindale-Hubbell, 1931 to date. 5 v. Annual.
Directory of United States and Canadian attorneys, and digests of state, Canadian, and foreign laws.

Pollack, Ervin H.   *Fundamentals of Legal Research*, 4th ed. Ed. by J. Myron Jacobstein and Roy M. Mersky. Mineola, N.Y.: Foundation Press, 1973. 565 pp.
A useful guide to the literature of law.

Price, Miles O., and Bitner, Harry. *Effective Legal Research.*
New York: Prentice-Hall, 1953. 633 pp.
Methods of legal research and types of legal reference books.
Robinson, Jacob. *International Law and Organization: General
Sources of Information.* Leiden, Netherlands: Sijthoff, 1967.
560 pp.
Lists reference works and periodicals, with guide to study
and research in the field.
*The Time-Life Family Legal Guide: What You Need to Know
about the Law.* New York: Time-Life Books, 1971. 400 pp.
Clearly written, up-to-date guide for the layman.
United States Code, 1970 Edition. Washington, D.C.: G.P.O.,
1971. 15 v. Supplement, 1971–72. 1973. 5 v.
"Containing the general and permanent laws of the United
States, in force on January 20, 1971." Popular name index and
general index.
United States Code Congressional and Administrative News.
Acts of 76th Congress, Jan. 3, 1939———. St. Paul, Minn.:
West Pub. Co., 1942———.
Published semimonthly in pamphlet form when Congress is
in session, with annual cumulations. Includes public laws,
the legislative history of important bills, executive orders and
proclamations of the president, and administrative rules of
general interest.
United States Supreme Court Reports. Lawyers' Edition. Book
1–100 [1790]–1955; 2d ser. v. 1———, 1956———. Rochester,
N.Y.: Lawyers Coop. Pub. Co.
Reprint edition of the United States Supreme Court opinions.
Includes annotations, summaries of briefs of counsel, and
advance sheets published biweekly while Court is in session.
U.S. Department of State. *Treaties in Force; a List of Treaties
and Other International Agreements of the United States in
Force.* Washington, D.C.: G.P.O., c1929?———. Irregular.
(Annual since 1958.)
Whiteman, Marjorie M. *Digest of International Law.* Washing-
ton, D.C.: G.P.O., 1963–73. 15 v.
Arranged by broad fields.

LIBRARIES

American Library Directory, 28th ed.   New York: Bowker, 1972.
1,212 pp. Biennial.
"A classified list of libraries in the United States and Canada,
with personnel and statistical data, plus a selected list of
libraries around the world." Lists 24,100 libraries in the
United States, and 2,285 in Canada.

The Bowker Annual of Library and Book Trade Information, 18th
ed.   New York: Bowker, 1973. 634 pp. Annual.
Statistical and directory information for United States and
other countries; also covers library and book trade developments and trends during preceding year. Index.

Kruzas, Anthony T., ed.   *Directory of Special Libraries and Information Centers*, 2d ed. Detroit, Mich.: Gale Research Co.,
1968. 1,048 pp.
Lists more than 13,000 libraries and information centers.
Semiannual supplements.

Library and Information Science Abstracts.   London: Library
Assoc., 1969 to date. Bimonthly.
Supersedes *Library Science Abstracts*, 1950–68. International
coverage; abstracts in English from about 200 journals in
field of library science and technology. Classified arrangement; author-subject index cumulates annually.

Library Literature.   New York: Wilson, 1934 to date. Bimonthly
with annual and biennial cumulations.
Subject index to domestic and foreign materials on library
and information science.

World Guide to Libraries, 3d ed.   New York: Bowker, 1971. 4 v.
Gives addresses, indicates subject specialties and size for
36,000 public, academic, and special libraries in 158 countries. Subject index.

MATHEMATICS

Abramowitz, Milton, and Stegun, Irene A.   *Handbook of Mathematical Functions with Formulas, Graphs, and Mathematical
Tables*. New York: Dover, 1965. 1,046 pp.

Akademiia Nauk SSSR, Mathematicheskii Institut. *Mathematics,*

Its Content, Methods, and Meaning. Cambridge, Mass.: M.I.T. Press, 1964. 3 v.

Burington, Richard S.   *Handbook of Mathematical Tables and Formulas,* 5th ed. New York: McGraw-Hill, 1973. 500 pp. By the same author: *Handbook of Probability and Statistics with Tables,* 2d ed. New York: McGraw-Hill, 1970. 462 pp.

Contents of Current Mathematical Journals.   Providence, R.I.: Amer. Mathematical Soc., 1969 to date. Biweekly.

Courant, Richard, and Robbins, Herbert.   *What Is Mathematics? An Elementary Approach to Ideas and Methods.* Oxford: Oxford Univ. Press, 1963. 521 pp.

Dick, Elie M.   *Current Information Sources in Mathematics: An Annotated Guide to Books and Periodicals, 1960–1972.* Littleton, Colo.: Libraries Unlimited, 1973. 280 pp.
More than 1,600 English language entries; author and subject indexes.

Fang, Joong.   *A Guide to the Literature of Mathematics Today.* Hauppauge, N.Y.: Paideia, 1972. 267 pp.
Directed toward "philosophers and historians interested in the development of mathematics in this century." Coverage to about 1967 for most material.

Grazda, Edward E., and others.   *Handbook of Applied Mathematics,* 4th ed. New York: Van Nostrand Reinhold, 1966. 1,119 pp.

Handbook of Mathematical Tables, 4th ed.   Cleveland, Ohio: Chemical Rubber Co., 1970. 1,120 pp.

Howson, A. G.   *A Handbook of Terms Used in Algebra and Analysis.* Cambridge: Cambridge Univ. Press, 1972. 238 pp. Modern definitions for the undergraduate student and school teacher.

International Dictionary of Applied Mathematics.   Princeton, N.J.: Van Nostrand, 1960. 1,173 pp.
"Defines the terms and describes the methods in the application of mathematics to thirty-one fields of physical science and engineering."

James, Glenn and Robert C., eds.   *Mathematics Dictionary,* 3d ed. Princeton, N.J.: Van Nostrand, 1968. 517 pp.

About 8,000 entries reflect current viewpoints and concepts in mathematics. Foreign language indexes: French, German, Russian, and Spanish.

Jansson, Martin E. *Handbook of Applied Mathematics,* 4th ed. Princeton, N.J.: Van Nostrand, 1966. 1,119 pp.
Covers basic principles of mathematics and their applications in practical arts and sciences.

Korn, Granino A. and Theresa M. *Manual of Mathematics.* New York: McGraw-Hill, 1967. 391 pp.
"Outlines of basic mathematical subjects for reference and review" with references to text materials.

Korn, Granino A. and Theresa M. *Mathematical Handbook for Scientists and Engineers,* 2d ed. New York: McGraw-Hill, 1968. 1,130 pp. Mathematical definitions, theorems, and formulas and their applications.

Kuipers, Lauwerens, and Timan, R., eds. *Handbook of Mathematics.* Oxford: Pergamon, 1969. 782 pp.
Translated from the Dutch by I. N. Sneddon. Well-written articles on a variety of mathematical topics.

Mathematical Reviews. Providence, R.I.: Amer. Mathematical Society, 1940 to date. Monthly.
Classified arrangement with signed abstracts of articles in many languages; semiannual author indexes.

May, Kenneth O. *Bibliography and Research Manual of the History of Mathematics.* Toronto: Univ. of Toronto Press, 1973. 818 pp.
"Classified, indexed and annotated bibliography of the secondary literature on the history of mathematics." Includes an extensive biographical section.

Pemberton, John E. *How to Find Out in Mathematics,* 2d ed. Oxford: Pergamon, 1969. 193 pp.
Guide to mathematics literature; includes an appendix on sources of Russian mathematical information.

Rektorys, Karel, ed. *Survey of Applicable Mathematics.* Cambridge, Mass.: M.I.T. Press, 1969. 1,369 pp.
Compendium of results from all fields of mathematics, with examples and explanations of theorems and formulas.

Universal Encyclopedia of Mathematics. New York: Simon and
Schuster, 1964. 715 pp.
  Covers from high school level through calculus, with tables
  and formulas.

MEDICINE

American Hospital Directory. Chicago, Ill.: Amer. Hospital
Assoc., 1945 to date. Annual.
  Published as Part 2 of the August 1 issue of *Hospitals.* Geo-
  graphical listing of hospitals in the United States and
  Canada; includes statistics and directory information.
American Medical Association. *Today's Health Guide.* Chicago,
Ill.: Amer. Medical Assoc., 1965. 640 pp.
  "A manual of health information and guidance for the Amer-
  ican family."
American Medical Directory. Chicago: Amer. Medical Assoc.,
1906 to date. Biennial.
  "A register of physicians who possess a degree of Doctor of
  Medicine; are located in the United States, Isthmian Canal
  Zone, Puerto Rico, Virgin Islands, certain Pacific Islands, or
  are temporarily located in foreign countries." Includes alpha-
  betical index and geographical register of physicians.
Andrews, Matthew. *The Parents' Guide to Drugs.* Garden City,
N.Y.: Doubleday, 1972. 192 pp.
  Includes state-by-state directory of sources of emergency aid
  for those with drug problems; also lists of organizations
  active in drug education; describes each of major drugs (use,
  composition, symptoms, etc.).
Blake, John B., and Roos, Charles. *Medical Reference Works,
1679–1966; a Selected Bibliography.* Chicago, Ill.: Medical
Library Assoc., 1967. 343 pp. *First Supplement,* 1970, then
biennial supplements.
  Classified arrangement with brief annotations. Author-title-
  subject index.
Blakiston's Gould Medical Dictionary, 3d ed. New York:
McGraw-Hill, 1972. 1,828 pp.

Authoritative dictionary of current terms in all branches of medicine, allied health sciences, and related disciplines.

Chatton, Milton J., ed. *Handbook of Medical Treatment,* 13th ed. Los Altos, Calif.: Lange Medical Pub., 1972. 648 pp.

Covers innovations in medical therapy, new drugs, and recommended dosages. Chapters by specialists arranged by organ or system affected, and by disease-causing agents. Index.

Clark, Randolph L., Jr., and Cumley, Russell W. *The Book of Health; a Medical Encyclopedia for Everyone,* 3d ed. New York: Van Nostrand, 1973. 975 pp.

Illustrated guide for the layman to human diseases, physiology, and treatment. Index.

Dental Abstracts: A Selection of World Dental Literature. Chicago, Ill.: Amer. Dental Assoc., 1956 to date. Monthly with annual subject and author indexes.

Abstracts in English from dental periodicals of the world.

Deutsch, Albert, and Fishman, Helen. *The Encyclopedia of Mental Health.* New York: Franklin Watts, 1963. 6 v.

Includes 170 articles by authorities, to provide information useful to the general public.

Directory of Medical Specialists Holding Certification by American Specialty Boards. Chicago, Ill.: Marquis, 1939 to date. Biennial.

Brief biographical and professional data; arranged by specialty, then geographically by state and city.

Dorland's Illustrated Medical Dictionary, 24th ed. Philadelphia, Pa.: Saunders, 1965. 1,724 pp.

Dictionary of terms used in medical sciences and related fields, and medical biography.

Fishbein, Morris, ed. *The New Illustrated Medical and Health Encyclopedia.* New York: Stuttman, 1970. 4 v.

Alphabetically arranged; nontechnical, comprehensive coverage of human anatomy, diseases, and current modes of treatment. Illustrated with photographs, drawings, diagrams. Index.

Index Medicus. Washington, D.C.: National Library of Medicine, 1960 to date. Monthly with annual cumulations.
Indexes about 2,500 journals by author and subject. Also includes bibliography of medical reviews. Published regularly since 1879 under various titles. *Abridged Index Medicus.* Washington, D.C.: National Library of Medicine, 1970 to date. Monthly with annual cumulations. Indexes articles from 100 English-language journals.

Krupp, Marcus A., and Chatton, Milton J. *Current Diagnosis and Treatment.* Los Altos, Calif.: Lange Medical Pub., 1962 to date. Annual.
Desk reference for "technics currently available for diagnosis and treatment" of, primarily, internal medical disorders. Includes current references to the clinical literature. Index. Supplemented by: Kempe, C. Henry, and others. *Current Pediatric Diagnosis and Treatment,* 2d ed. Los Altos, Calif.: Lange Medical Pub., 1972. 1,008 pp.

Lingeman, Richard R. *Drugs from A to Z: A Dictionary.* New York: McGraw-Hill, 1969. 277 pp.
Definitions and data for terms relevant to drugs and drug use.

Major, R. H. *A History of Medicine.* Springfield, Ill.: Chas. C. Thomas, 1954. 2 v.

Menditto, Joseph. *Drugs of Addiction and Non-Addiction: Their Use and Abuse, a Comprehensive Bibliography, 1960–1969.* Troy, N.Y.: Whitston Pub. Co., 1970. 315 pp.
Includes general and scientific books, dissertations, and periodical literature.

Merck Manual of Diagnosis and Therapy, 12th ed. Rahway, N.J.: Merck & Co., Inc., 1972. 1,964 pp.
Current information on research in diagnosis and treatment of disease; classified arrangement. Index.

Miller, Benjamin F. *The Complete Medical Guide,* rev. ed. New York: Simon and Schuster, 1967. 633 pp.
Comprehensive home medical advisor and dictionary of medical terms for laymen.

Nourse, Alan E. *Ladies Home Journal Family Medical Guide.*
New York: Harper, 1973. 1,071 pp.
Covers body functions in health, patterns of illness as they
affect body systems, first aid, care of the invalid, etc. Glos-
sary; index.
*Physician's Desk Reference to Pharmaceutical Specialties and
Biologicals.*   Oradell, N.J.: Medical Economics, 1947 to date.
Annual with supplements.
Information on drug products in five sections: alphabetical
index; drug classification index; generic and chemical name
index; product identification section; product information
section.
Schmidt, Jacob E. *Medical Discoveries, Who and When.* Spring-
field, Ill.: Chas. C. Thomas, 1959. 555 pp.
Listing of medical and related scientific discoveries, with
pertinent data.
Stedman's Medical Dictionary, 22d ed.   Baltimore, Md.: Williams
& Wilkins, 1972. 1,533 pp.
Definitions of thousands of terms used in medicine and related fields; many illustrations.

MILITARY SCIENCE

*Abstracts of Military Bibliography/Resumenes Analiticos de
Bibliografía Militar.*   Buenos Aires, Argentina: National Security Council, 1967 to date. Quarterly.
In Spanish and English; abstracts arranged under fifty broad
subject headings. Includes periodical articles, books, reports,
and monographs relating to the military worldwide.
*Air University Library Index to Military Periodicals; a Subject
Index to Significant Articles, News Items and Editorials Ap-
pearing in Sixty-five Military and Aeronautical Periodicals
Not Indexed in Readily Available Commercial Indexing Services.*   Maxwell Air Force Base, Ala.: Air Univ. Library,
1949 to date. Quarterly.
Baldwin, Hanson W., ed. *The Great Battles of History Series.*
Philadelphia, Pa.: Lippincott, 1962——. In progress.

Thirteen volumes by various authors published 1962–70. Illustrated with maps and charts.

Dictionary of United States Military Terms for Joint Usage. Washington, D.C.: G.P.O., 1968. 322 pp.
Prepared under direction of Joint Chiefs of Staff; standardized definitions for military terms.

Dupuy, Richard E. and Trevor N. *The Encyclopedia of Military History; from 3500 B.C. to the Present.* New York: Harper, 1970. 1,406 pp.
Chronological and geographical treatment of wars, warfare, and military affairs. General index and index of battles and sieges. Illustrated with maps and drawings.

Eggenberger, David. *A Dictionary of Battles.* New York: Crowell, 1967. 526 pp.
Covers more than 1,560 major battles from ancient times to the present. Bibliography and index of names and places.

Luttwak, Edward. *A Dictionary of Modern War.* New York: Harper, 1971. 224 pp., 64 pp.
Up-to-date handbook of terms and data for the layman in three categories: hardware (weapons); organization; and concepts. Illustrated with sixty-four pages of photographs.

Matloff, Maurice. *American Military History.* Washington, D.C.: Office of the Chief of Military History, U.S. Army, 1969. 701 pp. (Army Historical Series.)
Historical survey of the organizations and accomplishments of the United States Army from its beginnings through 1967. Bibliography; index.

MOVING PICTURES

Academy of Motion Picture Arts and Sciences and Writers Guild of America, West. *Who Wrote the Movie and What Else Did He Write?* Los Angeles, Calif.: The Academy, 1970. 491 pp.
An index of screenwriters and their film works, 1936–69. Includes about 2,000 authors and 13,000 film titles.

Educators Guide to Free Films. Randolph, Wis.: Educators Progress Service, 1941 to date. Annual.

Annotated guide, arranged by subject, gives source, availability, etc. Subject, title, and source indexes.

Enser, A. G. S. *Filmed Books and Plays; a List of Books and Plays from which Films Have Been Made, 1928–1967, Revised and with a Supplementary List for 1968 and 1969.* New York: Seminar Press, 1971. 509 pp.

Halliwell, Leslie. *The Filmgoer's Companion*, 3d ed. New York: Hill & Wang, 1970. 1,071 pp.

Coverage through 1969 for players, directors, and producers; films, technical terms, and film-related topics.

International Encyclopedia of Film. New York: Crown, 1972. 574 pp.

Over 1,000 alphabetic entries cover actors, directors, producers, films, and countries; chronological outline of film history. Bibliography; indexes of title changes, films, and names.

International Motion Picture Almanac. New York: Quigley, 1929 to date. Annual.

Contains biographies of moving picture personalities, lists moving pictures of all types produced during the year covered, reviews codes and censorship developments, and other data relating to the industry.

International Television Almanac. New York: Quigley, 1956 to date. Annual.

Information on the television industry: performers, producers, distributors, feature releases, stations, codes, awards, etc., during preceding year.

Kone, Grace Ann. *8mm Film Directory.* New Haven, Conn.: Readers Press, 1969. 532 pp.

Limbacher, James L. *Feature Films on 8mm and 16mm; a Directory of Feature Films Available for Rental, Sale, and Lease in the United States,* 3d ed. New York: Bowker, 1971. 269 pp.

Michael, Paul. *The American Movies Reference Book: The Sound Era.* Englewood Cliffs, N.J.: Prentice-Hall, 1969. 629 pp.

Includes sections for actors and actresses, films, directors, and producers. Also, brief history of the American film, chronological listing of awards, selected bibliography. Name index.

Munden, Kenneth W., ed. *The American Film Institute Catalog of Motion Pictures Produced in the United States.* New York: Bowker, 1971–76. In progress.

First two compilations are: *Feature Films, 1961–1970;* and *Feature Films, 1921–1930.* Film entries include producer and distributor, date, credits, cast, and synopses. Subject and credit indexes.

National Information Center for Educational Media. *Index to 16mm Educational Films.* New York: McGraw-Hill, 1967. 955 pp.

Resource guide to films recorded in the Master Data Bank at the University of Southern California since 1958.

Pickard, R. A. E. *Dictionary of 1,000 Best Films.* New York: Association Press, 1971. 496 pp.

Selection of silent and sound productions, domestic and foreign. Listed alphabetically by title, with synopses.

Rehrauer, George. *Cinema Booklist.* Metuchen, N.J.: Scarecrow Press, 1972. 473 pp.

Critical annotations cover books published between 1940 and 1970 devoted to films and filmmaking; author and subject index.

Sadoul, Georges. *Dictionary of Films.* Berkeley: Univ. of California Press, 1972. 400 pp.

Selection of 1,200 films from fifty countries produced during past seventy years, with descriptive and critical information provided for each. Companion volume is *Dictionary of Film Makers.* Berkeley: Univ. of California Press, 1972. 350 pp. Provides biographical data and critical appraisals of 1,000 filmmakers.

MUSEUMS

Christensen, Erwin O. *A Guide to Art Museums in the United States.* New York: Dodd, 1968. 320 pp.

"Basic information about 88 major and regional art museums in 59 cities of the U.S."

Directory of Museums and Art Galleries in the British Isles. South Kensington: Museums Assoc., 1948. 392 pp.

Listing of museums of all types in England, Scotland, Wales, and Ireland; includes basic information.

Faison, Samson L. *A Guide to the Art Museums of New England.* New York: Harcourt, 1958. 270 pp.

Brief descriptions of museums, arranged by states and localities, followed by discussion of selected art treasures in each.

Katz, Herbert and Marjorie. *Museums, U.S.A.: A History and Guide.* Garden City, N.Y.: Doubleday, 1965. 395 pp.

Encyclopedic coverage of all types of museums, with full directory appended.

McDarrah, Fred W. *Museums in New York.* New York: Dutton, 1967. 319 pp.

Descriptive guide to seventy-nine museums of all types, libraries, botanical and zoological gardens, and historic mansions open to the public in New York City.

Museums of the World; a Directory of 17,000 Museums in 148 Countries, Including a Subject Index. New York: Bowker, 1973. 762 pp.

Emphasis on Europe and North America, with information on all types of museums. Subject, name, and geographical indexes.

The Official Museum Directory. New York: Crowell-Collier Educational Corp./Amer. Assoc. of Museums, 1971. 1,022 pp.

Information on 6,657 institutions of art, history, and science in United States and Canada. Lists institutions by states and provinces, by names, by names of directors and department heads, and by categories.

MUSIC (*see also* FOLKLORE AND FOLK MUSIC)

Ammer, Christine. *Harper's Dictionary of Music.* New York: Harper, 1972. 414 pp.

For the nonspecialist; approximately 2,800 entries cover composition of music, performance, instruments, famous composers, musical terms, etc.

Apel, Willi. *Harvard Dictionary of Music,* 2d ed. Cambridge, Mass.: Harvard Univ. Press, 1969. 935 pp.

A standard reference for music terminology, history, theory, and relationship to other fields. Illustrated; bibliography.

Baker, Theodore. *Biographical Dictionary of Musicians,* 5th ed. New York: Schirmer, 1958. 1,855 pp. *Supplement,* 1965. *Supplement,* 1971.

Includes musicians of all periods and countries.

Barlow, Harold, and Morgenstern, Sam. *Dictionary of Musical Themes.* New York: Crown, 1948. 656 pp.

Contains about 10,000 themes of standard instrumental works, with location and identification guide.

Blom, Eric. *Everyman's Dictionary of Music.* New York: St. Martin's, 1972. 793 pp.

Brief biographical sketches of famous musicians; includes living performers.

Chilton, John. *Who's Who of Jazz; Storyville to Swing Street.* London: Bloomsbury Book Shop, 1970. 447 pp.

Biographies of over 1,000 jazz men born before 1920; their major activities and contributions to the field.

Duckles, Vincent H. *Music Reference and Research Materials; an Annotated Bibliography,* 2d ed. New York: Free Press of Glencoe, 1967. 385 pp.

Eisler, Paul E. *World Chronology of Music History.* Dobbs Ferry, N.Y.: Oceana, 1972————. In progress.

V. 1: 4000 B.C.–A.D. 1594. Planned multivolume set will present year-by-year account of Western music history.

Ewen, David. *Encyclopedia of Concert Music.* New York: Hill & Wang, 1959. 566 pp.

Articles on "1500 of the best known compositions in all branches of instrumental music, past and present"; also, biographies of musical figures, etc. By the same author: *The World of Twentieth Century Music.* Englewood Cliffs, N.J.: Prentice-Hall, 1968. 989 pp. Arranged by composer, with annotated chronological listing of works for each.

Feather, Leonard G. *The Encyclopedia of Jazz.* New York: Horizon Press, 1960. 527 pp.

Biographies of leading jazzmen, list of basic jazz records, history of terms, etc. Supplemented by same author's *The Encyclopedia of Jazz in the Sixties*. New York: Horizon Press, 1966. Unpaged.

Fuld, James J. *The Book of World-Famous Music; Classical, Popular and Folk,* rev. ed. New York: Crown, 1971. 688 pp. Detailed information about familiar music.

Grove's Dictionary of Music and Musicians, 5th ed. New York: Macmillan, 1954–61. 10 v.
The standard encyclopedia of music, comprehensive of all subjects since 1450.

Malone, Bill C. *Country Music, U.S.A.: A Fifty-Year History.* Austin: Univ. of Texas Press, 1968. 422 pp.

Music Index. Detroit, Mich.: Information Coordinators, Inc., 1949 to date. Monthly with annual cumulations.
Author and subject index to about 270 periodicals in principal fields of music.

The Musician's Guide, 1972; the Directory of the World of Music, 5th ed. New York: Music Information Service, 1972. 1,013 pp. Annual.
Compendium of directory information for music field. Covers education and scholarships, associations, music industry, periodicals, contests, festivals, etc. A comparable work for Great Britain is *The Music Yearbook: A Survey and Directory with Statistics and Reference Articles for 1972–73.* New York: St. Martin's, 1972. 750 pp. Annual.

The New Oxford History of Music. Oxford: Oxford Univ. Press, 1954———. In progress, to be completed in eleven volumes.
Comprehensive, scholarly survey of music history from earliest times.

Records in Review. Great Barrington, Mass.: Wyeth Press, 1955 to date. Annual.
Reviews of classical and semiclassical music recordings which appeared in *High Fidelity* magazine during preceding year.

Roxon, Lillian. *Rock Encyclopedia.* New York: Grosset & Dunlap, 1969. 611 pp.

Rust, Brian. *Jazz Records, A–Z, 1897–1931,* 2d ed. Hatch End,

Middlesex, England, 1962. 736 pp. Supplemented by same author's *Jazz Records A–Z, 1932–1945.* Hatch End, 1965. 680 pp.

Scholes, Percy A.   *The Oxford Companion to Music,* 10th ed. Oxford: Oxford Univ. Press, 1970. 1,189 pp.
Dictionary of music, including articles on all phases of subject and numerous biographies of musicians. Same publisher issues *The Concise Oxford Dictionary of Music,* 2d ed., 1964. 636 pp.

Slonimsky, Nicolas.   *Music since 1900,* 4th ed. New York: Scribner, 1971. 1,595 pp.
Emphasis on classical music; includes eighty-page dictionary of terms.

Stambler, Irwin.   *Encyclopedia of Popular Music.* New York: St. Martin's, 1965. 359 pp.
Articles on musicians, songs, and topics in the field. Omits jazz, folk, and classical music. Discography, bibliography, and section on awards.

Thompson, Oscar.   *The International Cyclopedia of Music and Musicians,* 9th ed. New York: Dodd, 1964. 2,476 pp.
Emphasizes American music; covers individual compositions, types of music, music criticism, opera plots, etc.

Westrup, Jack A., and Harrison, F. C.   *The New College Encyclopedia of Music.* New York: Norton, 1960. 739 pp.
Includes brief articles on composers, performers, titles, musical terms, etc.

MYTHOLOGY

Brewer, E. Cobham.   *Brewer's Dictionary of Phrase and Fable,* centenary ed. New York: Harper, 1971. 1,175 pp.
A vast miscellany of information; new edition of a reference work standard since 1870.

Encyclopedia of Classical Mythology.   Englewood Cliffs, N.J.: Prentice-Hall, 1965. 150 pp.
Mainly concerned with Greek and Roman mythology.

Evans, Bergen.   *Dictionary of Mythology, Mainly Classical.* Lincoln, Nebr.: Centennial Press, 1970. 293 pp.

Also some coverage of Celtic and Norse mythology. Entries for mythological characters, with brief retelling of their stories.

Frazer, James. *The Golden Bough*, 3d ed. New York: St. Martin's, 1958. 13 v.

"A study in magic and religion"; a classic in its field.

Gray, Louis H. *The Mythology of All Races*. Boston, Mass.: Marshall Jones, 1916–32. 13 v.

Myths arranged by race, with general index.

Larousse World Mythology. New York: Putnam, 1965. 560 pp. Comprehensive survey of world mythologies from prehistory to present, including folklore, legend, and religious customs.

Oswalt, Sabine G. *Concise Encyclopedia of Greek and Roman Mythology*. Chicago, Ill.: Follett, 1969. 313 pp.

About 1,000 articles with many cross-references; illustrated with maps, genealogical tables, and 200 photographs of ancient art.

Tripp, Edward. *Crowell's Handbook of Classical Mythology*. New York: Crowell, 1970. 631 pp.

Encyclopedic treatment of characters, places, and events in Greek and Roman mythology, with brief retelling of myths. Includes maps of classical world; pronouncing index.

NAMES

Gannett, Henry. *American Names, a Guide to the Origin of Place Names in the United States*. Washington, D.C.: Public Affairs Press, 1947. 334 pp.

Lists 15,000 United States place names with locations and origins.

Loughead, Flora H. *Dictionary of Given Names*. Glendale, Calif.: Arthur H. Clark, 1966.

Gives origins and meanings.

New Century Cyclopedia of Names. New York: Appleton, 1954. 3 v.

Includes more than 100,000 names of places, persons, literary and mythical characters, etc.

Shankle, George E. *American Nicknames,* 2d ed. New York: Wilson, 1955. 524 pp.

Origins and meanings of nicknames of cities, states, sports, heroes, politicians, institutions, etc.

Sharp, Harold S. *Handbook of Pseudonyms and Personal Nicknames.* Metuchen, N.J.: Scarecrow Press, 1972. 1,104 pp.

Covers pseudonyms, stage names, appellations, nicknames, pen names, and sobriquets of people living and dead from all occupations and countries. About 40,000 entries; emphasis on Western world.

Smith, Elsdon C. *The New Dictionary of American Family Names.* New York: Harper, 1973. 570 pp.

The origin and meaning of thousands of family names.

Stewart, George R. *American Place Names: A Concise and Selective Dictionary for the Continental United States of America.* Oxford: Oxford Univ. Press, 1970. 550 pp.

Selective listing of 12,000 well-known, repeated, and unusual place names, with brief notes on origin and derivation.

Webster's Dictionary of Proper Names. Springfield, Mass.: Merriam, 1970. 752 pp.

Includes personal and place names, fictional names, acronyms, etc.; nearly 10,000 entries from sixty-seven categories.

NURSING

Cumulative Index to Nursing Literature. Glendale, Calif.: Glendale Adventist Hospital, 1956 to date. Bimonthly with annual and five-year cumulations.

Author and subject index to articles in English-language journals. Also includes book reviews, pamphlets, and audiovisual materials.

Hansen, Helen F. *Pocket Encyclopedic Guide to Nursing.* New York: McGraw-Hill, 1960. 423 pp.

Defines technical terms, discusses principles of nursing care, techniques, and procedures.

International Nursing Index. New York: International Nursing Index, 1966 to date. Quarterly with annual cumulations.

Two main sections: subject and name. Indexes over 200 nursing journals worldwide, and nursing articles in over 2,300 non-nursing journals indexed in *Index Medicus*.

Olson, Lyla M. *A Nurses' Handbook for the Hospital, School and Home*, 10th ed. Philadelphia, Pa.: Saunders, 1960. 548 pp.

Young, Helen. *Lippincott's Quick Reference Book for Nurses*, 8th ed. Philadelphia, Pa.: Lippincott, 1967. 813 pp.
Techniques of nursing care in major branches of medicine, e.g., pharmacology, nutrition, medical, surgical, and obstetrical nursing.

OCEANOGRAPHY

Fairbridge, Rhodes W., ed. *The Encyclopedia of Oceanography*. New York:Reinhold, 1966. 1,021 pp.
Signed articles range from general introductory material to more technical discussions. Illustrated, many charts, tables, and diagrams. Index.

Firth, Frank E., ed. *The Encyclopedia of Marine Resources*. New York: Van Nostrand Reinhold, 1969. 740 pp.
Signed articles by specialists; emphasis on fisheries and marine biology.

Ocean Research Index; a Guide to Ocean and Freshwater Research, Including Fisheries Research. Guernsey, Channel Islands: F. Hodgson, 1970. 507 pp.
Arranged by country, with directory information on "organisations throughout the world which conduct, promote or encourage research in marine and freshwater science and related fields."

Oceanic Index. La Jolla, Calif.: Pollution Abstracts, Inc., 1964 to date. Bimonthly.
Key to worldwide literature of ocean sciences and related fields. Author and "keytalpha" permuted index. Each issue includes feature article on recent development in field.

U.S. Naval Oceanographic Office. *Glossary of Oceanographic Terms*, 2d ed. Washington, D.C.: The Office, 1966. 204 pp.
Includes appendix of oceanographic institutions, agencies, activities, and groups.

OPERAS AND OPERETTAS

Cross, Milton. *Complete Stories of the Great Operas.* Garden
City, N.Y.: Doubleday, 1955. 688 pp.
Summaries of plots of seventy-six operas, and other operatic
information. Supplemented by: Cross, Milton, and Kohrs,
Karl. *More Stories of the Great Operas.* Garden City, N.Y.:
Doubleday, 1971. 752 pp.

Ewen, David. *The New Encyclopedia of the Opera.* New York:
Hill & Wang, 1971. 759 pp.
Contains stories of operas, characters, biographies of persons
associated with opera, history, terms, etc.

Kobbe, Gustave. *Kobbe's Complete Opera Book*, rev. ed. New
York: Putnam, 1972. 1,262 pp.
Detailed information on 260 different operas.

Lubbock, Mark H., and Ewen, David. *The Complete Book of
Light Opera.* New York: Appleton, 1963. 953 pp.
Contains plot synopses, casts of characters, etc., for about 250
standard works from 1850 to present.

Moore, Frank L. *Crowell's Handbook of World Operas.* New
York: Crowell, 1961. 683 pp.
Covers opera's background, story, cast, composers, and char-
acters.

Rosenthal, Harold D., and Warrack, John. *Concise Oxford Dictionary of Opera.* Oxford: Oxford Univ. Press, 1964. 446 pp.
Brief account of virtually every known opera and related
topics.

Seltsam, William H. *Metropolitan Opera Annals; a Chronicle of
Artists and Performances.* New York: Wilson, 1947. 751
pp. *First Supplement: 1947–1957*, 1957. *Second Supplement:
1957–1966*, 1968.
Documents performances in the old Metropolitan Opera
House, 1883–1966. Illustrated with portraits. Index to artists,
operas, composers, and reviewers.

Victor Book of the Opera, 13th ed.   New York: Simon and Schuster, 1968. 475 pp.

Guide to 120 operas, with historical background and plot summaries; includes discography.

Westerman, Gerhart von. *Opera Guide.* New York: Dutton, 1965. 584 pp.

Reviews individual composers and their works in approximately chronological order.

PARLIAMENTARY PROCEDURE

Robert, Henry M. *Robert's Rules of Order Newly Revised,* rev. ed. by Sarah C. Robert and others. Chicago, Ill.: Scott, Foresman, 1970. 594 pp.

Authority for parliamentary rules governing procedures for societies, conventions, and other organizations. Special section of charts, tables, and lists.

Sturgis, Alice F. *Sturgis' Standard Code of Parliamentary Procedure,* 2d ed. New York: McGraw-Hill, 1966. 283 pp.

Clear explanations based on advice of legal authorities. Appendixes include suggested by-law provisions and model minutes. Lists of references and definitions.

PHILOSOPHY

Baldwin, James M. *Dictionary of Philosophy and Psychology.* New York: Macmillan, 1901–5. 3 v.

Standard work in field for past seventy years, though out-of-date for recent developments.

Borchardt, Dietrich H. *How to Find Out in Philosophy and Psychology.* New York: Pergamon, 1968. 97 pp.

Guide for the layman to reference sources in philosophy. Somewhat more specialized is: Koren, Henry J. *Research in Philosophy; a Bibliographical Introduction to Philosophy and a Few Suggestions for Dissertations.* Pittsburgh, Pa.: Duquesne Univ. Press, 1966. 203 pp.

The Encyclopedia of Philosophy. New York: Macmillan, 1967. 8 v.

Comprehensive coverage of entire field of philosophy and

related disciplines in nearly 1,500 signed articles. Includes biographies of individual philosophers. Index.

Magill, Frank N. *Masterpieces of World Philosophy in Summary Form.* New York: Harper, 1961. 1,166 pp.

Digests 200 classic works of philosophy, chiefly Western, in chronological order.

Philosopher's Index: An International Index to Philosophical Periodicals. Bowling Green, Ohio: Bowling Green Univ., 1967 to date. Quarterly with annual cumulations.

Author and subject index to articles from over 175 "major American and British philosophical periodicals, selected journals in other languages, and related interdisciplinary publications." Includes abstracts of articles; separate book review index.

Urmson, James O. *The Concise Encyclopaedia of Western Philosophy.* New York: Hawthorn, 1960. 431 pp.

Articles explain technical terms, describe well-known "isms," deal with individual philosophers, and discuss main fields of philosophical inquiry.

PHOTOGRAPHY

American Annual of Photography. Boston, Mass.: Amer. Photographic Pub. Co., 1887 to date. Annual.

Features prize-winning photographs of year and discussions of new techniques.

British Journal Photographic Almanac. London: Greenwood, 1861 to date. Annual.

Similar in scope to American annual.

Focal Encyclopedia of Photography, rev. ed. New York: Focal Press, 1965. 2 v.

Definitions of terms and articles on history, techniques, art, and applications of photography.

Haselgrove, Maurice L. *Photographers' Dictionary.* New York: Archer House, 1963. 202 pp.

Useful source for beginners.

The Life Library of Photography. New York: Time-Life Books, 1970–72. 15 v.

Each volume covers different aspect of photography: types of cameras, light and film, developing and printing, subjects, photography as art, special problems, etc. Fully documented with illustrative photographs.

Sussman, Aaron. *The Amateur Photographer's Handbook*, 8th ed. New York: Crowell, 1973. 562 pp.

Illustrated guide to cameras, films, picture composition, developing, printing, etc. Glossary of terms and general index.

PHYSICS

American Institute of Physics. *Handbook*, 3d ed. New York: McGraw-Hill, 1972. Various pagings.

Deals with mathematical aids to computation, mechanics, acoustics, heat, electricity and magnetism, optics, and atomic, molecular, and nuclear physics.

Besancon, Robert M., ed. *The Encyclopedia of Physics*. New York: Reinhold, 1966. 832 pp.

Entries of varying complexity from general introductory articles to detailed discussions of physical phenomena. Index.

Gray, H. J. *Dictionary of Physics*. New York: Longmans, 1958. 544 pp.

Comprehensive dictionary of general and applied physics.

Hogerton, John F. *The Atomic Energy Deskbook*. New York: Reinhold, 1963. 673 pp.

Over 1,000 alphabetically arranged entries cover energy development and applications; emphasis on peaceful uses in United States.

International Dictionary of Physics and Electronics, 2d ed. Princeton, N.J.: Van Nostrand, 1961. 1,355 pp.

Planned especially for biophysicists, chemical engineers, and engineers.

Physics Abstracts (Science Abstracts, Series A). London: Institution of Electrical Engineers, 1898 to date. Biweekly.

Classified arrangement for abstracts in English of literature in all fields of physics. Author and subject indexes cumulate semiannually.

Thewlis, J. *Encyclopaedic Dictionary of Physics.* New York: Pergamon, 1961–64. 9 v.

Alphabetically arranged articles showing fundamental advances in field since 1922. Kept up-to-date by supplements: supplement 1, 1966; supplement 2, 1967; supplement 3, 1969; supplement 4, 1971.

Whitford, Robert H. *Physics Literature; a Reference Manual,* 2d ed. Metuchen, N.J.: Scarecrow Press, 1968. 272 pp.

Annotated, selected list of periodicals, articles, and books. Author and subject indexes.

PICTURES AND PORTRAITS

A.L.A. Portrait Index; Index to Portraits Contained in Printed Books and Periodicals. Washington, D.C.: G.P.O., 1906. 1,601 pp.

Indexes some 120,000 portraits of about 40,000 persons through 1904.

Cirker, Hayward and Blanche. *Dictionary of American Portraits; 4,045 Pictures of Important Americans from Earliest Times to the Beginning of the Twentieth Century.* New York: Dover, 1967. 756 pp.

Alphabetically arranged, well-reproduced portraits with brief identifying captions; indexes of variant names and by profession or occupation. Bibliography.

Ellis, Jessie C. *Index to Illustrations.* Boston, Mass.: Faxon, 1966. 682 pp.

Subject arrangement, indexes selective list of books and periodicals.

Lee, Cuthbert. *Portrait Register.* Asheville, N.C.: Biltmore Press, 1968. 725 pp.

Lists, by subject and by painter, about 8,000 portraits owned in the United States. Indicates location.

Vance, Lucile E., and Tracey, Esther M. *Illustration Index,* 2d ed. Metuchen, N.J.: Scarecrow Press, 1966. 527 pp.

Subject index to illustrations in popular periodicals and books, 1950 through June, 1963.

POSTAGE STAMPS

Cabeen, Richard M. *Standard Handbook of Stamp Collecting*, 2d ed. New York: Crowell, 1965. 628 pp.
Concerns identification, classification, and preservation of all kinds of stamps; worldwide in scope.

Patrick, Douglas and Mary. *The International Guide to Stamps and Stamp Collecting*. New York: Dodd, 1962. 488 pp.
Answers 1,200 numbered questions, arranged under broad topics.

Scott's Standard Postage Stamp Catalogue. New York: Scott Pub. Co., 1867 to date. Annual.
Illustrations, descriptions, denominations, and values of principal stamps of all countries.

Standard Catalogue of Postage Stamps of the World. Ipswich, England: Whitfield King, 1899 to date. Approximately annual.
Listing with about 10,000 illustrations of practically all stamps ever issued throughout world.

U.S. Postal Service. *Postage Stamps of the United States; an Illustrated Description of All United States Postage and Special Service Stamps.* Washington, D.C.: G.P.O., 1970. 287 pp.
Covers period July 1, 1874, through June 30, 1970. Issued in looseleaf form, frequently revised.

POSTAL SERVICE

U.S. Postal Service. *Directory of International Mail.* Washington, D.C.: G.P.O., 1971. 574 pp.
Looseleaf, kept up-to-date with correction sheets. Gives rates and regulations governing mail to foreign countries.

U.S. Postal Service. *National Zip Code Directory.* Washington, D.C.: G.P.O., 1967 to date. Annual.
Gives zip code numbers for all addresses in the United States.

U.S. Postal Service. *Postal Service Manual.* Washington, D.C.: G.P.O., 1970. 614 pp.
Looseleaf, kept up-to-date with supplements. Complete man-

ual of American postal information: rules and regulations, rates, list of post offices, etc.

PRIZES AND AWARDS

Henderson, Jeanne J., and Piggins, Brenda G., eds. *Literary and Library Prizes*, 8th ed. New York: Bowker, 1973. 454 pp.

Information on literary prizes, library awards, fellowships, and grants in the United States, Canada, and Great Britain; also awards of international significance. Index.

Wasserman, Paul, and others. *Awards, Honors and Prizes*, 2d. ed. Detroit, Mich.: Gale Research Co., 1972. 579 pp.

About 3,000 entries with emphasis on awards available in United States and Canada; excludes scholarships and fellowships. Arranged by sponsoring organizations. Subject and award-title indexes.

PSYCHOLOGY AND PSYCHIATRY

Annual Review of Psychology. Stanford, Calif.: Annual Reviews, Inc., 1950 to date.

Reviews current psychological literature and discusses research in progress.

Brussel, James A., and Cantzlaar, George L. *The Layman's Dictionary of Psychiatry*. New York: Barnes & Noble, 1967. 269 pp.

Nontechnical definitions for about 1,500 psychiatric terms. Also contains entries for prominent psychiatrists and psychoanalysts.

Deutsch, Albert. *Encyclopedia of Mental Health.* New York: Franklin Watts, 1963. 6 v.

Articles by numerous authorities on various aspects of mental health field.

Drever, James. *A Dictionary of Psychology*, rev. ed. Baltimore, Md.: Penguin Books, 1964. 320 pp.

Good small dictionary defining terms.

English, Horace B. and Ava C. *A Comprehensive Dictionary of*

Psychological and Psychoanalytical Terms; a Guide to Usage.
New York: Longmans, 1958. 594 pp.

Eysenck, H. J., ed. *Encyclopedia of Psychology.* New York:
Herder & Herder, 1972. 3 v.

Survey of psychological knowledge in some 5,000 articles of
varying length.

Goldenson, Robert M. *The Encyclopedia of Human Behavior;
Psychology, Psychiatry and Mental Health.* Garden City,
N.Y.: Doubleday, 1970. 2 v.

About 5,000 entries in dictionary arrangement. Articles cover
various aspects of mental health and human behavior; definitions given for over 1,000 terms. Bibliography of references
cited. Illustrated; index.

Harriman, Philip L. *Handbook of Psychological Terms.* Totowa,
N.J.: Littlefield, 1965. 222 pp.

Harvard List of Books in Psychology, 4th ed. Cambridge, Mass.:
Harvard Univ. Press, 1971. 108 pp.

Compilation of 744 recent titles with annotations; listed alphabetically under thirty-one subject divisions. Author index.

Hinsie, Leland E., and Campbell, Robert J. *Psychiatric Dictionary,* 4th ed. Oxford: Oxford Univ. Press, 1970. 928 pp.

Defines about 9,600 psychiatric terms.

Menninger, Karl. *A Guide to Psychiatric Books in English,* 3d
ed. New York: Grune and Stratton, 1972. 238 pp.

Classified up-to-date list; unannotated. Author index.

Psychological Abstracts. Washington, D.C.: Amer. Psychological Assoc., 1927 to date. Monthly.

Abstracts in English of world's literature in psychology and
related fields. Arranged by subject with author index. Semiannual and annual author-subject index. *Cumulated Subject
Index to Psychological Abstracts, 1927–1960.* Boston, Mass.:
G. K. Hall, 1965. 863 pp.

PUBLIC SPEAKING

Braude, Jacob M. *Speaker's Encyclopedia of Stories, Quotations, and Anecdotes.* Englewood Cliffs, N.J.: Prentice-Hall,

1955. 476 pp. (Followed by same author's *Second Encyclopedia,* 1957. 468 pp.; and *Lifetime Speaker's Encyclopedia,* 1962. 2 v.)

Anthologies of stories, jokes, proverbs, etc., suitable for use in speeches.

Crosscup, Richard. *Classic Speeches: Words that Shook the World.* New York: Philosophical Library, 1965. 496 pp.

Famous speeches from ancient to modern times.

Friedman, Edward L. *The Speechmaker's Complete Handbook.* New York: Harper, 1955. 401 pp. (Followed by same author's *Toastmaster's Treasury.* New York: Harper, 1960. 366 pp.; *Speaker's Handy Reference.* New York: Harper, 1967. 388 pp.) Collection of material useful in speech preparation: anecdotes, introductions, responses, welcomes, and complete talks for various occasions.

Representative American Speeches. New York: Wilson, 1938 to date. Annual. Part of *Reference Shelf* series. Includes biographical notes on speakers and editorial introductions to addresses.

Sutton, Roberta B. *Speech Index,* 4th ed. Metuchen, N.J.: Scarecrow Press, 1966. 947 pp.

"An index to 259 collections of world famous orations and speeches for various occasions." Replaces earlier editions published in 1935, 1956, and 1962; extends coverage through 1965.

Vital Speeches of the Day. New York: City News Pub. Co., 1934 to date. Monthly.

Full texts of speeches by leaders in politics, economics, education, business, labor, etc.

RACES

Coon, Carleton S. *Origin of Races.* New York: Knopf, 1962. 724 pp.

A detailed history of evolution of the five major races.

Hammerton, J. A. *Peoples of All Nations.* London: Fleetway House, 1922–24. 7 v.

Articles on individual countries and dictionary of races; contains about 5,000 photographs and 150 maps.

Seligman, Charles G. *Races of Africa,* 4th ed. Oxford: Oxford Univ. Press, 1966. 170 pp.
Deals with nine major races indigenous to African continent, chiefly on tribal customs and social organization.

RAILROADS AND MOTOR COACHES

Jane's World Railways 1972–73, 15th ed. New York: McGraw-Hill, 1972. 590 pp.
Complete coverage with tabulated data for world's railroad systems and separate railways; arranged by continent, then country. Also covers railway manufacturing industry. Illustrated with maps, diagrams, and photographs. Index to railways.

Official Guide of the Railways. New York: National Railway Pub. Co., 1868 to date. Monthly.
Covers United States, Puerto Rico, Canada, Mexico, Central America, and Cuba; includes timetables, maps, and indexes of stations.

Russell's Official National Motor Coach Guide; Official Publication of Bus Lines for United States, Canada, and Mexico. Cedar Rapids, Iowa: Russell's Guides, 1927 to date. Monthly. Detailed bus schedules.

Sampson, Henry. *World Railways 1960 to 1961–62.* New York: Simmons-Boardman, 1960–62. 2 v.
A worldwide survey of railway operation and equipment.

RELIGION

Adams, Charles J., ed. *A Reader's Guide to the Great Religions.* New York: Free Press, 1965. 364 pp.
Bibliographic essays survey works dealing with history and beliefs of world's religions. Author and subject indexes.

Ballou, Robert O. *The Bible of the World.* New York: Viking, 1939. 1,415 pp.
Extended selections from the sacred scriptures of the eight great living religions.

Berry, Gerald L. *Religions of the World,* rev. ed. New York: Barnes & Noble, 1956. 136 pp.
> Brief, though comprehensive, information on world's principal religions.

Brandon, S. G. F., ed. *A Dictionary of Comparative Religion.* New York: Scribner, 1970. 704 pp.
> Signed articles deal with various aspects of world's religions from prehistoric times to present. List of terms relating to each major religion; general and synoptic indexes.

Catholic Encyclopedia. New York: Gilmary Society, 1907–22. 17 v.
> Authoritative, scholarly work dealing with medieval history, literature, philosophy, and art, in addition to Catholic doctrine and history.

Catholic Encyclopedia for School and Home. New York: Mc-Graw-Hill, 1965. 12 v.
> "The first completely new Catholic encyclopedia in half a century." Contains thousands of original illustrations, photographs, art reproductions, and maps.

Encyclopaedia Judaica. New York: Macmillan, 1972. 16 v.
> Emphasis is on twentieth-century Jewish scholarship; will be kept up-to-date with annual yearbook. Signed articles; over 8,000 illustrations. Index.

Hastings. James. *Encyclopaedia of Religion and Ethics.* New York: Scribner, 1908–27. 13 v.
> Comprehensive of all religions, ethical systems and movements, philosophy, etc.

Index to Religious Periodical Literature. Chicago, Ill.: Amer. Theological Library Assoc., 1949 to date. Annual with triennial cumulations.
> International in scope, indexes 135 periodicals in fields of theology, church history, and biblical literature. Separate book review section. A similar service, restricted to American periodicals, is *Religious Periodicals Index.* New York: Jarrow Press, 1970 to date. Quarterly.

Jewish Encyclopedia. New York: KTAV Pub. House, 1964. 12 v. (Reprint of edition published 1901–6.)

Covers Jewish history, religion, literature, and customs; numerous biographies.

Mayer, Frederick E. *The Religious Bodies of America*, 5th ed. St. Louis, Mo.: Concordia Pub. House, 1972.

Concerns doctrines, practices, and historical development of churches of America. In same field is: Hudson, Winthrop S. *Religion in America; an Historical Account of the Development of American Religious Life*, 2d ed. New York: Scribner, 1973. 463 pp.

Mead, Frank S. *The Encyclopedia of Religious Quotations*. New York: Revell, 1965. 544 pp.

Over 10,000 quotations on religious and related topics of all periods. By the same author: *Handbook of Denominations in the United States*, 5th ed. Nashville, Tenn.: Abingdon, 1970. 265 pp. Describes history, doctrines, organizations, and present status of over 250 religious bodies.

New Catholic Encyclopedia. New York: McGraw-Hill, 1967. 15 v.

Prepared by editorial staff at the Catholic University of America. About 17,000 signed articles with emphasis on second half of twentieth-century knowledge, outlook, and interests. Index.

Official Catholic Directory. New York: Kenedy, 1886 to date. Annual.

Detailed information on churches, clergy, missions, schools, religious orders, etc., of Catholic church in United States and other parts of the world.

Oxford Dictionary of the Christian Church. Oxford: Oxford Univ. Press, 1957. 1,492 pp.

Includes some 6,000 articles relating to historical and doctrinal development; also numerous biographies and definitions of ecclesiastical terms and customs.

Religious and Theological Abstracts. Myerstown, Pa., 1958 to date. Quarterly.

Nonsectarian; abstracts in English of articles from selected international list of religious periodicals. Author, subject, and biblical index.

Richardson, Alan.   *A Dictionary of Christian Theology*. Philadel-
phia, Pa.: Westminster, 1969. 364 pp.
  Emphasizes contemporary theological issues; also covers his-
  tory of Christian ideas. Bibliographies.
Sacred Books of the East.   Oxford: Clarendon Press, 1885–1910.
50 v.
  Translations into English of all important religious texts of
  principal Oriental religions.
Schaff, Philip.   *New Schaff-Herzog Encyclopedia of Religious
Knowledge*. New York: Funk & Wagnalls, 1908–12. 13 v. (Re-
printed, 1949–50.)
  Inclusive of all religions; biblical, historical, and modern the-
  ology; church history and biography, etc. Supplemented by
  Twentieth Century Encyclopedia of Religious Knowledge.
  Grand Rapids, Mich.: Baker, 1955. 2 v.
Standard Jewish Encyclopedia.   Garden City, N.Y.: Doubleday,
1962. 991 pp.
  Concise factual and biographical information, with emphasis
  on recent developments in Jewish history, the American com-
  munity, and Israel.
Yearbook of American Churches.   New York: National Council
of the Churches of Christ in America, 1916 to date. Annual.
  Directory and statistical information on the organizations
  and activities of all faiths in United States.
Zaehner, Robert C.   *The Concise Encyclopedia of Living Faiths*.
New York: Hawthorn, 1959. 431 pp.
  Descriptions of world's major religions.

REPTILES

Cochran, Doris M., and Goin, Coleman J.   *The New Field Book
of Reptiles and Amphibians*. New York: Putnam, 1970.
359 pp.
  Guide to identification of all presently known living amphibians and reptiles in United States; illustrated with photographs. Index.
Ditmars, Raymond L.   *The Reptiles of North America*. Garden
City, N.Y.: Doubleday, 1936. 476 pp.

Field guide to United States and Canadian reptiles, with 135 illustrations. By same author: *Reptiles of the World.* New York: Macmillan, 1933. 321 pp., covering crocodilians, lizards, snakes, turtles, and tortoises, with 200 illustrations; and *Snakes of the World.* New York: Macmillan, 1931. 207 pp., with illustrations from life.

Leviton, Alan. *Reptiles and Amphibians of North America.* Garden City, N.Y.: Doubleday, 1970. 250 pp.

Stebbins, Robert C. *A Field Guide to Western Reptiles and Amphibians: Field Marks of All Species in Western North America.* Boston, Mass.: Houghton, 1966. 279 pp.

Describes and illustrates 207 species of reptiles and amphibians found in the eleven western states, Alaska, and five western Canadian provinces.

Wright, Albert H. *Handbook of Frogs and Toads in the United States and Canada,* 3d ed. Ithaca, N.Y.: Comstock Pub. Co., 1949. 640 pp.

Identification and description of 102 species and subspecies, with illustrations. Same publisher issues similar handbooks on snakes and turtles.

ROCKS AND MINERALS

Kemp, J. F. *Handbook of Rocks,* 6th ed. Princeton, N.J.: Van Nostrand, 1940. 300 pp.

Classification and identification of rocks.

Nicolay, H. H., and Stone, A. V. *Rocks and Minerals; a Guide for Collectors of the Eastern United States.* South Brunswick, N.J.: Barnes, 1967. 255 pp.

Arranged by states and counties; indicates types of rocks and minerals found in each area.

Pearl, Richard M. *How to Know the Minerals and Rocks.* New York: McGraw-Hill, 1955. 200 pp.

Field guide to identification and collecting of common rocks; fully illustrated.

Pough, Frederick H. *A Field Guide to Rocks and Minerals,* 3d ed. Boston, Mass.: Houghton, 1960. 349 pp.

Describes various types of rocks with many illustrations, some in color.

Zim, Herbert S., and Shaffer, Paul R. *Rocks and Minerals; a Guide to Familiar Minerals, Gems, Ores, and Rocks.* New York: Simon and Schuster, 1957. 160 pp.

SCIENCE AND TECHNOLOGY

American Men and Women of Science, 12th ed. New York: Bowker, 1971–73. 8 v.

Who's who of American science: v. 1–6, physical and biological sciences; v. 1–2, social and behavioral sciences.

Applied Science and Technology Index. New York: Wilson, 1958 to date. Monthly with annual cumulations.

Subject index to about 225 journals in aeronautics and space science, automation, chemistry, construction, earth science, electricity and electronics, engineering, industrial and mechanical arts, machinery, materials, mathematics, metallurgy, petroleum, physics, telecommunications, transportation, and related subjects.

Asimov, Isaac. *Asimov's Biographical Encyclopedia of Science and Technology: The Lives and Achievements of 1,195 Great Scientists from Ancient Times to the Present, Chronologically Arranged,* rev. ed. Garden City, N.Y.: Doubleday, 1972. 805 pp.

Collocott, T. C., ed. *Dictionary of Science and Technology.* New York: Barnes & Noble, 1972. 1,328 pp.

Successor to *Chambers Technical Dictionary* (3d ed., 1958). Comprehensive coverage of some 60,000 terms in 100 subject areas; also includes tables and charts.

Dictionary of Scientific Biography. New York: Scribner, 1970 ———. To be completed in twelve volumes.

Published under the auspices of the American Council of Learned Societies. Will cover lives and contributions of over 4,500 scientists and mathematicians from all areas and periods. Selective bibliographies with each entry.

Government Reports Announcements. Springfield, Va.: National Technical Information Service, U.S. Dept. of Commerce, 1938 to date. Semimonthly.

Formerly titled *United States Government Research and Development Reports.* Abstracts reports produced under sponsorship of government agencies in all fields of science and technology. Companion publication is *Government Reports Index*, semimonthly with annual cumulations. Indexes by subject, personal and corporate author, contract number, and accession/report number.

Grogan, Denis J. *Science and Technology; an Introduction to the Literature.* Hamden, Conn.: Archon, 1970. 231 pp.

Selective coverage of English-language source materials in science and technology.

Henderson, Isabella and W. D. *A Dictionary of Scientific Terms*, 7th ed. Princeton, N.J.: Van Nostrand, 1960. 595 pp.

Definitions of terms in biology, botany, zoology, anatomy, cytology, genetics, embryology, and physiology.

Herner, Saul. *A Brief Guide to Sources of Scientific and Technical Information.* Washington, D.C.: Information Resources Press, 1969. 102 pp.

Annotated listing of basic reference and research tools. Index.

Jenkins, Frances B. *Science Reference Sources*, 5th ed. Cambridge, Mass.: M.I.T. Press, 1969. 231 pp.

Guide to reference works in all branches of science and technology.

Jordan, Emil L. *Hammond's Nature Atlas of America.* Maplewood, N.J.: Hammond, 1952. 256 pp.

Maps of United States showing distribution of minerals, flowers, birds, fishes, etc., with descriptions and illustrations.

McGraw-Hill Encyclopedia of Science and Technology, 3d ed. New York: McGraw-Hill, 1971. 15 v.

A monumental work; 7,200 articles covering all natural sciences, and such applied technologies as engineering, agriculture, forestry, industrial biology, and food. Supplemented by *McGraw-Hill Yearbook of Science and Technology.*

Newman, James R., ed. *The Harper Encyclopedia of Science,* rev. ed. New York: Harper, 1967. 1,379 pp.

Nearly 4,000 signed articles cover major scientific fields. Bibliography and index.

Science Citation Index. Philadelphia, Pa.: Institute for Scientific Information, 1963 to date. Quarterly with annual cumulations.

Indexes about 2,500 journals, plus United States and foreign patents, in mathematical, natural, physical, and behavioral sciences. Provides access to related articles by indicating sources in which a known article by a given author has been cited. In five sections: citation index; patent citation index; corporate index; source index; and permuterm subject index.

Scientific and Technical Books in Print. New York: Bowker, 1972 to date. Annual.

Books from United States publishers are listed alphabetically under author, title, and subject.

Scientific and Technical Societies of the United States, 8th ed. Washington, D.C.: National Academy of Sciences, 1968. 221 pp.

For each group, includes information on purpose, history, membership, publications, meetings, and other professional activities. Annual supplements.

Singer, Charles, and others. *A History of Technology.* Oxford: Clarendon Press, 1954–58. 5 v.

Covers from prehistoric times to 1900.

Uvarov, E. B., and Chapman, D. R. *The Penguin Dictionary of Science,* 4th ed. New York: Schocken, 1972. 443 pp.

Nearly 5,000 entries cover terminology of all scientific fields; accurate, brief definitions.

Van Nostrand's Scientific Encyclopedia, 4th ed. Princeton, N.J.: Van Nostrand, 1968. 2,008 pp.

Comprehensive in scope, covering both basic and applied sciences, including such new fields as planetary exploration, rocketry, and space travel. About 16,500 entries; well illustrated.

World Guide to Science Information and Documentation Services. Paris: UNESCO, 1965. 211 pp.

Includes resources, services, publications, etc., of 144 institutions in sixty-five countries for natural sciences, agriculture, and medicine. Companion volume is *World Guide to Technical Information and Documentation Services*. Paris: UNESCO, 1969. 287 pp. Covers 273 centers in seventy-three countries and territories.

SECRETARIAL SCIENCE

Doris, Lillian, and Miller, Besse M.   *Complete Secretary's Handbook*, 3d ed. Englewood Cliffs, N.J.: Prentice-Hall, 1970. 528 pp.
    Comprehensive guide to secretarial practices, techniques, and business etiquette. Index.

Gavin, Ruth E., and Sabin, W. A.   *Reference Manual for Stenographers and Typists*, 4th ed. New York: McGraw-Hill, 1970. 286 pp.

Hutchinson, Lois I.   *Standard Handbook for Secretaries*, 8th ed. New York: McGraw-Hill, 1969. 638 pp.
    Emphasizes correct use of English language and letter writing. Includes information on postal and telephone services, business and banking, insurance, etc. Index.

Janis, J. Harold, and Thompson, Margaret H.   *New Standard Reference for Secretaries and Administrative Assistants*. New York: Macmillan, 1972. 801 pp.
    Covers meetings, report preparation, publicity, letter writing, financial and tax considerations, etc. Includes dictionary of business terms and list of standard abbreviations. Index.

Klein, A. E., ed.   *The New World Secretarial Handbook*, rev. ed. New York: World Pub. Co., 1972. 659 pp.
    Procedures, techniques, dress, and etiquette, and duties of executive secretary. Includes guide to spelling and syllabification of 33,000 most used words.

Mager, Nathan H. and Sylvia K.   *The Office Encyclopedia*. New York: Pocket Books, 1969. 500 pp.

Secretary's Desk Book.   West Nyack, N.Y.: Parker Pub. Co., 1965. 327 pp.

Taintor, Sarah A., and Monro, Kate M.   *The Secretary's Hand-*

book; a Manual of Correct Usage, 9th ed. New York: Macmillan, 1969. 530 pp.

SHIPS AND SHIPPING

Albion, Robert G. *Naval and Maritime History; an Annotated Bibliography,* 3d ed. Mystic, Conn.: Marine Historical Assoc., 1963. 230 pp. *First Supplement: 1963–65.* 62 pp.; *Second Supplement: 1966–68.* 60 pp.

Classified listing, primarily of books in English.

Harnack, E. P. *All about Ships and Shipping,* 10th ed. Hollywood-by-the-Sea, Fla.: Transatlantic, 1960. 729 pp.

A handbook of popular nautical information.

Jane's Fighting Ships. New York: McGraw-Hill, 1898 to date. Annual.

Detailed data on world's navies, with plans, pictures, dimensions, weights, etc.

McEwen, W. A., and Lewis, A. H. *Encyclopedia of Nautical Knowledge.* Cambridge, Md.: Cornell Maritime Press, 1953, 618 pp.

Practical, theoretical, and historical articles on sea and ships and related topics.

Merchant Ships, World Built. Tuckahoe, N.Y.: John DeGraff, 1952 to date. Annual.

Describes new merchant vessels built throughout world each year; extensively illustrated.

Motor Ship Reference Book, 20th ed. New York: St. Martin's, 1960. 231 pp.

Tryckare, Tre. *The Lore of Ships.* New York: Crescent Books, 1963. 279 pp.

Profusely illustrated guide to all types of ships, ancient and modern, with signed commentaries by experts. Shows details of construction and equipment. Index.

U.S. Naval History Division. *Dictionary of American Naval Fighting Ships.* Washington, D.C.: The Division, 1959——. In progress.

Multivolume work giving historical information for ships of Continental and United States navies. Illustrated.

SOCIAL SCIENCES

Encyclopaedia of the Social Sciences. New York: Macmillan, 1937. 8 v.

Covers entire field of social sciences, including political science, economics, law, anthropology, sociology, penology, social work and related subjects; scholarly and authoritative.

Gould, Julius, and Kolb, William L. *A Dictionary of the Social Sciences.* New York: Free Press of Glencoe, 1964. 761 pp.

Sponsored by UNESCO; most important one-volume dictionary of social sciences.

Hoselitz, Berthold F. *A Reader's Guide to the Social Sciences,* rev. ed. New York: Free Press, 1970. 425 pp.

Bibliographic essays by specialists cover history and current trends in sociology, anthropology, psychology, political science, economics, and geography. General bibliography includes page references to text.

Hoult, Thomas F. *Dictionary of Modern Sociology.* Totowa, N.J.: Littlefield, 1969. 408 pp.

Definitions reflect "current concept usage" in sociological and related literature. Bibliography of works and authors cited. Also for general reader: Theodorson, George A. and Achilles, G. *A Modern Dictionary of Sociology.* New York: Crowell, 1969. 469 pp.

International Encyclopedia of the Social Sciences. New York: Macmillan, 1968. 17 v.

"Designed to complement, not to supplant" the *Encyclopaedia of the Social Sciences.* Emphasis is on social sciences in 1960s, with topical signed articles devoted to theory, methodology, concepts, and principles for various disciplines. Index.

Public Affairs Information Service Bulletin. New York: Public Affairs Information Service, 1915 to date. Weekly, cumulated five times a year and annually.

Subject index to current books, government publications, and periodical articles in social sciences. Supplemented by: *Foreign Language Index.* New York: Public Affairs Information

Service, 1972 to date. Quarterly with annual cumulations. Volume 1 covers period from 1968–71. Indexes writings on public and economic affairs in French, German, Italian, Portuguese, and Spanish languages.

Social Sciences and Humanities Index. New York: Wilson, June, 1965, to date. Quarterly with annual cumulations.

Replaced *International Index.* New York: Wilson, 1907– March, 1965.

For social sciences, includes periodical articles in anthropology, area studies, economics, folklore, geography, history, political science, and sociology.

Social Work Year Book. New York: National Assoc. of Social Workers, 1929–64. 14 v. Biennial. Continued by *Encyclopedia of Social Work.* New York: National Assoc. of Social Workers, 1965 to date.

Deals with history and current developments in social work and social welfare, including biographies of leading social workers. Directory of international, national, and Canadian agencies.

Sociological Abstracts. Brooklyn, N.Y.: Sociological Abstracts, Inc., 1952 to date. Seven times a year.

International coverage of journals in sociology and related fields; classified arrangement.

Stevens, Rolland E. *Reference Books in the Social Sciences and Humanities,* 3d ed. Champaign, Ill.: Illini Union Bookstore, 1971. 188 pp.

Annotated list of about 540 most useful bibliographies, periodical indexes, dictionaries, encyclopedias, and other reference books, arranged by subjects.

White, Carl M., and others. *Sources of Information in the Social Sciences; a Guide to the Literature,* 2d ed. Chicago, Ill.: Amer. Library Assoc., 1973. 702 pp.

Annotated guide to extensive literature of social sciences; each section prepared by specialist.

Zadrozny, John T. *Dictionary of Social Science.* Washington, D.C.: Public Affairs Press, 1959. 367 pp.

Defines terms relating to principal social sciences.

SONGS

Coffin, Berton. *The Singer's Repertoire*, 2d ed. Metuchen, N.J.: Scarecrow Press, 1960–62. 5 v.

Lists some 8,000 songs, arranged by vocal classification, then by nationality, mood, etc.

Cushing, Helen Grant. *Children's Song Index*. New York: Wilson, 1936. 798 pp.

Indexes more than 22,000 songs in 189 colections.

Ewen, David. *American Popular Songs from the Revolutionary War to the Present*. New York: Random House, 1966. 507 pp.

Arranged by title, with information on more than 3,600 popular songs.

Sears, Minnie Earl. *Song Index*. New York: Wilson, 1926. 650 pp.

Indexes about 12,000 songs in 177 collections. *Supplement*, 1934, adds 7,000 songs in 104 collections; by author, composer, title, or first line. Supplemented further by de Charms, Desiree, and Breed, Paul F. *Songs in Collections*. Detroit, Mich.: Information Service, 1965. 590 pp., indexing 9,400 songs in 411 collections for period 1940–57.

Shapiro, Nat. *Popular Music; an Annotated Index of American Popular Songs*. New York: Adrian Press, 1964——. In progress. V. 1, 1950–59; v. 2, 1940–49; v. 3, 1960–64; v. 4, 1930–39; v. 5, 1920–29. Selective list, arranged by year, then title. Information on composers, publishers, performers, and recordings.

SOVIET RUSSIA

Florinsky, Michael T. *McGraw-Hill Encyclopedia of Russia and the Soviet Union*. New York: McGraw-Hill, 1961. 624 pp.

Deals broadly with Russian history and civilization, including biography, geography, economics, government, culture, and science.

Gilbert, Martin. *Russian History Atlas*. New York: Macmillan, 1972. 146 pp., 29 pp.

Black and white maps with brief textual commentary depict

history of Soviet Union from tribal beginnings to present time.

Maxwell, Robert. *Information U.S.S.R.; an Authoritative Encyclopedia about the Union of Soviet Socialist Republics.* New York: Pergamon, 1962. 982 pp.

Arranged by broad fields, with detailed index.

Schopflin, George, ed. *The Soviet Union and Eastern Europe; a Handbook.* New York: Praeger, 1970. 614 pp.

Covers history, economics, politics, society, arts, and literature of the U.S.S.R. and Communist countries of Eastern Europe. Emphasis on post–World War II period.

Taaffe, Robert N. *An Atlas of Soviet Affairs.* New York: Praeger, 1965. 143 pp.

Economic geography of U.S.S.R., including many historical and political maps.

Utechin, Sergej. *A Concise Encyclopedia of Russia.* New York: Dutton, 1964. 623 pp.

General dictionary of Russian subjects, emphasizing social sciences; biographical and geographical articles included.

Who Was Who in the USSR: A Biographic Directory Containing 5,015 Biographies of Prominent Soviet Historical Personalities. Metuchen, N.J.: Scarecrow Press, 1972. 677 pp.

Covers period 1917–67; includes individuals prominent in Soviet political, intellectual, scientific, social, and economic life.

SPORTS

Blue Book of College Athletics for 1972–1973. Cleveland, Ohio: Rohrich Corp., 1973. 419 pp.

Burton, Bill. *The Sportsman's Encyclopedia.* New York: Grosset & Dunlap, 1971. 638 pp.

Comprehensive of all major and many minor sports.

Georgano, G. N. *The Encyclopedia of Motor Sport.* New York: Viking, 1971. 656 pp.

Concerned with organization, circuits, races, drivers, cars, etc.

SPECIALIZED SUBJECT REFERENCE BOOKS

Golf Magazine's Encyclopedia of Golf.   New York: Harper, 1970. 424 pp.
   Historical, biographical, and statistical information; also covers equipment, rules, and terms.
Hickok, Ralph J. *Who Was Who in American Sports.* New York: Hawthorn, 1971. 256 pp.
   Selective biographical listing for all major, and most minor, sports in United States.
Hollander, Zander, ed.   *The Modern Encyclopedia of Basketball.* New York: Four Winds Press, 1973. 547 pp.
   Covers history, rules, records, teams, and outstanding players.
McCallum, John, and Pearson, Charles H. *College Football, U.S.A., 1869–1972; Official Book of the National Football Foundation.* New York: McGraw-Hill, 1972. 564 pp.
Menke, Frank G.   *The Encyclopedia of Sports,* 4th ed. New York: A. S. Barnes, 1969. 1,100 pp.
   Wide coverage of field, including history, rules, championship records, statistics, etc.
Miracle, Leonard, and Trefethen, James B., eds. *New Hunter's Encyclopedia,* 3d ed. Harrisburg, Pa.: Stackpole, 1966. 1,131 pp.
   Arranged in sections; deals with types of game animals and birds, guns and ammunition, hunting dogs, hunting laws and regulations, etc.; numerous illustrations.
New York Times Sports Almanac. New York: Franklin Watts, 1965 to date. Annual. United States and international sports records and schedules.
Official Encyclopedia of Sports. New York: Franklin Watts, 1964. 344 pp.
   Deals with thirty-three sports and games; many action photographs, diagrams, and rules.
Quercetani, Roberto L. *A World History of Track and Field Athletics, 1864–1964.* Oxford: Oxford Univ. Press, 1964. 370 pp.
   Records of twenty events, photographs, and index of persons.
Spalding's Official Athletic Almanac. New York: American Sports Pub. Co., 1893–1941.

Detailed data on athletic records in various fields; Olympic, A.A.U., etc.

Treat, Roger. *Official Encyclopedia of Football,* 10th ed. New York: A. S. Barnes, 1972. 672 pp.
Data on collegiate and professional football: teams, players, coaches; also rules and records.

Turkin, Hy, and Thompson, S. C. *The Official Encyclopedia of Baseball,* 6th ed. New York: A. S. Barnes, 1972.
Historical and current information on baseball and baseball players. In same field: *Baseball Encyclopedia; the Complete and Official Record of Major League Baseball.* New York: Macmillan, 1969. 2,337 pp. Compilation of statistics, including batting and pitching records for all major league players.

United States Lawn Tennis Association. *Official Encyclopedia of Tennis.* New York: Harper, 1972. 472 pp.

White, Jess R. *Sports Rules Encyclopedia.* Palo Alto, Calif.: National Press, 1961. 563 pp.
Official rules for thirty-eight sports and games.

Wilt, Fred, and Ecker, Tom. *International Track and Field Coaching Encyclopedia.* West Nyack, N.Y.: Parker Pub. Co., 1970. 350 pp.
Concerned with instruction, teaching, and techniques.

STATISTICS

Andriot, John L. *Guide to United States Government Statistics,* 3d ed. Arlington, Va.: Documents Index, 1961. 402 pp.
Arranged by departments and agencies, annotated guide to publications containing statistical data. Subject index.

UNESCO Statistical Yearbook. Louvain, Belgium: UNESCO, 1972. 890 pp.
Contains statistics from over 200 countries and territories: population, education, science and technology, libraries and museums, book production, newspapers and other periodicals, paper consumption, films and cinema, radio and television, and cultural expenditures.

United Nations. *Demographic Yearbook.* New York: United Nations, 1949 to date. Annual.

Various types of world population data.

United Nations. *Statistical Year Book.* New York: United Nations, 1948 to date. Annual.

Summary of international statistics for population, agriculture, mining, manufacturing, finance, trade, education, etc.

U.S. Bureau of the Census. *Census of Population, 1960.* Washington, D.C.: G.P.O., 1961. Fifty-seven parts.

Eighteenth decennial census of population of United States; Census Bureau also publishes special censuses for agriculture, manufactures, business, housing, mineral industries, etc.

U.S. Bureau of the Census. *Census of Population: 1970.* Washington, D.C.: G.P.O., 1971——. In progress.

U.S. Bureau of the Census. *Directory of Non-Federal Statistics for States and Local Areas; a Guide to Sources, 1969.* Washington, D.C.: G.P.O., 1970. 678 pp.

Lists published sources of social, political, and economic statistics. Companion volumes: Bureau's *Directory of Federal Statistics for Local Areas; a Guide to Sources,* 1966. 156 pp.; *Directory of Federal Statistics for States; a Guide to Sources,* 1967. 372 pp.

U.S. Bureau of the Census. *Historical Statistics of the United States: Colonial Times to 1957.* Washington, D.C.: G.P.O., 1960. 789 pp.

Covers population, vital statistics, immigration, finance, railroads, commerce, etc. Supplemented by *Continuation to 1962 and Revisions.* Washington, D.C.: G.P.O., 1965. 154 pp.

U.S. Bureau of the Census. *Statistical Abstract of the United States.* Washington, D.C.: G.P.O., 1879 to date. Annual.

Compilation of statistics gathered by all government and some private agencies; includes population, vital statistics, immigration, finance, railroads, commerce, etc. References to sources.

Wasserman, Paul, and others. *Statistics Sources: A Subject Guide to Data on Industrial, Business, Social, Educational, Financial, and Other Topics for the United States and Selected Foreign Countries,* 3d ed. Detroit, Mich.: Gale Research Co., 1971. 647 pp.

TEXTILES

American Fabrics. *AF Encyclopedia of Textiles,* 2d ed. Englewood Cliffs, N.J.: Prentice-Hall, 1972. 636 pp.

Provides trend, design, and technical development reports in textile field.

American Home Economics Association. *Textile Handbook,* 4th ed. Washington, D.C.: The Association, 1970. 115 pp.

Guide for consumer, covering fibers, yarns, fabric construction and finishes, maintenance, labeling, etc.

Backer, Stanley, and others. *Thesaurus of Textile Terms; Covering Fibrous Materials and Processes,* 2d ed. Cambridge, Mass.: M.I.T. Press, 1969. 448 pp.

Cook, J. Gordon. *Handbook of Textile Fibres,* 4th ed. Herts, England: Merrow, 1968. 2 v.

V. 1, natural fibers; v. 2, handmade fibers.

Hall, Archibald J. *The Standard Handbook of Textiles,* 7th ed. Metuchen, N.J.: Textile Book Service, 1970. 369 pp.

Deals with natural and synthetic textile fibers, their processing, and textile machinery; numerous photographs.

Hollen, Norma, and Saddler, Jane. *Textiles,* 3d ed. New York: Macmillan, 1968. 243 pp.

Covers types of fibers, fabrics, and finishes; charts show historical development in each area. Illustrated with drawings and photographs; index.

Klapper, Marvin. *Fabric Almanac,* 2d ed. New York: Fairchild, 1971. 191 pp.

Glossary includes names of new fibers and companies; tables show statistics of textile production worldwide.

Linton, George E. *The Modern Textile and Apparel Dictionary,* 4th ed. Metuchen, N.J.: Textile Book Service, 1972.

Defines over 10,000 terms relating to fabrics and textile manufacture; illustrated. By same author: *Applied Basic Textiles.* New York: Duell, Sloan and Pearce, 1966. 472 pp. *Natural and Man-made Textile Fabrics.* New York: Duell, Sloan and Pearce, 1966. 420 pp.

Press, J. J.   *Man-made Textile Encyclopedia.* New York: Textile Book Pub., 1959. 913 pp.

Describes processing and properties of synthetic fibers.

Sommar, Helen G.   *A Brief Guide to Sources of Fiber and Textile Information.* Washington, D.C.: Information Resources Press, 1973. 138 pp.

Descriptive annotations for reference works, documents, current awareness services, etc. Includes information on research and development projects. Name and subject index.

Wingate, Isabel B., ed.   *Fairchild's Dictionary of Textiles.* New York: Fairchild, 1967. 662 pp.

Concise definitions for terms used in textile industry; includes trade names.

Wingate, Isabel B.   *Textile Fabrics and Their Selection,* 6th ed. Englewood Cliffs, N.J.: Prentice-Hall, 1970. 657 pp.

Standard work in field; illustrations and bibliography.

THEATER AND DRAMA

Anderson, Michael, and others.   *Crowell's Handbook of Contemporary Drama.* New York: Crowell, 1971. 512 pp.

"A critical handbook of plays and playwriting since the Second World War." Covers drama in Europe, North and South America.

Breed, Paul F., and Sniderman, Florence M.   *Dramatic Criticism Index; a Bibliography of Commentaries on Playwrights from Ibsen to the Avant-Garde.* Detroit, Mich.: Gale Research Co., 1972. 1,022 pp.

About 12,000 citations to critical writings on more than 300 modern playwrights. Indexes for play titles and critics.

Chicorel, Marietta, ed.   *Chicorel Theater Index to Plays in Anthologies, Periodicals, Discs and Tapes.*   New York: Chicorel Library Pub. Co., 1970———. In progress.

First two volumes index plays appearing in anthologies and selected periodicals. "Subject indicators" index provides access by type of play, nationality, and period.

Drury, Francis K. W. *Drury's Guide to Best Plays,* 2d ed. Metuchen, N.J.: Scarecrow Press, 1969. 512 pp.

Arranged alphabetically by playwright; includes plot synopses and pertinent data. Bibliography of collections of
plays. Title, cast, and subject indexes.

Gassner, John, and Quinn, Edward. *The Reader's Encyclopedia
of World Drama.* New York: Crowell, 1969. 1,030 pp.
Covers plays, playwrights, types of drama, and development
of theater in individual countries. Appendix: basic documents in dramatic theory.

Geisinger, Marion. *Plays, Players, and Playwrights: An Illus-
trated History of the Theatre.* New York: Hart, 1971. 767 pp.
Brief encyclopedic entries cover period from Greek and
Roman theater to present day; many illustrations.

Hartnoll, Phyllis. *The Oxford Companion to the Theatre,* 3d ed.
Oxford: Oxford Univ. Press, 1967. 1,088 pp.
International handbook, covering all periods of theater history through 1964; thousands of articles on biography, famous plays, famous theaters, theatrical techniques, schools
of drama, etc.

Keller, Dean H. *Index to Plays in Periodicals.* Metuchen, N.J.:
Scarecrow Press, 1971. 558 pp.
Index to over 5,000 plays in 103 periodicals from 1900
through 1969.

Lewine, Richard, and Simon, Alfred E. *Songs of the American
Theatre: 1900–1971.* New York: Dodd, 1973. 820 pp.

Logasa, Hannah, and Ver Nooy, Winifred. *Index to One-Act
Plays, 1900–1924.* Boston, Mass.: Faxon, 1924. 327 pp. Four
supplements issued covering 1924–57. Boston, Mass.: Faxon,
1932–58. 4 v.

McGraw-Hill Encyclopedia of World Drama. New York:
McGraw-Hill, 1972. 4 v.
Emphasis on European and American drama with biographical and critical data on 910 playwrights and brief essays on
general subjects such as tragedy and comedy. Over 2,000
photographs; title index.

Matlaw, Myron. *Modern World Drama; an Encyclopedia.* New
York: Dutton, 1972. 960 pp.
Comprehensive survey of modern drama includes eighty

countries, 688 playwrights, 1,058 plays; emphasis on Western world.

Melchinger, Siegfried. *The Concise Encyclopedia of Modern Drama.* New York: Horizon Press, 1964. 288 pp.
Record of first performances, biographical dictionary of playwrights, outlines of plays; illustrated with photographs.

Ottemiller, John H. *Ottemiller's Index to Plays in Collections: An Author and Title Index to Plays Appearing in Collections Published between 1900 and Mid-1970,* 5th ed. Metuchen, N.J.: Scarecrow Press, 1971. 452 pp.
Includes 3,049 plays from 1,047 collections published in United States and Great Britain.

Palmer, Helen H., and Dyson, Anne J. *American Drama Criticism; Interpretations, 1890–1965 Inclusive, of American Drama since the First Play Produced in America.* Hamden, Conn.: Shoe String Press, 1967. 239 pp.
Supplement (1970, 101 pp.) extends coverage through 1968. By the same compilers is *European Drama Criticism.* Hamden, Conn.: Shoe String Press, 1968. 460 pp.
Covers the period 1900–66.

Rigdon, Walter. *The Biographical Encyclopedia and Who's Who of the American Theatre.* New York: Heineman, 1965. 1,100 pp.
Comprehensive treatment, not only of biography, but other aspects of American theater, past and present.

Shank, Theodore, Jr. *A Digest of 500 Plays.* New York: Crowell-Collier Educational Corp., 1963. 475 pp.
Arranged by country; author and title index.

Sobel, Bernard. *The New Theatre Handbook and Digest of Plays,* 8th ed. New York: Crown, 1959. 749 pp.
Several thousand articles on biography, national drama, definitions of theatrical terms, synopses of famous plays, etc.

West, Dorothy H., and Peake, Dorothy N. *Play Index, 1949–1952.* New York: Wilson, 1953. 239 pp. Supplemented by *Play Index, 1953–1960; an Index to 4,592 Plays in 1,735 Volumes.* New York: Wilson, 1963. 404 pp. *Play Index, 1961–1967.* New York: Wilson, 1968. 464 pp. *Play Index, 1968–1972.* New York: Wilson, 1973.

Who's Who in the Theatre; a Biographical Record of the Contemporary Stage, 15th ed.   New York: Pitman, 1972. 1,752 pp.
Biographies of persons associated with modern theater; genealogies of famous theatrical families; list of notable productions on London stage from earliest times; and long-run productions on New York stage.

Young, William C.   *American Theatrical Arts; a Guide to Manuscripts and Special Collections in the United States and Canada*.   Chicago, Ill.: Amer. Library Assoc., 1971. 166 pp.
Lists and describes theater collections in 138 institutions. Indexed by personal names, subjects, and geographic locations.

TREES

Forbes, Reginald D.   *Forestry Handbook*. New York: Ronald Press, 1955. Various pagings.
Sponsored by Society of American Foresters.

Grimm, William C.   *The Book of Trees*, 2d ed. Harrisburg, Pa.: Stackpole, 1962. 487 pp.
Grouped by families; profusely illustrated.

Harrar, Ellwood S. and George J.   *Guide to Southern Trees*, 2d ed. New York: Dover, 1962. 709 pp.
Guide to identification and study of trees found in southern United States; 200 full-page illustrations.

Hough, Romeyn Beck.   *Hough's Encyclopedia of American Woods*. New York: R. Speller, 1957. 6 v. and 13 atlases.
Shows actual specimens of woods.

Little, Elbert L., Jr.   *Check List of Native and Naturalized Trees of the United States*. Washington, D.C.: G.P.O., 1953. 472 pp. (U.S. Forest Service.)
Gives both scientific and common names and scientific data on all trees found in United States, including Alaska.

Montgomery, F. H.   *Trees of the Northern United States and Canada*. New York: Warne, 1970. 144 pp.
Field guide with keys for determining genus and for keying down to species; 136 illustrations. Index of scientific and common names.

Peattie, Donald C. *A Natural History of Trees of Eastern and Central North America,* 2d ed. Boston, Mass.: Houghton, 1966. 606 pp.

Common and Latin names, complete descriptions; grouped by families; illustrated.

Peattie, Donald C. *A Natural History of Western Trees.* Boston, Mass.: Houghton, 1953. 751 pp.

Guide to identification of over 200 kinds of trees, economic facts, and full descriptions; detailed drawings and illustrations.

Petrides, George A. *A Field Guide to Trees and Shrubs,* 2d ed. Boston, Mass.: Houghton, 1972. 428 pp.

Field marks of 646 species of trees, shrubs, and woody vines growing wild in northeastern and north-central United States and in southeastern and south-central Canada. Illustrated; index.

Platt, Rutherford. *Discover American Trees,* rev. ed. New York: Dodd, 1968. 256 pp.

Arranged by regions of United States; illustrated with drawings and photographs.

U.S. Dept. of Agriculture. *Yearbook, 1949: Trees.* Washington, D.C.: G.P.O., 1949. 944 pp.

Articles on trees, their cultivation, and uses in agriculture.

UNITED NATIONS

Everyman's United Nations; a Complete Handbook of the United Nations during Its First Twenty Years, 1945–1965, 8th ed. New York: United Nations, 1968. 634 pp.

Frequently revised. Deals with structure, functions, and work of United Nations and its agencies.

United Nations Documents Index. New York: United Nations, 1950 to date. Monthly with annual cumulations.

A checklist and subject index to all United Nations publications, except restricted material and internal papers.

Winton, Harry N. M., ed. *Publications of the United Nations System; a Reference Guide.* New York: Bowker, 1972. 202 pp.

Annotated listing of reference works and periodicals published by United Nations and its related agencies. Subject index.

Worldmark Encyclopedia of the Nations, 4th ed. New York: Worldmark Press/Harper, 1971. 5 v.

V. 1, United Nations, covers organization, operation, and agencies. Remaining volumes provide data for countries in Africa, North and South America, Asia and Australasia, and Europe.

Yearbook of the United Nations. New York: United Nations, 1946 to date. Annual.

Report on activities of United Nations and affiliated agencies, texts of important documents, lists of United Nations publications, and biographies of United Nations personnel. Subject and name indexes.

VOCATIONS

Career for the College Man; the Annual Guide to Business Opportunities. New York: Careers, Inc., 1950 to date.

Based on data from leading United States companies and information on various other phases of vocational guidance.

Forrester, Gertrude. *Occupational Literature: An Annotated Bibliography.* New York: Wilson, 1971. 619 pp.

Approximately 6,000 references are listed under 500 occupational titles.

Hopke, William. *The Encyclopedia of Careers and Vocational Guidance,* rev. ed. Garden City, N.Y.: Doubleday, 1972. 2 v.

Guidance for career planning and information about specific careers.

McKay, Ernest A. *The Macmillan Job Guide to American Corporations for College Graduates, Graduate Students, and Junior Executives.* New York: Macmillan, 1967. 374 pp.

Information on career opportunities in over 250 corporations, their subsidiaries and affiliates.

Occupational Index. Jaffrey, N.H.: Personnel Services, Inc., 1936 to date. Quarterly.

Each issue lists about 100 annotated references relating to

occupations and vocational counseling; includes books, pamphlets, periodical articles, government publications.

U.S. Bureau of Labor Statistics. *Occupational Outlook Handbook.* Washington, D.C.: G.P.O., 1949 to date. Biennial.
Information for more than 800 occupations: nature of work, earnings, job prospects, education and training requirements. Kept up-to-date and supplemented by *Occupational Outlook Quarterly,* 1957 to date.

U.S. Employment Service. *Dictionary of Occupational Titles,* 3d ed. Washington, D.C.: G.P.O., 1965. 2 v.
V. 1, definitions of titles; v. 2, occupational classification and industry index.

WEATHER

Kendrew, W. G. *The Climates of the Continents,* 5th ed. Oxford: Oxford Univ. Press, 1961. 608 pp.
Concerns climates of various areas of world, including such special topics as wind directions, temperature, sunshine, and fog.

Meteorological Office. *Observer's Handbook,* 3d ed. London: H.M.S.O. (dist. by British Information Services), 1969. 242 pp. Guide for making weather observations; routine and procedures primarily based on international convention established by World Meteorological Organization.

U.S. Dept. of Agriculture. *Yearbook, 1941: Climate and Man.* Washington, D.C.: G.P.O., 1941. 1,248 pp.
Articles on climate and weather, particularly as they relate to agriculture.

U.S. Environmental Data Service. *Climatic Atlas of the United States.* Washington, D.C.: G.P.O., 1968. 80 pp.
Depicts climate of United States in terms of distribution and variation of climatic elements.

Visher, Stephen S. *Climatic Atlas of the United States.* Cambridge Mass.: Harvard Univ. Press, 1954. 403 pp.
Deals with temperature, winds, atmospheric pressure, storms, sunshine, humidity and evaporation, precipitation, and climatic regions and changes; contains 1,031 maps and charts.

WOMEN'S MOVEMENT

Barrer, Myra E., ed. *Women's Organizations and Leaders: 1973 Directory.* Washington, D.C.: Today Publications & News Service, 1973. 452 pp.
Over 5,000 main entries for women's organizations and prominent individuals in the United States, the Canal Zone, Guam, Puerto Rico, and the Virgin Islands. Subject, geographical, and alphabetical indexes. Annual editions planned.

Chamberlin, Hope. *A Minority of Members: Women in the U.S. Congress.* New York: Praeger, 1973. 374 pp.
Well-documented biographies of eighty-five congresswomen, using much primary material. Index.

Drake, Kirsten, and others. *Women's Work and Women's Studies, 1971.* New York: Women's Center, Barnard College, 1972. 160 pp.
Annual classified abstracting service for books, articles, and research relating to women's studies. Includes information on current feminist activism. Author index.

Ford, L. S., and Maddigan, R. J. *Directory of Women Attorneys in the United States,* 2d ed. Butler, Ind.: Ford Associates, 1973. 142 pp.

Hughes, Marija M. *The Sexual Barrier; Legal and Economic Aspects of Employment.* San Francisco: The Author, 1970. 35 pp. Supplement No. 1, 1971. 33 pp. Supplement No. 2, 1972. 72 pp.
Bibliographical guide to books, pamphlets, and government documents covering laws and conditions relating to the employment of women. Author index to all three lists in second supplement.

Ireland, Norma O. *Index to Women of the World from Ancient to Modern Times; Biographies and Portraits.* Westwood, Mass.: Faxon, 1970. 573 pp.
Alphabetical listings of some 13,000 women, with citations to material and portraits in 945 collective biographies and serial publications. Includes list of collections analyzed.

James, Edward T. and Janet W., eds. *Notable American*

Women, 1607–1950; a Biographical Dictionary. Cambridge, Mass.: Belknap Press of Harvard Univ., 1971. 3 v.

Signed articles with bibliographies evaluate contributions in all fields made by prominent American women. Introduction surveys history of women in America.

Krichmar, Albert. *The Women's Rights Movement in the United States 1848–1970: A Bibliography and Sourcebook.* Metuchen, N.J.: Scarecrow Press, 1972. 436 pp.

Partially annotated bibliography organized under such topics as economic status, education, religion, and biography. Includes books, articles, dissertations, and government publications. Special sections on manuscript sources and women's liberation serials. Author and subject indexes.

The New Woman's Survival Catalog. New York: Coward, McCann & Geoghegan, Berkley Pub. Corp., 1973. 223 pp.

"Self-help tool for all women" in an informal layout with much useful information arranged under such topics as communications (including feminist presses), health, learning, work and money, legal rights, and building the movement. Includes list of women's centers. No index.

Stimpson, Catharine R., ed. (In conjunction with the Congressional Information Service.) *Discrimination against Women; Congressional Hearings on Equal Rights in Education and Employment.* New York: Bowker, 1973. 568 pp.

Well-organized and edited version of the 1970 hearings of the Special Subcommittee on Education. Includes oral testimonies and substantiating documents. Index of persons and organizations.

Stimpson, Catharine R., ed. (In conjunction with the Congressional Information Service.) *Women and the "Equal Rights" Amendment; Senate Subcommittee Hearings on the Constitutional Amendment.* New York: Bowker, 1972. 538 pp.

Edited transcript of the Senate Judiciary Committee's hearings in May, 1970, with documentary material reassembled in pro and con sequences. Index of persons and organizations.

Westervelt, Esther M., and Fixter, Deborah A. *Women's Higher and Continuing Education; an Annotated Bibliography with Selected References on Related Aspects of Women's Lives.* New York: College Entrance Examination Board, 1971. 67 pp. Descriptive annotations for over 300 readily available books and articles on women's education, roles, and employment. Also lists bibliographies on related topics.

Wheeler, Helen. *Womanhood Media: Current Resources about Women.* Metuchen, N.J.: Scarecrow Press, 1972. 335 pp. Annotated basic book list of over 300 titles with author and title index; also section on non-book resources and directory of sources which includes listing of women's liberation groups. Evaluates treatment of women in general reference works.

Who's Who of American Women. Chicago: Marquis, 1958 to date. Biennial. Brief biographical data on living American women "outstanding as women."

Women Studies Abstracts. New York: Women Studies Abstracts, 1972 to date. Quarterly. Summarizes books, articles, and studies on such topics as education, employment, women in history and literature, and the Women's Movement.

WRITING

Burack, Abraham S., ed. *The Writer's Handbook.* Boston, Mass.: The Writer, 1972. 819 pp. Frequently revised. Deals with writer's craft, commercial aspects of writing, and lists markets for various types of literary productions.

Literary Market Place. New York: Bowker, 1940 to date. Annual. Concerns promotion and advertising of literary property, lists literary agents, artists, and book services, book clubs, publishers, book reviewers, magazines, news services, etc., in United States. Complemented by *International Literary Market Place.* New York: Bowker, 1965 to date. Biennial. Lists publishers and book-trade organizations by country.

Turabian, Kate L. *A Manual for Writers of Term Papers, Theses, and Dissertations,* 3d ed. Chicago, Ill.: Univ. of Chicago Press, 1967. 164 pp.

U.S. Government Printing Office. *Style Manual.* Washington, D.C.: G.P.O., 1973. 548 pp.

Useful guide to copy preparation, with rules for capitalization, punctuation, abbreviations, etc. Includes section on foreign languages.

University of Chicago Press. *A Manual of Style; for Authors, Editors, and Copywriters,* 12th ed. Chicago, Ill.: Univ. of Chicago Press, 1969. 546 pp.

Clearly written, stresses simplicity and fundamentals of style, with examples of principles.

Writers' and Artists' Year Book. New York: Macmillan, 1906 to date. Annual.

"A directory for writers, artists, playwrights, film writers, photographers, and composers," English and American.

Writer's Market. Cincinnati, Ohio.: Writer's Digest, 1930 to date. Annual.

Data on agents and markets for free-lance writers, artists, and photographers; includes subject listing of special interest markets. Emphasis on magazines and trade journals.

Additional Sources
of Information

Ash, Lee. *Subject Collections: A Guide to Special Book Collections and Subject Emphases as Reported by University, College, Public, Museum, and Special Libraries in the United States and Canada,* 4th ed. New York: Bowker, 1973. 1,800 pp.
Locates and evaluates some 45,000 subject collections in about 2,000 museums and 15,000 academic, public, and special libraries.

Besterman, Theodore. *A World Bibliography of Bibliographies and of Bibliographical Catalogues, Calendars, Abstracts, Digests, Indexes, and the Like,* 4th ed. Lausanne: Societas Bibliographica, 1965–66. 5 v.
Records bibliographies published through 1963; 117,000 items grouped under some 16,000 headings and subheadings. Cross-references.

Bibliographic Index. New York: Wilson, 1937 to date.
Alphabetical subject arrangement of bibliographies in both English and foreign languages. Published in April and August, with annual cumulation in December.

Courtney, Winifred F. *The Reader's Adviser,* 11th ed. New York: Bowker, 1969. 2 v.
V. 1, the best in literature (including drama and poetry); v. 2, religion, science, philosophy, social sciences, history, and other subject areas.

Downs, Robert B. *American Library Resources, a Bibliographi-*

cal Guide. Chicago, Ill.: Amer. Library Assoc., 1951. 428 pp. *Supplement, 1950–1961.* Chicago, Ill.: Amer. Library Assoc., 1962. 226 pp. *Supplement, 1961–1970.* Chicago, Ill.: Amer. Library Assoc., 1972. 244 pp.

Annotated list of a total of 11,817 library catalogs, union lists, descriptions of collections, manuscript calendars, etc.

Hamer, Philip M. *A Guide to Archives and Manuscripts in the United States.* New Haven, Conn.: Yale Univ. Press, 1961. 775 pp.

Arranged by depositories, alphabetically by state, then by city. Describes holdings of "source materials for the study of the history of the United States and its relations with other nations and peoples."

International Federation for Documentation. *Abstracting Services,* 2d ed. The Hague: The Federation, 1969. 2 v.

V. 1, science, technology, medicine, agriculture; v. 2, social sciences and humanities. An international directory listing about 1,500 abstracting journals and card services.

Kruzas, Anthony T., ed. *Encyclopedia of Information Systems and Services.* Ann Arbor, Mich.: Edwards Brothers, 1971. 1,108 pp.

Directory of 833 information-oriented services and organizations (e.g., data banks, research centers, professional associations) in United States and Canada. Twelve indexes provide access to descriptive entries.

Murphey, Robert W. *How and Where to Look It Up; a Guide to Standard Sources of Information.* New York: McGraw-Hill, 1958. 721 pp.

Sternberg, Virginia A. *How to Locate Technical Information.* Waterford, Conn.: National Foreman's Institute, 1964. 111 pp.

Sunners, William. *How and Where to Find the Facts; an Encyclopedic Guide to All Types of Information.* New York: Arco Pub. Co., 1963. 442 pp.

U.S. Library of Congress. *The National Union Catalog of Manuscript Collections.* Washington, D.C.: Library of Congress, 1959 to date. Annual.

Describes manuscript collections housed permanently in

United States repositories open to researchers. Cumulative
name and subject indexes.

Walford, Albert J., ed. *Guide to Reference Material,* 2d ed.
London: Library Assoc., 1966–70. 3 v. (Third edition in progress, 1973———.)

Similar to Winchell's *Guide to Reference Books,* with British
perspective. V. 1, science and technology; v. 2, philosophy,
psychology, and religion, social and historical sciences; v. 3,
generalia, language and literature, arts.

Winchell, Constance M. *Guide to Reference Books,* 8th ed. Chicago, Ill.: Amer. Library Assoc., 1967. 741 pp. Sheehy, Eugene P. *First Supplement, 1965–1966.* Chicago, Ill.: Amer.
Library Assoc., 1968. 122 pp. *Second Supplement, 1967–1968.*
Chicago: Ill.: Amer. Library Assoc., 1970. 165 pp. *Third Supplement, 1969–1970.* Chicago, Ill.: Amer. Library Assoc.,
1972. 190 pp.

Standard bibliography of field; classified and annotated
entries.

Wynar, Bohdan S., ed. *American Reference Books Annual.*
Littleton, Colo.: Libraries Unlimited, 1970 to date. Annual.

Comprehensive listing of reference books published in United
States during preceding year with brief descriptive reviews.
Arranged by subject, then by type of reference work. Index.

Index

Baird, W. R., *Baird's Manual of American College Fraternities*, 154
Baker, E. A., 108–9
Baker, Theodore, 208
Balanchine, George, *Balanchine's . . . Stories of the Great Ballets*, 159
Baldwin, H. W., 114, 203–4
Baldwin, J. M., 215
Ball, V. K., 178
Ballentine, J. A., *Ballentine's Law Dictionary*, 195
Ballou, R. O., 223
Baly, Denis, 141
Barlow, Harold, 208
Barnhart, C. L., 103
Barone, Michael, 184
Barraclough, E. M. C., 174
Barrer, M. E., 248
Barron's Guide to the Two-Year Colleges, 155
Barron's Profiles of American Colleges, 155
Bartholomew, John, 80
Bartlett, John, 104, 110
Barton, Roger, 122
Baseball Encyclopedia, 238
Basic Books in the Mass Media, 64
Baskin, Wade, 145
Baumeister, Theodore, 168
Baumgardt, J. P., 180
Beaumont, C. W., 159–60
Beilstein, Friedrich, 150
Benet, W. R., 101
Bengtson, Hermann, 114
Bennett, Harry, 177
Bergman, P. M., 145
Bernstein, T. M., 73
Berrey, L. V., 76
Berry, G. L., 224
Besancon, R. M., 217
Besterman, Theodore, 252

Best's Insurance Reports: Life-Health, 190
Best's Key Ratings Guide: Property-Liability, 190
Bible, 139–41
Bible of the World, 223
Bibliographic Index, 252
Bibliography: national, 47–49
Bibliography and Index of Geology, 183
Bibliography and Research Manual of the History of Mathematics, 199
Bibliography of Agriculture, 125
Bibliography of American Literature, 105–6
Bibliography of Bibliographies in American Literature, 106–7
Bibliography of Modern History, 116
Bibliography of North American Folklore and Folksong, 176
Bibliography of North American Geology, 183
Bibliography of United States–Latin American Relations since 1810, 194
Bibliography on Oral History, 69
Bibliography . . . on the History of Agriculture in the United States, 125–26
Bibliotheca Americana, 48
Bibliothèque Nationale, *Catalogue Général des Livres Imprimés*, 46
Bier, J. A., 148
Biographical Dictionaries, 86
Biographical Dictionary of Musicians, 208
Biographical Directory of the American Congress, 186
Biographical Directory of the American Psychiatric Association, 91